PEPYS'S

LATER DIARIES

PEPYS'S
LATER DIARIES

EDITED BY C.S. KNIGHTON

SUTTON PUBLISHING

First published in the United Kingdom in 2004 by
Sutton Publishing Limited · Phoenix Mill
Thrupp · Stroud · Gloucestershire · GL5 2BU

British Library Cataloguing in Publication Data
A catalogue record for this book is available from the British Library.

ISBN 0-7509-3656-8

Typeset in 11/14.5pt Sabon.
Typesetting and origination by
Sutton Publishing Limited.
Printed and bound in England by
J.H. Haynes & Co. Ltd, Sparkford.

Contents

Acknowledgements   vii

Abbreviations and Symbols   ix

Chronological Table   xvii

General Introduction   xix

One   The Brooke House Journal 1670   1

Two   The King's Bench Journal 1679–80   35

Three   Proceedings with James and Harris 1680   65

Four   The Tangier Journal 1683   113

Five   Diary of the Special Commission 1686   173

Diplomatic Notes   203

Index   207

Acknowledgements

I am indebted to the Master and Fellows of Magdalene College Cambridge, and to the Pepys Librarian, Dr R. Luckett, for permission to print three diaries from manuscripts in their custody, and for allowing the reproduction of illustrations from the Pepys Library. I am grateful to the Council of the Navy Records Society and its Hon. Secretary, Professor A.D. Lambert, for permitting me to reuse two texts published by the Society. Mr R.A.M. Dale and his sister Mrs Puttick kindly gave their blessing to my use of the NRS text of the Tangier Journal edited by their late great-uncle, Edwin Chappell. By kind permission of the literary executors of the late Professor William Matthews I have also been able to make use of his transcript of the journal. I must also thank Mrs Fitzsimons, Assistant Librarian at Magdalene, for help with the illustrations, and Mrs Duchin, the Library Assistant, for the like with the Chappell papers. I am obliged once again to Mr G.D. Bye for his expertise with the camera, especially in dealing with the large coloured engravings of Tangier. I am also grateful to the staff members of Cambridge University Library, the Bodleian Library, and the Codrington Library of All Souls College, Oxford, the Public Record Office and the National Maritime Museum for assisting my research. I am further obliged to the NMM and to the National Portrait Gallery for permission to reproduce illustrations. For particular points I am grateful to Mr P. Barber (British Library), Dr I.G. Brown (National Library of Scotland), Dr J.D. Davies, Mr A.V. Griffiths (British Museum), and Dr R. Mortimer (Westminster Abbey).

Cambridge, Michaelmas 2003   C.S.K.

Abbreviations and Symbols

(i) Bibliographical Abbreviations

Works listed here and cited in the notes were published in London or by issuing societies unless otherwise stated

Baxter, *Treasury*	S.B. Baxter, *The Development of the Treasury, 1660–1702* (1957)
BL	British Library
Bodl.	Bodleian Library, Oxford
Bryant, *SN*	Sir A. Bryant, *Samuel Pepys: The Saviour of the Navy* (1938)
Bryant, *YP*	Sir A. Bryant, *Samuel Pepys: The Years of Peril* (1935)
Chandaman, *Revenue*	C.D. Chandaman, *The English Public Revenue 1660–1688* (Oxford, 1975)
Collinge	*Navy Board Officials, 1660–1832*, comp. J.M. Collinge (Office-Holders in Modern Britain, VII, 1978)
CJ	*Journals of the House of Commons*
CSO	*The Commissioned Sea Officers of the Royal Navy, 1660–1815*, ed. D. Syrett and R.L. DiNardo (NRS, Occasional Publications, I, 1994)
CSPD	*Calendar of State Papers, Domestic Series*
CTB	*Calendar of Treasury Books*
Davies, *Gentlemen and Tarpaulins*	J.D. Davies, *Gentlemen and Tarpaulins: The Officers and Men of the Restoration Navy* (Oxford, 1991)

Diary	*The Diary of Samuel Pepys*, ed. R.C. Latham and W. Matthews (1970–83)
EHR	*English Historical Review*
Evelyn, *Diary*	*The Diary of John Evelyn*, ed. E.S. de Beer (Oxford, 1955)
Foss	E. Foss, *Biographia Juridica: A Biographical Dictionary of the Judges of England . . . 1066–1870* (1870)
Foster, *Alumni Oxon.*	*Alumni Oxonienses . . . 1500–1714*, ed. J. Foster (Oxford, 1891–2)
Fox, *Great Ships*	F.L. Fox, *Great Ships: The Battlefleet of King Charles II* (Greenwich, 1980)
Further Corr.	*Further Correspondence of Samuel Pepys, 1662–1679*, ed. J.R. Tanner (1929)
Grey, *Debates*	*Debates of the House of Commons, from the year 1667 to the year 1694*, ed. A. Grey (1769)
Haley, *Shaftesbury*	K.H.D. Haley, *The First Earl of Shaftesbury* (Oxford, 1968)
Heath	*The Letters of Samuel Pepys and his Family Circle*, ed. H.T. Heath (Oxford, 1955)
Hist. Parl.	*The House of Commons, 1660–1690*, ed. B.D. Henning (The History of Parliament, 1983)
Hist. Parl. 1690–1715	*The House of Commons, 1690–1715*, ed. E. Cruickshanks, S. Handley and D.W. Hayton (The History of Parliament: Cambridge, 2002)
HMC	Historical Manuscripts Commission
HMC, *Dartmouth*	*The Manuscripts of the Earl of Dartmouth* (HMC, 1887–96)
HMC, *Lindsey*	*Supplementary Report on the Manuscripts of the late Montague Bertie, twelfth Earl of Lindsey, formerly preserved at Uffington House, Stamford, Lincolnshire, A.D. 1660–1702*, ed. C.G.O. Bridgeman and J.C. Walker (HMC, 1942)

HMC, *Ormonde*	*Calendar of the Manuscripts of the Marquess of Ormonde, K.P., preserved at Kilkenny Castle*, new series (1902–20)
Hornstein, *Navy*	S.R. Hornstein, *The Restoration Navy and English Foreign Trade, 1674–1688* (Aldershot, 1991)
Houblon, *Houblon Family*	Lady A. Archer Houblon, *The Houblon Family: Its Story and Times* (1907)
Howarth	*Letters and the Second Diary of Samuel Pepys*, ed. R.G. Howarth (1932)
Kenyon, *Popish Plot*	J.P. Kenyon, *The Popish Plot* (1972)
LJ	*Journals of the House of Lords*
McGowan	*The Jacobean Commissions of Enquiry, 1608 and 1618*, ed. A.P. McGowan (NRS, CXVI, 1971)
MCMR	*Magdalene College Magazine and Record*
MM	*The Mariner's Mirror*
Naval Minutes	*Samuel Pepys's Naval Minutes*, ed. J.R. Tanner (NRS, LX, 1926)
NRS	Navy Records Society
NWB	*Samuel Pepys and the Second Dutch War: Pepys's Navy White Book and Brooke House Papers*, ed. R.C. Latham (NRS, CXXXI, 1995)
ODNB	*Oxford Dictionary of National Biography*
Ollard, *Pepys*	R.L. Ollard, *Pepys: A Biography* (1974)
Pepys, *Memoires*	Samuel Pepys, *Memoires relating to the State of the Royal Navy of England for ten years detemin'd December 1688* (1690), repr. ed. J.R. Tanner as *Pepys' Memoires of The Royal Navy, 1679–1688* (Oxford, 1906)
PL	Pepys Library, Magdalene College, Cambridge
PLB	Pepys Library Buffet [secondary material; not part of Pepys's bequest]

Priv. Corr.	*Private Correspondence and Miscellaneous Papers of Samuel Pepys, 1679–1703*, ed. J.R. Tanner (1926)
Routh, *Tangier*	E.M.G. Routh, *Tangier: England's Lost Atlantic Outpost, 1661–1684* (1912)
Sainty	*Admiralty Officials, 1660–1870*, comp. J.C. Sainty (Office-Holders in Modern Britain, IV, 1975)
Sainty, *Treasury*	*Treasury Officials 1660–1870*, comp. J.C. Sainty (Office-Holders in Modern Britain, I, 1972)
Sainty and Bucholz	*Officials of the Royal Household 1660–1837*, comp. J.C. Sainty and R.O. Bucholz (Office-Holders in Modern Britain, XI–XII, 1997–8)
STC	*A Short-Title Catalogue of Books Printed in England, Scotland, and Ireland, and of English Books Printed Abroad, 1475–1640*, comp. A.W. Pollard and G.R. Redgrave, 2nd edn by W.A. Jackson, F.S. Ferguson and K.F. Pantzer (1976–91)
PRO	Public Record Office
Tanner, *Naval MSS*	*A Descriptive Catalogue of the Naval Manuscripts in the Pepysian Library at Magdalene College, Cambridge* (NRS, XXVI–VII, XXXVI, LV, 1903–23)
Tomalin, *Pepys*	C. Tomalin, *Samuel Pepys: The Unequalled Self* (2002)
TP	*The Tangier Papers of Samuel Pepys*, ed. E. Chappell (NRS, LXXIII, 1935)
WAM	Westminster Abbey Muniments
Wing	*Short-Title Catalogue of Books Printed in England, 1641–1700*, comp. D. Wing, 2nd edn by J.J. Morrison, C.W. Nelson and M. Seccombe (New York, 1972–98)

See also head-note to the diplomatic notes

(ii) General Abbreviations

AG   Attorney-General
CJCP   Chief Justice of Common Pleas
JCP   Puisne Justice of Common Pleas
JKB   Puisne Justice of King's Bench
KC   King's Counsel
Kt   Knight
LCJ   Lord Chief Justice (of King's Bench)
PC   Privy Councillor
SG   Solicitor-General

(iii) Pepys's Own Abbreviations as Reproduced in this Edition

Persons denoted by intitals (generally expanded in the first instance; the prefixes Mr and Sir are not always used).
This list does not include occasional local abbreviations.

Mr A.G.	Attorney-General
	Sir William Jones to October 1679, then Sir
	Creswell Levinz
Sir R.B.	Rear Adm. Sir Richard Beach
	Navy Commissioner, Portsmouth 1679–92
Sir J.B.	Rear Adm. Sir John Berry
	Navy Commissioner 1686–90
Sir W.B.	Sir William Booth
	Captain of the Grafton *in 1683*
Lord B./Br.	Viscount Brouncker
	Navy Commissioner 1664–80, Admiralty
	Commissioner 1681–4
Lord Do.	George Legge, 1st Baron Dartmouth
	Admiral commanding Tangier squadron 1683–4
Sir A.D.	Sir Anthony Deane
	shipwright; Navy Commissioner 1675–80, 1686–9
Sir J.G.	Sir John Godwin
	Navy Commissioner 1679–86, Commissioner 1686–8

Sir R.H.	Sir Richard Haddock
	Comptroller of the Navy 1682–6, 1688–1715,
	Commissioner 1686–8
Hd./Harbd.	William Harbord
	MP; Chairman of Naval Enquiry Committee 1679
A.H.	Alexander Harris
	Head messenger, Admiralty 1676–82
J.H.	John Harris
	Porter, Admiralty 1676–8; Alexander's brother
W.H./Mr H.	William Hewer
	Clerk to Pepys at Navy Board and Admiralty
	1660–79; Navy Commissioner 1686–9; Treasurer
	of Tangier 1679–84; with whom Pepys latterly lived
S.H.	Sarah Houblon
	wife of James Houblon, a close friend of Pepys
J.J.	John James
	formerly Pepys's butler
Dr K.	Thomas Ken
	senior Chaplain to the fleet at Tangier 1683–4;
	later Bishop of Bath & Wells
K.	Col. Percy Kirke
	Governor of Tangier
Dr L.	Adam Littleton
	Canon of Westminster 1674–94
Sir T.L.	Sir Thomas Lee
	Admiralty Commissioner 1679–81, 1689–91
Sir J.N.	Rear Adm. Sir John Narbrough
	Navy Commissioner 1680–88
S.P./Mr P.	Samuel Pepys
	Clerk of the Acts 1660–73; Admiralty Secretary
	1673–9, 1684–9
Sir P.P.	Sir Phineas Pett
	shipwright; Navy Commissioner 1680–88
B.St M./Mr St M.	Balthasar St Michel ('Balty')
	Navy Commissioner 1686–8; Pepys's brother-in-law

Mr Sh.	Henry Sheres *military engineer; Surveyor-General of the* *Ordnance 1685–9*
Mr S.	James Southerne *Clerk of the Acts 1677–86, 1688–90; Navy* *Commissioner 1686–8; Admiralty Secretary* *1690–4*
Sir J.T.	Sir John Tippets *shipwright; Surveyor of the Navy 1672–86,* *1688–92; Commissioner 1686–8*
Dr Tr.	William Trumbull ('the Doctor') *civil lawyer; later Secretary of State*
Sir W.W.	Sir William Warren *timber merchant*
D./D.Y.	James, Duke of York *Lord High Admiral c. 1649–73; King James II &* *VII 1685–8*

also

N.O./N.Bd	Navy Office/Board *also* Navy Commissioners, Navy Officers *responsible for shipbuilding, supplies and* *manning*
T.	Tangier

(iv) Typographical Devices

| | indicates section of text omitted in this edition
* | indicates a comment in the diplomatic notes (pp. 203–5)

Chronological Table

public events	Pepys's life	diaries
1633 *[Charles I's personal rule]*	born in London	
1640s *civil wars*	at Huntingdon Grammar School and St Paul's School	
1649 *execution of Charles I*		
1650	goes up to Magdalene College Cambridge	
1653 *Oliver Cromwell becomes Lord Protector*		
1654	graduates BA; enters service of his cousin Edward Mountagu	
1655	marries	
1658 *Richard Cromwell succeeds his father*	sets up house in Westminster	
1660 *Restoration of Charles II*	appointed to the Navy Board as Clerk of the Acts	*The great Diary begun*
1661 *Tangier ceded by Portugal*		
1662	appointed to Tangier Committee	
1664 *hostilities with Dutch begin*		
1665 *First Dutch War declared* *Great Plague of London*	appointed Treasurer of Tangier	
1666 *Great Fire of London*		
1667 *Medway raid; war ends; enquiries begin*		
1668	major speech at Commons enquiry	
1669	death of his wife	*Diary ends*

1670	*Brooke House Commission report debated before Privy Council*	defends Navy Board's wartime management	*Brooke House Journal*
1672	*Third Dutch War begins*		
1673	*Test Act; Duke of York resigns as Lord High Admiral; Admiralty Commission established*	appointed Secretary of Admiralty elected MP for Castle Rising	
1674	*Third Dutch War ends; French threat replaces Dutch*		
1677		convinces Parliament of need to build 30 new ships	*Parliament Notes*
1679	*Popish Plot agitation continues; new Admiralty Commission*	elected MP for Harwich; resigns as Secretary of Admiralty and Treasurer of Tangier; accused of treason and imprisoned; gathers evidence for defence	*King's Bench Journal/ Proceedings with James & Harris*
1680		discharged by court	
1683	*Tangier abandoned*	accompanies Lord Dartmouth to assist evacuation	*Tangier Journal*
1684	*new Admiralty Commission*	reappointed Secretary of Admiralty	
1685	*accession of James II*	elected MP for Harwich; plans overhaul of Navy	
1686	*Navy Board replaced by temporary Commission*	persuades King to appoint Commissioners of his choosing	*Diary of Special Commission*
1688	*Commission stood down James II flees Revolution*		
1689	*William III & Mary II joint-sovereigns*	resigns from Admiralty	
1690s		plans history of Navy; completes Library	
1702	*accession of Anne*		
1703		dies at Clapham	

General Introduction

The great Diary for which Pepys is universally known was closed on 31 May 1669. For some while his eyesight had been weakening, and he feared that complete blindness was imminent. He suspected that the Diary, written in shorthand and usually by candlelight, had been much to blame, and with great reluctance he decided not to continue it. Although his eyes recovered after a few months' rest, and in time he resumed his habitual shorthand, he never again kept a comparable diary. It would be as churlish to complain that he gave us no more than those nine and a half years as to berate eminent composers who did not deliver a tenth symphony. Even so, we must regret that Pepys did not leave us a record, of whatever artistic merit, of those great events of the 1670s and 1680s in which he was an active participant: the Third Dutch War, the Exclusion Crisis and the development of party politics, the Revolution of 1688. This is indeed one of the most important and interesting books never written.[1]

There are nevertheless a few sketches for this unachieved masterpiece. Pepys did revert to the diary format on several later occasions, though always restricted to some particular business of special importance. This volume includes the five most cohesive of these texts, presented as far as possible in a uniform style. Two have been printed before. The Tangier Journal of 1683 is Pepys's record of the winding-up of Britain's first African colony. Of these later pieces it is the nearest to a general diary, and has been issued in popular editions. These versions were revealed as defective with the publication of a scholarly version by the Navy Records Society; the present collection includes a slightly trimmed version of the Society's text with a new commentary. The NRS has more recently published

Pepys's Brooke House Journal of 1670, chronicling the proceedings of a royal Commission into alleged mismanagement by the Navy Board during the Second Dutch War. Here a much more substantial reduction is made, because the full text contains a daunting mass of technical data which overflows from the diurnal framework. Three previously unpublished diaries are printed from MSS in the library which Pepys bequeathed to his old Cambridge college, Magdalene. Two concern his troubles during the Popish Plot in 1679–80: a formal journal of his appearances before the court of King's Bench, where he stood accused of but was never tried for high treason; and a more particular journal of his attempts to obtain retractions from those who had deposed evidence against him. Finally there is a diary recording the setting up in 1686 of a special commission to reform the Navy, the culminating achievement of Pepys's professional life. These five diaries here stand in chronological order; and while they do not produce a sequence from 1670 to 1686, they allow us to follow Pepys day by day at key moments in those years.

The Tangier Journal is derived from Pepys's shorthand original. The other diaries exist only in copies made by Pepys's clerks, and each was written up as a piece after the events it described. Pepys's original daily notes were simply discarded when these fair copies were made. We know that Pepys built up his personal Diary in the same way.[2] None of these pieces has a convenient authentic name; in each case Pepys's own rather cumbersome title will be seen set before the text. The term 'Second Diary' has been applied both to the Tangier Journal (in R.G. Howarth's edition of 1932) and to the Brooke House Journal (as a chapter title in Sir Arthur Bryant's *Years of Peril*). For the 1683 diary 'Tangier Journal' is now well established. That of 1670 seems to have been christened the 'Brooke House Journal' by Richard Ollard, and the 'King's Bench Journal' suggests itself by comparison. For the third item I can offer nothing better than 'Proceedings with James and Harris'. The 1686 journal begins a volume which is stamped 'Diary Naval' on the spine; but this seems to claim too much, and I have invented 'Diary of the Special Commission' – though even that implies more than it delivers.

Pepys also kept a diary of sorts during the Commons debates of 1677, when he was promoting a programme for rebuilding the battlefleet. Although this has been mentioned together with the texts here printed, it is too fragmentary a document to be presented alongside them for general reading. There are also many outstanding problems in interpreting the MS. It is hoped, however, that a version will eventually be issued in an appropriate place.[3] The canon of 'Pepys diaries' could be extended to include several short chronological summaries of various pieces of business.[4] Such documents would not usually be included by diary bibliographers.[5]

It has always been recognised, but must nevertheless be repeated, that even the longer texts printed here are B-features. None approaches the stature of the Diary of 1660–9. The Tangier Journal, the best of the rest, has been called 'a worthy appendage to the great diary . . . written with all the old vitality' and abounding in 'incisive character sketches'.[6] The most recent and most severe verdict is that 'it could be almost anyone's'; the enthusiasm, the curiosity, even the literary invention which distinguished the first Diary are gone.[7] All these pieces nevertheless have the interest which attaches to minor works by a great artist, and they are unquestionably historical documents of considerable importance. Above all, many of Pepys's admirers will find here things to cherish, as we all value the company of old friends even when they have lost the sparkle which once delighted us.

Pepys's biographers have made use of some or all of these later diaries, but here Pepys tells his own stories, (more or less) uninterrupted, and it seemed desirable to present his narration in a consistent fashion. The governing factor was that the two texts taken from the Navy Records Society's editions appear there in modern spelling, in keeping with the Society's usual practice. For the Brooke House Journal it would have been absurd to turn the selections printed here back into their original spelling, when the full edition has modernised the whole. Similar considerations apply to the Tangier Journal, and the more so because the MS is in shorthand. Although some of Pepys's earlier editors attempted to render his shorthand into what they considered seventeenth-century orthography, there is no certain authority for the practice, and the definitive modern edition of the Diary makes modern British spelling its standard.[8] 'Tangier' apart, the spelling is that of the copyist, not of Pepys himself. From all this it follows that the three texts here newly published should also be presented in modern spelling. In all cases exceptions are allowed for words (e.g. 'hath') which have no precise modern equivalent. The names of persons and places are given throughout in their established modern forms (the MS variants being supplied in the index); unidentified persons and places appear in their MS forms. These conventions are commonly used in modern-spelling editions. A special feature here is the retention of the initials Pepys uses for familiar individuals and in a few other cases. In preparing the NRS volume where the Brooke House Journal appears, Robert Latham and I decided to retain most of these usages, by way of perpetuating something of the character of the original. I adopted the same practice in the texts here newly transcribed; and for consistency I have reintroduced it in the Tangier Journal, in place of the fully extended names given by the NRS editor. A few other inoffensive quirks and archaisms have also been left in place.

The dating formulae at the start of each entry generally follow Pepys's usage. Contemporary forms of abbreviation (as '22th' for 'two-and-twentieth') have been retained. The year of grace was calculated from 25 March, and the modern calendar year from 1 January, where variant is supplied editorially. All dating in the editorial matter follows modern usage in this respect; otherwise the old style (Julian calendar) is used throughout.

The newly published material is given in its entirety, though in all cases the 'diary' is detached from surrounding material. For the previously printed texts the symbol | is used to indicate an omission (less intrusive, it is hoped, than . . . , while clearly indicating the editorial knife). The nature of the editing is more particularly discussed in the introductions to the Brooke House and Tangier Journals. Wherever possible the cuts have been made in a way which allows Pepys's own words to be read consecutively; but occasionally it has been necessary to insert [*editorial words thus*] for fluency. The same device is occasionally used to expand abbreviations, or to explain obscure words or constructions. Rather longer editorial links have been found necessary in the Brooke House Journal. Diplomatic notes (recording MS corrections or problematic readings) are flagged in each case by *; the notes themselves appear separately from the general footnotes, on pp. 203–5. These apply chiefly to the Tangier Journal, as again more fully discussed in its separate introduction.

Although the spelling has been modernised, the language has not, and remains that of the seventeenth century. This will be found at greatest remove from modern usage in the Brooke House Journal, where Pepys is at his most formal, and intentionally so. The grinding construction of his sentences was an essential part of his defensive armoury, and he makes no concessions to the faint-hearted. Here and elsewhere a few technical terms are explained in the annotation. The modern reader must chiefly beware of simple words which have changed in meaning over the past 300 years. Generally it is a matter of emphasis or insinuation which we now detect where Pepys knew and intended none. 'Extraordinary', for example, means no more than its modern contraction 'extra'; an 'extraordinary expense' was one not occurring regularly, without any suggestion of excess. 'Foul' (of a written text) means a rough version but not necessarily a messy one. When Pepys says a paper is read 'deliberately' he means 'carefully, deliberatively', not 'on purpose'. To 'pretend' means merely to claim, with no implication of falsity. Most of those who read these pages will already know Pepys's style; any who now make his acquaintance for the first time will soon have an ear for the rhythms of his language. Guidance is therefore given only in the most difficult passages.

Since all these diaries were kept at moments of great personal significance, their circumstances are by definition prominent in all versions of Pepys's life. It is therefore unnecessary to preface them with lengthy recapitulation of what may be read elsewhere. The most fully documented account remains that of Sir Arthur Bryant, who quotes extensively from these texts.[9] There have since been several biographies, most recently that by Mrs Tomalin from which I have already quoted.[10] The full versions of the Brooke House and Tangier Journals are lucidly prefaced by their respective editors. In introducing and annotating these five texts I have therefore not given authority for well-established elements in Pepys's curriculum vitae.

1. Paraphrasing R.C. Latham's concluding remarks in *The Illustrated Pepys* (1978), p. 231, and *The Shorter Pepys* (1985), p. 1024.
2. W. Matthews in *Diary*, I, pp. c–cvi.
3. Bodl. MS Rawlinson C. 859a (as now detached from the larger MS containing the Tangier Journal and related papers). The 'Parliament Notes' were transcribed by William Matthews along with the Tangier material, all from shorthand, and a copy of his typescript was deposited in the Pepys Library reference collection. The full corpus of Pepys's literary remains is laid out in *Diary*, X, pp. 89–91.
4. E.g. 'A journal of my proceedings in the business of the prizes', 17 September–13 November 1665, printed as an appendix to *TP* (pp. 335–7). It concerns Pepys's share of cargoes unlawfully seized during the Second Dutch War.
5. Cf. W. Matthews, *British Diaries: An Annotated Bibliography of British Diaries written between 1442 and 1942* (Berkeley, CA, 1950); *Unpublished London Diaries*, comp. H. Creaton (London Record Soc., XXXVII (2003), pp. 2–3.
6. C. Lloyd in *Diary*, X, p. 412.
7. C. Tomalin, *Samuel Pepys: The Unequalled Self* (2002), p. 334.
8. Cf. W. Matthews in *Diary*, I, pp. lvii–lviii.
9. A. Bryant, *Samuel Pepys: The Years of Peril* (1935) [for Brooke House and Popish Plot]; *Samuel Pepys: The Saviour of the Navy* (1938) [for Tangier and the Special Commission]. The first volume of the trilogy [*The Man in the Making* (1933)] covers the period of the great Diary.
10. R.L. Ollard, *Pepys: A Biography* (1974). V. Brome, *The Other Pepys* (1992). S. Coote, *Samuel Pepys: A Life* (2000). In passing I should say that Mr Coote's book had not reached me when I wrote *Pepys and the Navy* (Stroud, 2003), and I now find I used a chapter title which he had already put to the same purpose. I apologise for this accidental collision.

ONE

The Brooke House Journal
3 January–21 February 1670

The first of the later diaries is a record of proceedings before the Privy Council in the first weeks of 1670, when Pepys defended the management of the Navy during the Second Dutch War. Coming as it does just six months after the closure of the great Diary, it involves issues and personalities familiar to those who have followed Pepys through the 1660s. Indeed it may be said to close one of its principal storylines. The contrast with the personal Diary is therefore all the more striking and possibly disconcerting. It is better to see it as a polished version of one of the many ancillary records which Pepys was already keeping in the Diary years, and from which the Diary itself was in part compiled. While most of these were discarded when they ceased to be of current use, 'Brooke House' was carefully revised, and left *en clair* as a permanent record.

The Second Dutch War (1665–7) was the first great challenge of Pepys's professional career. When he was brought into the Navy Board as Clerk of the Acts (or secretary) in 1660 he had some experience of public administration but none at all of the workings of the Navy. He was greatly outranked by his colleagues at the Board: Sir George Carteret, the Treasurer; Sir William Batten, the Surveyor; Sir John Mennes, the Comptroller, and Sir William Penn were all past or current flag officers with a wealth of collective expertise. But they were also quite old, and unenthusiastic for the desk work at which Pepys excelled. So by the time the war came, Pepys had been able to make his mark in the naval administration to a much larger degree than his position as Clerk strictly entailed. Equally, of course, his position became the more exposed when things went badly, which after a promising start the war certainly did. The Dutch were beaten at Lowestoft in 1665, but not swept from the sea. They returned to fight two massive engagements in 1666, without a clear victor emerging. In 1667, when the English had decided to settle for peace and had laid up the great ships, the Dutch executed the daring raid on the

Medway anchorage which remains the most humiliating episode in the history of the Royal Navy.

Parliament had voted unprecedented sums of money to fight the war, and soon began to complain loudly of the poor return on its investment. The earlier Dutch war, under Cromwell's protectorate, appeared to be much more satisfactory in military and economic terms. Charles II's regime had clearly failed to achieve the same effect. There were some criticisms of the operational command, and of the King himself, but for the most part Parliament suspected the naval administration was inefficient and corrupt, and had somehow withheld the ships, men and supplies necessary for victory. All this was the responsibility of the Navy Board and its subdepartment the Navy Treasury; and as a result the file of accusations would land squarely in Pepys's in-tray.

Pepys first had to face the House of Commons Committee on Miscarriages, which was set up in October 1667. This was something of a blunt instrument, with a wide but imprecise remit. Two of its most prominent concerns did not directly affect Pepys or his Navy Board colleagues: the allegation that the English fleet had failed to pursue the Dutch after Lowestoft, and the criticism of the division of the fleet in the following year. The Medway raid was a different matter, because it raised questions about hardware which the Navy Board supplied – notably the defensive iron chain which had presented so inconsiderable an obstacle to the Dutch. However, it proved possible to focus blame on the resident Navy Commissioner at Chatham, Peter Pett, and the Ordnance Office. Pepys's principal business before the Miscarriages Committee was on the subject of seamen's tickets. These were vouchers issued by the Navy Treasury when ships were discharged and pay was due. The tickets could only be cashed at the Treasury Office in London, and many seamen sold them below value to brokers rather than journey to the office. It fell to Pepys to explain time after time why a credit system was necessary: often there simply was no cash in hand; at other times it might be dangerous to carry large sums to the dockside. There were also accounting complexities, as when seamen transferred from one ship to another without touching land. Pepys's most extensive dissertation on the subject was delivered in a three-hour speech at the bar of the Commons on 5 March 1668.[1] This also marked Pepys's emergence as the public spokesman for the Navy Board, and stimulated his ambitions to enter the Commons chamber in his own right. These aspirations received a further boost after the second stage of the post-war enquiry.

Introduction

The Brooke House Commission has a separate but parallel history to
that of the Miscarriages Committee. In September 1666 the Commons,
already worried by the disappearing war chest, appointed a committee to
examine the accounts of the Navy, Army and Ordnance. The MPs
attempted to give teeth to their enquiry by associating with the Lords, and
so acquiring the Upper House's ability to examine witnesses on oath. When
this failed they tried another procedural wheeze, the tack, writing proposals
for their own judicial enquiry into an existing money bill. The King
managed to defuse the ensuing argument for a while with a tactic of his
own, proroguing the session. His position was much less confident after the
Medway raid, and in October he agreed to an enquiry with the powers of
scrutiny for which the Commons had been asking. This body was
established by statute, and is therefore designated a commission rather than
a committee. Its nine members were, however, chosen by an ad hoc
Commons committee, and by the House's own resolve no sitting members
were nominated. The Commissioners were themselves paid, and were
provided with a staff of three and premises at Brooke House in Holborn.
There they set to work to discover how the parliamentary vote for the war
had been spent, and by their statutory authority they sent for all relevant
accounts and interrogated the accountants. Pepys was an early visitor at
their office, and started to keep his own separate records of dealings with
them.[2] Their very first demand he thought 'contains more then we shall
ever be able to answer while we live'.[3]

So the Commissioners proceeded on their laborious way. As they did,
Pepys shadowed them, anticipating their moves and conducting his own
evaluation of the naval administration at the Duke of York's request. In
October 1669 the Commission finally submitted its report to the King and
Parliament, making ten 'Observations' against the accounts of the Navy
Treasurer, Carteret, and a further eighteen 'Observations' on administrative
procedures of the whole Navy Board. The Commissioners had sent advance
copies of their report to the Board at the end of September, but Pepys did
not see it until he returned to the Navy Office on 20 October. He had been
on leave since August, recovering from the eyestrain and general fatigue
which made him abandon the Diary at the end of May. He and his wife
had been visiting France and the Netherlands; and although the trip
restored Pepys's health, his wife developed a fever and died soon after their
return. Despite or perhaps because of this blow, and the additional
disappointment of failing in his first attempt to enter Parliament, Pepys
immersed himself in responding to the Brooke House report. Within a

3

week he had produced a detailed rebuttal of the eighteen 'Observations', covering fifty pages as now printed. He followed this up immediately after Christmas with a briefer defence of his own conduct, and then sent the King and the Duke of York copies of the longer reply.

Meanwhile the venue for public debate of the Commission report had been crucially shifted. Initially the Lords and Commons each appointed committees, which began by considering the charges against Carteret. Pepys was twice summoned to the Lords, but this was not a very intimidating tribunal; Carteret himself, though manifestly not in control of his books, emerged uncensured. The Commons were less complacent, and voted for the Treasurer's dismissal. At this point the King again prorogued Parliament, and during the recess found a much safer course, summoning the Commissioners to continue their examination of the Navy Officers at special sessions of the Privy Council, chaired by himself. It is these meetings, in January and February 1670, which the Brooke House Journal reports.

Pepys begins with a brief summary of events since his return from France in October 1669, and of his appearances before the Lords' committee. The daily record opens on 3 January with a visit to the Treasury; proceedings in the Council Chamber at Whitehall get under way two days later. At first the matter under discussion is still the accounting of Sir George Carteret, held over from the Commons committee which the new forum had superseded. Still nobody could explain where Parliament's £5 million had gone, and the suspicion lurked that Carteret had siphoned off half a million to support the King's private pleasures. This was not Pepys's battle, but he was ready with an exercise in creative accounting. He argued that 'war expenses' could be backdated beyond the day declared by statute to mark the outbreak of hostilities; and when challenged he claimed as much right to interpret an Act of Parliament as anyone else. This delighted the King, who invited Pepys to publish a refutation of the whole 'other uses' allegation. Pepys never took up the suggestion, but he is keen to demonstrate how from this moment the King warmed to him, and how together they ran the show.

Pepys and his colleagues take a more prominent role from 12 January. The debate over Carteret's accounts has been concluded, and now the Commission opens its 'Observations' on the Navy Board's conduct. The Navy Officers are sworn in and provided with chairs; this was itself an improvement on standing at the bar of the House of Commons. Pepys says nothing more of the practical arrangements, but we may imagine the King and the Privy Councillors seated on one side of a table, with the Brooke

House Commissioners facing them from another, and the Navy Officers somewhere in between. Surprisingly, the general public are also admitted. At the next meeting (17 January) Pepys arranges the procedure to his and the King's satisfaction. After the Commissioners have presented each 'Observation', Pepys would read the response he had already prepared as the Board's general answer. The other Navy Officers would then be called upon to speak for their particular responsibilities. But if the journal is anything like a fair record, it appears that Pepys's colleagues were rarely called upon to supplement his answers. The Commissioners are seen to wilt under the barrage of Pepys's relentless statistics, and the Privy Councillors rarely intervene as details of contracts and stores are raked over. One can almost hear the collective groan as Pepys reaches for another file, then continues. It should be kept in mind that the journal, even in its complete form, cannot tell the whole story. After each phase of the debate had opened with an 'Observation' (a few sentences, alleging some misconduct in general terms), the Commission presented specific instances, to which Pepys had to respond in addition to his prepared answer. The 'Observations' and Pepys's formal written answers are extant, but Pepys has not preserved the Commission's supporting evidences or his responses to them.

The journal distils the whole proceedings into a contest between Pepys and two Commissioners: the chairman, Lord Brereton and the chief naval spokesman Col. George Thomson. Brereton was a Cheshire squire who had sat in Richard Cromwell's Parliament and the Convention of 1660 before inheriting an Irish barony. Yet he was also a noted algebraist and a founding Fellow of the Royal Society. As such he commanded respect, but his main qualification for the chairmanship seems to have been distance from the political arena.[4] At one point Pepys hoped to establish a rapport with him on the basis of a shared love of music, but their relationship was progressively dissonant. He had been wary of Col. Thomson from the outset, and rightly so, because the colonel had served in the republican Admiralty, and was well able to make damning comparisons between the current naval administration and that of the 'late times'.[5] Pepys acknowledged his expertise, but put the knife in all the same. None of the other seven Commissioners has more than a walk-on part in Pepys's drama. Lord Halifax, easily the most prominent, had declined to sign the report, and in the whole journal Pepys mentions him only once as present.[6] Pepys and Halifax are so renowned as commentators on their times that it is disappointing there is no exchange between them here.[7]

The Commission directed its attention to three main areas: the making and satisfactory performance of contracts for stores; the Board's own book-keeping; and the payment of seamen by ticket. The first was potentially awkward for Pepys, because at an early stage in his career he received a handsome *douceur* from a leading timber merchant, Sir William Warren. This led to further deals, including a major contract for Swedish masts which Pepys personally arranged. In doing so he usurped the function of the Surveyor (Batten), who had a family interest in a rival firm of timber-shippers. The other merchants complained they had been given inadequate opportunities to tender, and that they could have supplied the Navy better and more cheaply than Warren had done. None of this had much bearing on why the Dutch fleet had not been sunk, but it suggested wastage of public money by the Navy Office, if not actual peculation. Pepys responded with a rehearsal of the Office's general responsibilities, as laid out by the Duke of York's Instructions of 1662, and by a crisp particularity as to the details of the contract and the dimensions of the merchandise. On the more routine details of administration Pepys was on surer ground; he had after all created much of the archive which the Commissioners had been examining. Again he defended the Office by reference to the Duke's regulations, while pointing out that some of the surveys and stock-taking procedures were impossible in the course of a war. There was still the suggestion that things had been done better under the Commonwealth. In his written submissions Pepys was able to make satisfactory comparisons between the administrative costs of the Second War against the First; in the debate it was left to the King to close out the matter with a sweeping statement of how much more the war had cost the Dutch.[8]

The King entered the discussion on several occasions, sometimes appealed to directly by Pepys, and always supportively. Pepys milks these moments for all they are worth, and no doubt the King did stand by his man. But Charles needed no prompting, and his confident management of the Brooke House proceedings may well have encouraged him to take open government a stage further. In the following month he began to attend ordinary sessions of the House of Lords, and would do so regularly for as long as he summoned parliaments.[9] Pepys's journal captures something of Charles's famously easy public manner. At the same time his presence was intimidating, and the constant reference to the King's charges and the King's business must have been the more potent when the focus of it all was on the other side of the table. At an early stage Brereton discovered there was a limit to what could be said in the King's presence. Pepys, on the other hand, gets away with a wildly risky joke about Charles's failure to father a legitimate heir.

The King features prominently at the climax of Pepys's story. Having once again explained in general terms the need to pay seamen by ticket, Pepys grandly disclaimed personal connection to any particular payment. This was unwise, because Brereton then gleefully exhibited a ticket for £7 10s marked 'paid to Mr Pepys'. It will be seen that Pepys asserted rather than proved his innocence of pocketing this money. The King's endorsement (that Pepys would not have stolen so piffling a sum) was well intended, though oddly suggesting that he would not have been surprised by a larger fraud. The episode says much about the Brooke House proceedings; the more detailed the enquiry became, the more difficult it became to lay any substantial charge against the Navy Board. And even when damning evidence was exhibited, the King could dismiss it with 'a smile and a shake of his head'.

Since Pepys's journal is the only record we have of these proceedings, its authenticity cannot be tested. Pepys makes himself the central character, winning every round in the argument. Clearly it is an artfully constructed piece, worked up after the event from notes made at the time. It is evident from some of the scribal errors that it was written from dictation (probably one clerk reading to another from Pepys's draft). Pepys wanted it for his own reference, but he must also have known that he was creating a document of future historical importance. It is the best view we have of the beginnings of the modern public enquiry.

The only MS of the journal is Pepys Library 2874, pp. 385–504. This is in volume VI of 'A miscellany of matters historical, political and naval', a series of twelve large folios written by clerks at Pepys's direction. The MS was transcribed by the present editor and edited by Robert Latham for the Navy Records Society, along with other papers concerning the Brooke House Commission.[10] What follows is a selection of about one quarter of the original journal. The intention has been to provide a reading text which is representative of the whole, of approximately the same length as the other 'later diaries'. First to be jettisoned were supplementary notes which Pepys appended for further reference, and which are clearly not part of the reported proceedings. Beyond that, cuts have been most substantial where there was a prolonged discussion of technicalities. Some account of all the main issues has been retained, but several of the Commission's eighteen 'Observations' touched similar points, and not every one of them is featured here. I have retained most of the colourful matter and reflections of personality, the best of Pepys's oratorical flights, and the majority of his exchanges with the King. I am conscious that I have thereby exaggerated the egocentric nature of the document, and given a generous impression of its overall content. My defence is that Mr Latham and I have already made the complete text available for all who wish to use it. I must confess that in the process Pepys did not always hold my attention, and others may welcome this shorter version. A few errors in my previous transcription have here been silently corrected. The annotation largely follows Latham's, though I have occasionally ventured a new interpretation.

1. *Diary*, IX, pp. 102–4. *The Diary of John Milward, Esq., Member of Parliament for Derbyshire (September 1666 to May 1668)*, ed. C. Robbins (Cambridge, 1938), pp. 207–9.

2. PRO, ADM 106/2886, pt 1. Bodl. MS Rawlinson A. 185, ff. 315–16 (foliation defective).

3. *Diary*, IX, p. 34 & n. 4. This was in response to a comprehensive request for a statement of stores supplied, contracts made and ships hired during the three years of war.

4. *Hist. Parl.*, I, pp. 715–16. Cf. Evelyn, *Diary*, III, p. 232; J. Aubrey, *Brief Lives*, ed. A. Powell (1949), p. 312.

5. Cf. B. Worden, *The Rump Parliament, 1648–1653* (Cambridge, 1974), pp. 63, 256; B.S. Capp, *Cromwell's Navy: The Fleet and the English Revolution, 1648–1660* (Oxford, 1989), pp. 80, 123, 363.

6. *NWB*, pp. 343, 367 (neither detail included in the present selection).

7. The other Commissioners: John Gregory and Sir William Turner (noted as occurring below); Sir James Langham, Bt, and William Pierrepont, former MPs; Col. Henry Osborne, former Royalist officer, and Giles Dunster, subsequently Surveyor of Customs; all noted in *NWB*, pp. xxvii–xxviii (Langham mistakenly 'Sir John').

8. Cf. *Diary*, V, p. 328; VII, p. 307 & n. 5.

9. Charles began to attend the Lords on 21 March 1670. No monarch since Henry VIII had attended or spoken there save on formal occasions: A. Swatland, *The House of Lords in the Reign of Charles II* (Cambridge, 1996), pp. 96–8.

10. *NWB*, pp. 334–435. This volume also contains (pp. 271–333) the full texts of the 18 Observations made by the Brooke House Commissioners, and Pepys's responses to them, together with other submissions. The Navy White Book itself, occupying the first part of the NRS edition, is a separate item; the abbreviation *NWB* adopted here for the whole published volume follows the working title used by Latham and myself.

A JOURNAL OF WHAT PASSED BETWEEN THE COMMISSIONERS OF
ACCOUNTS AND MYSELF BEFORE HIS MAJESTY IN COUNCIL,
TOUCHING THEIR REPORTS AND OBSERVATIONS UPON SIR GEORGE
CARTERET AND THE NAVY OFFICE; AS ALSO THE PRETENDED
DIVERSION OF MONEYS TO OTHER USES THAN THE WAR'S.

At my return from France October 20, 1669 I met with a parcel of
Observations sent to this Office by the said Commissioners in my
absence. | I applied myself as soon and as far as my business of
Aldeburgh and with the sickness and death of my dear wife would
admit me to the preparing an answer thereto,[1] which I compassed by
the 27th of November, and carried it myself the 29th, where finding
the Commissioners out of the way, I left it with their clerk and my
old acquaintance Mr Symons, having communicated the foul copy
thereof only to the Duke of York, Lord Brouncker, and Sir Wm
Coventry, the last of whose advice I took through the whole.[2]

Once by order from the Committee of the House of Lords[3] and
another time by command of the Duke I attended their examination
of Sir G. Carteret's business, and as there was occasion informed the
Lords in what was before them, but never unasked, though even that
did not suffice to prevent the dissatisfaction of the Lord Brereton and
Col. Thomson with my appearance at all in this business.

December, I received order from the Clerk of the Council to
attend the King therein, to do the like office at the Council Board
upon occasion of his taking into examination of Sir Geo. Carteret's
matters. And was from day to day verbally directed to repeat my
attendance, which I did to the great satisfaction of the
Commissioners of Accounts as well as good success to Sir George,
who several times so far owned his obligations to me therein,
though assisted by Mr Ayloffe and my old chamber-fellow Mr
Sawyer, counsellors,[4] as to tell me that he had more reason to

9

present me with fees than his counsel; although I ever made it my care not to interpose in any wise between the said Commissioners and him upon any less warrant or inducement than the King's particular command, which I so far took care of and am able so far to justify, as to be able to appeal to the Commissioners themselves, among whom when the Lord Brereton did once or twice take occasion to stop me in my discourse, I ever replied that what I was doing was in obedience to the King's command, and therein appealing to His Majesty, he did always answer for me to my Lord Brereton that he had called upon me to speak and thereupon commanded me to proceed. |

January 3, 1669 [1670]. By letter from Sir G. Downing this day,[5] I was commanded from the Lords of the Treasury to meet with and assist Sir Robt Long and Sir Philip Warwick[6] in the preparing an answer to the exceptions made by the Commissioners of Accounts to several sums claimed in Sir G. Carteret's account to the value of £514,000, which (to use their own words) they most humbly conceive are for other uses than the war.

Accordingly I met them at Sir Philip Warwick's, where with Sir G. Carteret we run over the particulars, and I taking the minutes of the particular points wherein they could help me, though very unsatisfactory to me, give me matter of much wonder to find a case of such importance to the King no earlier studied nor at this day better understood. They committed it to me to digest, with the addition of my own thoughts thereupon, so as to be able to manage the matter on behalf of His Majesty before the Commissioners of Accounts at the Council Board.

January 4th. Sir Rt Long, Sir Philip Warwick and myself attended the Lords of the Treasury early this morning. Where Sir John Duncombe[7] only present, with whom having discoursed a little on this matter, he carried us up to the King, where present the Duke of York, the Lord Keeper, Duke of Ormond, both the Secretaries of State and others,[8] the manner of managing this matter was considered and the doing of it laid by the King upon me, to be assisted as there should be occasion by the said two knights in points relating to the Treasury.

Then going into the Council Chamber, and all persons called in, there was found to appear on behalf of the Commissioners of Accounts the Lord Brereton only, who informed His Majesty that Col. Thomson was come as far as Brooke House with intention of accompanying him to the Council, but that there he found himself so ill as not to be able to go further, and that for the rest of them, they were wholly strangers to the matter in hand, by reason that that part of the work of their Commission which respects the Navy was committed to and examined by Col. Thomson only of the whole number.[9] Upon which score the rest thought it unnecessary for them to attend here. Upon which the King judging it unfit to enter upon this matter without Col. Thomson, as being one heretofore conversant in matters of the Navy, the Board adjourned till the next morning if then Col. Thomson should be in condition to attend.

January 5. This morning Col. Thomson being present with others of their number besides my Lord Brereton, the King entered upon the debate. | The King commanded me to open their report by particulars relating to this £514,000, which I did in a manner greatly satisfactory to the King and audience, though the contrary to the Commissioners of Accounts at least in two particulars. The one, that wherein I greatly surprised them as well as the King's officers too, which was my denying the 1st of September 1664 to be reputed for the commencement of the war, or that the Act[10] did make either that day or any other day the bounds of the war's beginning, but that whatever was done by His Majesty and whenever preparative to the war, all was to be reckoned within the war and the intent of the Parliament's grants of money for the maintenance of the same. | Lord Brereton replied that he wondered that one Commissioner of the Navy should undertake the construction of an Act contrary to the judgement of nine Commissioners appointed by that Act, to which I replied that I look upon this Act like all other statutes penned for the information and therefore to the understanding of every Commissioner, and that therefore as an Englishman and as one principally concerned therein I did challenge [*claim*] a right of delivering my sense of it, especially in a matter wherein as I conceived there lay so little mystery, and therefore till His Majesty's learned counsel had delivered their opinion therein I desired mine might be admitted in behalf of His Majesty.

The other was upon occasion of my saying that the inferring (as is pretended) from an estimate of the Navy Office which would not amount to £90,000, that the ordinary charge of the Navy during the war did come up to £190,000, was an unjustifiable inference. To which my Lord Brereton very eagerly replied that he did believe that gentleman would not say what he had now said in another place;[11] which being an insolence more reflective on the honour of His Majesty and [the]* Board than myself, I silently suffered to pass, expecting that the King or some of the Lords would in their own honour have taken notice of it, as several of them afterwards told me it had been but fit they should. | But the King did afterwards at dinner call me his advocate, and made much sport with my Lord Brereton's manners and dissatisfaction with my opposing him and his eight brethren in the construction of their own lesson.

January 6. Waiting at noon upon His Royal Highness and praying his getting me opportunity of waiting upon His Majesty and himself to offer something relating to what passed yesterday at the Council, he directed me to attend the King and him at dinner, after which they were pleased with my Lord Arlington to withdraw with me to a corner of the room, where I began first to desire I might receive His Majesty's censure [*opinion*] of my performance yesterday, which His Majesty was pleased to tell me it was to his perfect satisfaction, giving me several times thanks for my care therein. | I humbly advised that his Majesty would be pleased to consider by what ways | to rectify the opinions of the world occasioned by this reporting of these gentlemen that His Majesty had employed to his private uses of pleasure, &c. not only the £514,000 here mentioned, but near £300,000 more in the moneys applied to the Ordnance and Guards. Here my Lord Arlington took occasion to put His Majesty in mind of what (as he said) he had the last night advised His Majesty, viz. that His Majesty would be pleased to cause the substance of this discourse to be put into writing, and that therefore as he did believe that Mr Pepys was the best informed of any man to do His Majesty this service, so (he added) that though Mr Pepys was by [*present*], yet he should not refrain to say that his style was excellent and the fittest to perform this work; though he would have it recommended to him to study the laying it down with all possible plainness, and with the least show of rhetoric if he could. Which motion the King embraced, and accordingly laid it upon me as a matter much importing him, | and so with expressions of his gracious opinion of my services dismissed me.|

January 7th. I attended this morning my Lord Arlington and received his letter to Sir Philip Warwick, making an advantageous mention of my discourse at the Council Board and bespeaking me in His Majesty's name both his own assistance, Sir R. Long's and the King's counsel. This done I do visit Sir W. Coventry. | I dined with him and find that both him and Sir John Duncomb did labour to bespeak my expectation of receiving all severe usage from the House of Commons, which I without much trouble do embrace the thoughts of, as being much more willing to be at ease than [hold]* my employment with so much trouble as I have of long done and must still look for, while yoked with persons who every day make work for future censure, while I am upon the tenters in their preservation from the blame due to their failures past.

Monday January 10th. By order of Council dated [7 *January*]¹² brought to the Board on Saturday, this Office was directed to attend the Council to answer to the Observations relating to their management. Before the Council met, [*I met*] the Duke of York walking in the Park, who upon seeing me told me that he had newly met Sir W. Coventry (who was walking in the Mall with Sir Philip Warwick), and that he had told them that he was concerned in this morning's work in the Council, to which I replied that I could wish he were concerned a little nearer us. Whereto the Duke publicly answered that that were too much in all conscience for the Commissioners of Accounts, Willm Coventry and me both upon them at once; and repeated the same aloud to Sir Wm Coventry when meeting him at his next turn, who answered that he reckoned himself safe enough in Mr Pepys alone. Thence to the Council Chamber, where, before the King and Board met, I by the Duke of York got the King to withdraw into his closet with the Duke and me, where I presented him with a copy not only of my general answer but of another bound up with it containing a particular answer relating to myself, dated the 6th inst. | I affixed an epistle to His Majesty, which at my presenting him the book, I took liberty to read.[13] | Wherein being seconded by His Royal Highness, His Majesty was pleased to own with great kindness his well liking of all I had done and said, and directing me to act accordingly, he went forth and so to the Council Chamber. |

Wednesday January 12. In pursuance of a warrant brought yesterday to the Board, we, viz. Lord Brouncker, Mennes, Middleton[14] and myself attended Brooke House, where having chairs set us, | they administered the usual oath to us. Which being done, they asked us each for himself whether the papers come from each of us were true, to which we separately swore that they were. | They then began to talk loosely of the want of Sir Wm Warren's account, asking when the same would be fully finished. | And so was running on (God knows whither) when Sir Wm Turner[15] desired that he might have a plain answer in whose charge the stating of Sir W. Warren's account lay. I then spoke, telling them that to give it them plainly and shortly, it lay, as Sir John Mennes had rightly told them, in his particular hand as Comptroller to state these as all other accounts. But that from a certain time upon petition of Sir W.W. to the Duke for better dispatch, His Highness had directed the Lord Brouncker to join with him in the stating of this particular account.[16] | Thomson run on to say that he wondered it should be thought Sir John Mennes's duty, when in the Hamburg business[17] Sir J.M. hath made oath that he never knew anything of that undertaking, neither in the beginning nor progress of it. To which nobody else making answer, I also was silent, leaving it to the having an answer more seasonable given to it, | showing the esteem that ought to be laid upon the words and performances of this weak gentleman. |

Monday January 17th. The King met again in the Council Chamber where | Brereton produced a paper containing an instance on the 1st Observation [*alleging merchants' failure to answer contract*], namely Sir W.W.'s Gothenburg contract for masts July 1664; which being read, I took upon me to speak to the King, beginning with the laying a foundation for his distinguishing between what we were accountable for as particular Officers and what as a joint Board. | I humbly submitted it to His Majesty to choose his own method, whether by examining us apart in reference to our particular duties, or summoning the whole Board to join in a general answer, or entering upon what I as a private man had presented His Majesty with as my conceptions touching what might be expected in defence of the whole.

To this His Majesty resolved to begin with my answer, as if it were the general answer of the Board, and as we come to any points relating to this or that particular Officer to call for satisfaction from that Officer. |

Here we entered into the merits of the cause, and I showing, first, the performing of this contract to have been solemnly already enquired into, and declared to have been performed on Sir W. Warren's part, by Sir W. Batten himself.

I appealed to the King and Duke, who both remembered their being particularly consulted with in the framing this contract.

To their objecting the great charge the King was at in convoy to fetch the masts home, the King himself answered that the convoy was not sent only for his goods, but to answer also the importunities of his merchants to bring home theirs. Which answer was not only useful but wholly new to me, and what Sir W.W. tells me is true, there coming under that convoy about forty merchantmen besides the King's goods.

To their urging the great numbers of small masts wherewith their stores were clogged, I showed them how soon after the delivery of each of the two great parcels of masts by Sir W. Warren, great demands of small masts under 14 hands were demanded in each yard; | Thomson most ignorantly urging that there was more use of great than small masts in a war, I appealed to Sir Jeremy Smith as a seaman, and run him down so as to make him laughed at. |

They brought also an affidavit of Mr Wood's charging us with making a prejudicial contract – that masts might have been had at better terms in the said time, [*and*] that we were forced afterwards to buy masts of him at dearer rates.

I showed that Mr Wood was invited with others when the contract was made,[18] that no terms so good were offered by him or anybody; that the masts he offered had been viewed and dubbed [*trimmed*] by Comr Pett and me and found sap-rotten and decayed in 1662. | I challenged any man to show where the service suffered any injury for the want of great masts during the war. I showed lastly that Mr Wood was a party in the complaint as having been greatly disappointed by our sending this merchant to market, we having in several years after the King came in not been able to serve ourselves with masts from any hands but his or Capt. Taylor's, so that he hath evermore endeavoured to bring disgrace upon this contract. |

Then Thomson started | a cavil about Sir W.W.'s not delivering to the King the right masts which were but a present to him from those of New England. The thing being wholly new as well as improper to the thing in hand, I told him that Sir W.W. ought to give satisfaction to those of New England, and that neither the King nor his officers were concerned in it, the King saying very well, that he thought it a very worthy present, and received what was given him without looking the given horse in the mouth. |

Thus ended this day's work with an adjournment till Thursday next, with appearance of most perfect satisfaction to the King, the Board and all bystanders. |

Thursday January 20. We attended His Majesty again at the Council Board, where the Commissioners of Accounts fell upon the second contract, viz. for New England masts,[19] insisting upon his [*Warren*] having delivered much short both in time, number and dimensions the quantity he undertook. Whereto I showed that | he did deliver | smaller masts from New England grounded upon the notice we had of the incertainty or rather improbability of our being supplied with the great masts we desired from Gothenburg, | and therein by the advice of the Surveyor [*we*] were more pressing to have these than the whole number of the great ones, and that not without reason, as may be collected from the number of great masts of New England now lying useless and perishing in stores, and the want of those of the lesser dimensions. |

They then proceeded to the last part, about imprests, pressing very earnestly the great value of the imprests granted to Sir W.W., | beyond what we were obliged to do by any contract appearing. I replied shortly that we are not bound to give imprests only pursuant to contract. | That ['tis]* true £34,000 worth of imprests lie at this day out against him, but that above £29,000 thereof is actually at this day discharged by bills perfectly adjusted between the King and him | and that there lie also before us pretences of his unadjusted to above £20,000 more, which, as it is too soon for us to assert their being all reasonable, so seems it no less too soon for the Commissioners of Accounts, till they had examined them to condemn any part of them – at least so as out of above £20,000 not to allow so much to be good as to secure His Majesty in four or five. Which seemed an answer wherein every man acquiesced, saving the Commissioners of Accounts, who took occasion thereupon to fly out upon the delay of his account, which I answer by saying in whose hand it lay, viz. Sir J. Mennes's, with the special assistance of the Lord Brouncker. | His Highness seconded me that Sir W. Warren had several times | applied | for the dispatch of his accounts, which he very well observed, and so did the King too, to be no sign of a merchant's desire of defrauding the King. | And so as I remember the matter ended without anything sticking upon of blame therein. |

Friday January 21 1669 [1670]. I was unexpectedly summoned with Sir P. Warwick and Sir Rt Long to attend the King in Council this morning, which I did, though by my endeavours of seeing Du Vall carried to his execution,[20] I happened to come after the business was over. But understand it to be the King's having called the Commissioners of Accounts before him | in order to their doing him and the government right in the mistake they had led the world into to his prejudice about his diverting so many hundreds of thousands of pounds to other uses than the war. Wherein the King was forwarded by my Lord Keeper, Duke of York, Lord Bridgwater, Lord Ashley and Sir Thom. Clifford, most of which prosecuted the motions I had started touching the Act's giving no ground either to the limiting the beginning of the war to the 1st of September 1664, or to the making any difference between ordinary and extraordinary charge of the Navy. | Lord Brereton answered that he should be ready to make His Majesty all reparation in anything wherein he had committed any mistake, but that he could not yet see that he had committed any. At which the King it seems grew very angry, and expressed in words of greater resentment than ever he did yet. | It at last came to this issue, that they would farther consider this matter, and set down the particular uses which they cannot allow to belong to the war, and attend the King with their resolutions therein this day seven-night.

Monday January 24th. The King and Council being met, and the Commissioners and we (viz. my Lord Brouncker and myself) called in, their 3rd Observation was read [*alleging the Navy Treasurer's accounts to be defective because payments to contractors were not dated*]. Upon which I read my written answer, and then in discourse showed them that the crime here charged upon us was our not doing what [*was*] never enjoined us; what in no age was ever practised; what we could not have attempted to have done without unfaithfulness; what in itself is impossible to be done; and lastly, what as soon as we were enjoined in and enabled thereto, has as far as it is possible been punctually executed.

To the first of which they wholly answered with silence.

To the second the like; saving that, I appealing | to Col. Thomson's observation as to the practice of the late times, he desired leave to be rightly understood | that he never was employed in the time of Oliver but only at the latter end under the Parliament.[21] | The third I proved by showing the Officers of the Navy not to be privy to the days of the Treasurer's payments as not being present, and therefore unable knowingly to sign to the same in his ledger. | The fourth I showed by laying open to them the practice of the Navy in bringing as far as possible all the wages upon the same ship under one head in the ledger, though the same be made up of several sums paid by tickets upon an hundred several days, and therefore that it is impossible truly to assign any one day for the payment of the gross sum as it lies in the ledger. |

Here being led also to take notice of the greatness of the action, | and therein the King also seconding me, Thomson replied that method might as easily be observed in a great action as in a little one, and instanced that a defect in architecture might be sooner observed in Paul's as Pancras;[22] at which position and instance the King and the Board seeming to make mirth of it, I thought it unnecessary for me to return any answer to it, though I had an instance in my mind [which]* my Lord Brereton as an understander of music would have allowed me for good, viz. that a theorbo is neither so soon put nor so easily or cheaply kept in tune as a violin or trump-marine, nor a harp as a Jew's trump.[23] |

And here it was that I first took occasion to object against their late declaring that they did not govern themselves by anything of what was practised in the time of usurpation, thinking it necessary to tell His Majesty that I thought we had reason in our defence to have reference to the management of that time. | To all which the King gave his full allowance, and the whole company discovered their doing the like, the King himself enlarging upon the liberty taken by people everywhere, in every coffee-house, and therein appealed to the company then present whether they had not met with discourses to the prejudice of his and his Officers' managements by quoting how much things were better done in the Navy in the late times, 'those pure angelical times' (saith the King), to which I added 'those times concerning which people discourse in matters of the Navy as historians do of the primitive times in reference to the church'. |

Friday January 28th 1669 [1670]. | The Commissioners of Accounts presented a paper going over the heads of that part of their report relating to the sums excepted against Sir G. Carteret's account as being for other uses than the war, | declaring that they did in their private opinions think it reasonable that His Majesty should be allowed the charge of his preparations, though they do yet adhere to their thinking themselves bound up to the allowing of nothing before Sept. 1, 1664. | This paper of theirs being read, a silence for a while remained, myself though prepared and expected by the King, and my papers in my hand ready for it, yet thought it unfit for me to begin the day until I had seen whether the King's counsel would first offer anything, or the King command me to speak. By and by the King spoke to Sir Hen. Finch[24] to deliver his opinion in point of law, who | did handsomely make a show of proving the King's right to any allowance for his preparation. |

I confess I was extremely sick of this day's passages, and particularly the Solicitor's speech, blessing my fortune that I happened not to begin the day, my discourse being likely to have been of a sense much contrary to the Solicitor's, | and being I confess, after so elaborate and elegant a discourse | unwilling to expose myself to the contradicting him with another so much inferior in the style of it, besides that I did not think it convenient for me to take upon me the justifying the point of law on His Majesty's side further than he had done, though I think he left me abundant room for so doing, and particularly where the Parliament | doth expressly require them to take the accounts of all moneys expended in the fitting &c. of His Majesty's Navy, which, if I mistake not, is a proof not inferior at least to any that he made use of. |

Tuesday February 1, 1669 [1670]. The King and Council being sat and the company called in, the Commissioners of Accounts | began their 5th Observation, proving by several particulars, chiefly as I remember consisting of ships' books and yard books, that [*we*] had signed the Treasurer[*'s*] ledger for payments where no bills had been first passed, amounting to above £50,000. |

To which, after reading my written answer, I had occasion among other discourses principally to insist | that what they herein charge us with is no more than our not doing what was never enjoined us, what our predecessors in former and later times never observed more than we, and what in itself is but an indifferent matter of form only. | I declared that whatever pretences I may have of having out-done any of their performances in the late times, yet I would be contented to stand by the issue of such a censure that I had done in this war as well as the like works were done in any other time. Besides, the King did add, that no time was so proper for us to be compared with as those times of action which came nearest in its burden to ours. | Col. Thomson, in the case of Sir G. Carteret's being allowed Exchequer fees, owned that he had looked back as far as Queen Elizabeth's time and could find no precedent for it, though

I find him mistaken, for in a ledger of her time which I have, there doth appear an ample precedent for this allowance.[25]

Saturday February 5th. The King and Council met, and company called in, the Commissioners of Accounts, after reading the 7th Observation, presented a paper containing instances, as they would have it, to prove | our overlooking and not punishing the faults of under-officers. But it contained nothing but instances of inmethodical and some double entries of goods received into His Majesty's stores, and particularly of Chatham and Harwich. | I observed them in this to have without exception condemned [*us*] in an universal neglect of looking to the behaviour of the under-officers, whereas I told the King I was ready to produce them a long list of instances to the contrary, if it were necessary to be done in a case where every leaf almost in our books gives a sufficient testimony thereof. | But besides, these are not officers of our own choice, and consequently we [*are*] not accountable for them otherwise than for the correcting them so far as we are made to understand their defaults. |

They then proceeded to the tender of a second paper containing instances of our providing and receiving goods otherwise than by contract, quoting that article of the General Instructions[26] wherein we are forbid to buy any goods otherwise than by a contract first made. To which I applied myself by making answer by discourse, without first reading my written answer thereto; which since my recollection I find to have been attended with the inconvenience of having forgot the mention of some things to advantage, which inconvenience I must hereafter labour to prevent by reading always my written answer first. But I proceeded very happily to show His Majesty | we have a full power of buying goods by commissions, purveyance and other ways than that of contract. To all which the King most fully agreeing, they offered nothing in opposition than that letter of the General Instructions, which I thereupon took up and showed it ought not to be interpreted to the contradicting the whole tenor of the rest of his Instructions and practice in all times.

Monday February 7th. | The 8th Observation being read, and by them opened by reading the articles of the Comptroller's and

Surveyor's duty obliging them to balancing of storekeepers' accounts and taking of surveys, | I began by craving leave in the first place to show the King and my Lords the nature of this work of balancing storekeepers' accounts, that it might be the better understood when we come to speak of its being performed or not performed; which being granted me, I shortly told them that it was no less than the taking an account of almost an infinite number of provisions, great and small, foreign and domestic, under perpetual receipts and issues to almost as numberless number of services, and these in distant places, both on sea and on shore, while at the same time the charge thereof also lay in a great variety of hands full of employment during a war, who must be all taken from the other indispensable works of their places to attend the making up of this balance. And not only so, but the whole service must stand still, for without seeing the remainder of the stores, no balance can be made up, and how the remainder of stores shall be taken at a time when every quarter of an hour or less goods of one sort or other are issuing or receiving, or both, and that in sundry places of the same yard, so as it were impossible without a total standstill of the service to take a general survey at any one time, so can no balance remain true at any time an hour together. |

I then | appealed particularly to Thomson not only for instance under the late times, but whether in those enquiries he hath formerly pretended to have made into the ancient practice of the Navy as far backward as Queen Elizabeth, whether he had ever even under the meanest action in any age heard of a balance of storekeepers' accounts taken.

I then went on | about the little prejudice this can be thought to have been of to His Majesty's service in the late war; where having read what I had written thereon, the King was so fully satisfied with the reason as to prevent any enlarging of mine thereon, by taking it upon himself in his own vindication as well as ours (as he was pleased to call it) the giving a summary account of the success of our endeavours in the late war; which he was pleased to say was such as, but for the unhappy business of Chatham,[27] we had no reason but to own to come up to the utmost of whatever was performed in the first Dutch war, or what the enemy could be said to have done in this; and so of his own accord run over the several instances of dispatch given by this Board in the fitting forth and the refitting forth of the fleets before and after fights, always sooner than the enemy could do, though the diversities of the Admiralties (as the King well observed) made it almost as easy to set out ten as two.[28] To which I humbly took leave to offer the consideration of the difference between the charge which the late war is owned to have cost them and us. Which the King very readily took upon him also to speak to by saying that he had made it his work to inform himself in the expense of the Dutch in the late war, and finds it upon very good information to have amounted to 11 millions sterling, whereas ours doth not come up to or at least exceeds not 6.[29] |

The King then called for the next Observation, viz. the 9th. Which being read, and their paper containing only the general article of our duties obliging us to musters in the Narrow Seas every three months, and a declaration that they find the same not to have been done, there seemed to need no more answer than just the reading of what I had wrote, wherein the King owned full satisfaction on our part, expressing his observation of the strangeness of their proceeding in charging us with a fault for the breach of one part of an instruction wherein the very next words of the same instruction wholly acquits us, directing himself to Col. Thomson and saying that he would be once in his life ingenuous and own his being satisfied. |

The King then called for the 10th Observation, which being read and a paper instancing two depositions of boatswains' and carpenters' accounts passed without any control made use of by the purser, there needed no other answer than what I had wrote thereon, which was done and proved fully satisfactory, without the help of what further matter I might have added out of my foul notes, which, not foreseeing our advantage [*progress*] so far this day, I had not prepared myself to apply to. |

To all which the Commissioners of Accounts remaining wholly silent, the King and Board broke up with most ample expressions at the Board, and much more afterwards, of the unanswerable satisfaction given them.

Saturday February 12, '69 ['70]. The King and Council sat, and we called in, the 11th Observation was read and their papers of instances, upon which I propounded the reading of the 12th and 13th, as relating all to the business of tickets,[30] for saving time capable of receiving a common answer. Which being agreed to, the other two were accordingly read, and then my written answer to the whole. | I then began with this question: whether the fault they here blame us with be a fault of breaking some written instructions of the Admiral's or the practice of the Navy, showing and appealing therein to Thomson that in the late times they never offered at the establishing or observing any rules of comparing tickets [*with*] their counterparts till after the end of the first Dutch war, they having not so much as invented, much less exercised, the printing of tickets till then. Here my Lord Brereton interposed, saying that he had often answered this sort of question, fully as he thought, by saying that they did not hold themselves obliged to report miscarriages arising only from breach of a known rule or practice, but also everything wherein His Majesty may be found to suffer any evil. | I answered his Lordship, first, that it is true they were not tied only to take notice of breaches of rule, but that they had a double work upon their hand – one to blame the guilty for defaults past against rules known, the other for the discovering any defects in our methods past in order to the rectifying the same for the time to come. | I then showed him that no blame can be done to us in this particular from breach of rule, there being none, nor ground of condemning the methods of the Navy as imperfect in this matter, in regard that the examination of tickets by their counterparts is a matter wholly impracticable in a time of war, | and this the State in the late times knew well enough, when they forbore either the enjoining or attempting the practising of it. But I showed them that | the examining of tickets by their counterparts was practised till the hurry of the war made it impracticable. I showed them also that it has been done together with the sending of lists to the Treasurer's office ever since the end of the war, and is at this day done. |

Here my Lord Brereton begun to enlarge upon the great number of errors now before them in tickets, finding no proper way of expressing it than by saying they alone would make a book as big or bigger than my answer now before them; and though it was in some sense unfit to speak anything but good of the dead, yet that they could not but take notice that they had found great number of tickets to great value paid by Sir W. Batten to himself, and that Mr Fenn[31] had done the like to much greater, insinuating that the like had been practised by others of the Board, but that they should be very ready to receive any satisfaction that should be offered them in reference to this matter. |

Upon which, finding that this discourse was like to end with some tincture at least of a possibility of blame upon the several members of this Office, which they would insinuate by an offer of a readiness in them to receive satisfaction from us, I thought it unfit for me in my particular to suffer it to rest so, and therefore took the boldness to tell them that whatever they would have the world think as to others, I did desire the whole world to show me to have been concerned directly or indirectly in any one ticket in reference either to any title to it or the payment or receipt of the moneys due upon it. At which my Lord Brereton, with a look full of trouble and malignity, answering 'How! Mr Pepys, do you defy the whole world in this matter?', I replied yea, that I defied both the whole world and my Lord Brereton in particular if he would be thought one of it. At which I could perceive the whole Board shaken with the surprise thereof, and my Lord Brereton himself struck dumb, so as no reply being at all made to it, nor further matter (as I remember) added on this subject, the King called after some pause for the next Observation. |

[*The 14th Observation blamed the Board for seamen being put on short rations because the Navy Victualler had supplied pursers with cash instead of provisions. As usual Pepys first read his prepared answer.*] I enlarged thereupon by discourse, showing first, that though it be unusual and may by the weakening men's bodies be in some measure found inconvenient for seamen to be put to short allowance in the Channel, yet that the King cannot be said to have suffered anything thereby in the case mentioned and in other places. | Secondly, that the want of provisions was not complained of anywhere more than in the Generals' own ships, where it is not to be thought but all care was used for seeing the same received on board in specie and well kept there. Thirdly, that the number of the supernumeraries in the fleet was such as to lead the Generals in '66[32] to demand one month's victuals extra in six to be sent them in consideration of supernumeraries. | Fourthly, that the ships happened in both years to fight presently after taking in their victuals, so as to be forced to fling over much provisions to make room for wounded men, and clear their wings to come at shot. Against the next time let me be ready with the instances hereof. Fifthly, that the seeing provisions brought on board in specie is by the Admiral made the sole duty of the commander. Here I forgot to have by me the old Additional Instruction as well as the General to prove it. | Whereto my Lord Brereton objected | the 11th General Instruction, where the Board is authorized to give instructions to all inferior officers, among which pursers are there reckoned, and to keep a strict watch over them that they do their duties. To which I made little other answer than that this was impossible for us to see done, being tied to attendance here while ships lay in victualling at the several ports far distanced at the same time. |

I appealed to them to inform His Majesty what service or design of His Majesty during the whole war had suffered any miscarriage by this want of provisions or the badness thereof, taking upon me the making some comparison between the management of victualling between this and the former war, wherein so many thousands of tuns and provisions were flung overboard, fleets come in for want, men mutiny, and the contractors but for friendship which the interest of some of them found, had probably been hanged for it, as it was threatened they should be. | In short I undertook to say that whoever shall hereafter come to tell the story of the management of this war, he will find more matter for wonder than censure in what relates to Sir Denis Gauden's[33] part therein. In which the King and Duke very amply joined with me, and in their owning a full satisfaction in what relates to the Board in this Observation, and especially in that which observed, viz. that though it may be thought that some misbehaviour there may have been possibly in some pursers in their disposal of their provisions, yet that nothing at all appears why these Commissioners should in this their Observation so peremptorily charge the fault thereof upon the want of care in this Board.

Thursday February 17, 1669 [1670]. This day being appointed for another hearing at the Council, I was by my Lord Brouncker first, then by Mr Slingsby,[34] then by the King himself, and lastly by my Lord Lauderdale, told that my Lord Brereton had given out that he would this day make good his challenge | touching my being concerned in the receiving money upon tickets, which therefore I expected, but in vain, nothing at all being mentioned of it at this meeting. But so soon as the King and Council were sat, the 15th Observation [*alleging the Board had paid merchants excessive prices for commodities*] was read, and after it my written answer. Which being ended, I by discourse summed up the force of it [*that the Board had made its own complaints to the Admiral, and in some of the instances the Commissioners now queried*]. | All that Brooke House offered in opposition hereto was the observing the date of the earliest of these our complaints, and the showing instances of our height of prices before those complaints, and quoting the prices given by private merchants at that time for those goods. Whereto I answered first by observing that these instances are wholly new, and as in other cases these Commissioners do not own any satisfaction in what is given to the instances there sent us, but labour still to surprise us with new ones not heard of before, though all to no purpose. | But that which I shut up all with, as what I insisted finally and principally upon in vindication of this Office, was that it was not our part to be accountable for the buying of goods at the prices now to be found in private merchants' books, in which all circumstances do not appear that should discover the difference between our bargain and theirs. | I did assert in behalf of this Office and invited them by any instances to disprove it, that the Office did never omit to buy as cheap as they could, much less did ever give a greater price while under the same circumstances of price, time and delivery, quantity and dimensions of the goods, &c., they would or were ever informed that they could have bought the same cheaper.

Whereto Brooke House not offering anything in answer, the King owned his full satisfaction and called for the next Observation.

[*The 16th Observation claimed that the Board favoured certain contractors, particularly Sir William Warren.*] | I do not remember they offered anything in objection to | my answer that was either extraordinary in itself or that did not receive a present full answer, saving two particulars touching Sir W. Warren's accounts, which the Lord Brouncker took upon him to give present answer to by denial of what they alleged, and referring himself to the justifying that denial against the next meeting. | The King owning with their Lordships complete satisfaction touching this Observation, with words several times put in by the King and Duke of the serviceableness of Sir W. Warren and readiness on all occasions to furnish the King with ships and goods [at]* greater hazards and lower prices than others, His Majesty concluded the meeting. |

Monday February 21, 1669 [1670]. [*Brouncker first gave a detailed explanation of the items in Warren's account which the Commissioners had queried.*] | Which being said by my Lord Brouncker, and improved as much as I held needful by my discourse thereon, to the satisfaction of His Majesty and the total silencing of those Commissioners, the 17th Observation was read, with a paper of instances of the loss the King was at upon several ships particularly enumerated by their lying in harbour unpaid off. In reply to which I read my written answer, and then proceeded to the discoursing largely thereon, grounded upon the | notes which for my memory I had prepared, though for shortness I spared the use of several (if not most) of the letters therein quoted, reserving their use to future occasions, and pressed the force of the whole by concluding with an observation of the unfortunate condition of the Officers of the Navy under the plain dilemma wherein by this charge from the Commissioners of Accounts they expressly stand, viz. ships coming in to be paid off, and we evermore under a want of money wherewith to do it; if we suffer them to lie in pay unemployed, we then fall under the censure of wasting His Majesty's treasure; if we discharge them into other ships, which cannot be done but by ticket, and this even at times when the King's service was at a stand for want of men in those other ships (which was the real case of most if not all discharges of ships by ticket |), we are then arraigned for occasioning discontent to the seamen. |

Having thus concluded without any further reply upon this Observation, the King called for the next, when my Lord Brereton interposed, saying that | the next falling within the care of another member of their number,[35] he desired before he took leave of His Majesty in this matter he might be heard in something relating to what had passed between him and Mr Pepys, and wherein he understood it to have been suggested that he had affirmed something touching Mr Pepys more than he was able to prove, namely that Mr Pepys had received moneys upon tickets, which he said he was prepared to prove by a ticket which he then produced for £7 odd money to one Capp of the *Lion*, upon which ticket it was writ 'paid to Mr Pepys'. Having said which, and the ticket being offered to the King and Duke, the King put it into my hand for my perusal; which while I was doing, Col. Thomson voluntarily took occasion to observe to His Majesty (as near as I can [*remember*] in these very words) that they had discovered two or three more; they should not have troubled His Majesty with the mention of it, being so small a matter, had it not been that Mr Pepys had so positively taken upon him to assert his having never been concerned in the receiving money upon a ticket, which being so asserted they thought themselves obliged to take notice of what they had found in disproof thereof. Which having been said, I betook myself to answer by observing, first, that in the many score thousands of pounds that had been paid in wages of seamen, and of that too great part in tickets, only one ticket could be found wherein any pretence could be of my being concerned therein. That nothing was offered to be objected either by my Lord Brereton or Col. Thomson against the truth of the ticket itself in any circumstance of it, but only a supposition that this one ticket, true as it is, was paid to me. Thirdly, that however these words 'paid to Mr Pepys', and by whom and whensoever they came to be writ, I did persist my defiance of any man to prove that this or any other ticket was ever paid to me.

Whereto my Lord Brereton answered that what he had said he was able to prove by the oath of Mr Stephen,[36] who had sworn the words to have been written with his hand, and that the money was paid to me. Upon which I replied that so much had been my constant resolution during the whole war to the having nothing to do with the payment or receipt of the money due upon any ticket or in any wise to be concerned for anything relating to a ticket more than the signing of them when brought to me by the clerks employed in the examination thereof, that it is not by any presumptuous guess but by a firm knowledge that I do take upon me to assert in defiance of the whole world my uninterestedness in anything of this matter, and therefore doubt not but the instance being now (and not before) given me, I shall be able even in this particular to show the little truth lying in this objection. Which having said, the King, with a smile and a shake of his head, told the Commissioners that he thought it a vain thing to believe that one having so great trust and therein acting without any exception therein in matters of the greatest moment should descend to the so poor a thing as the doing anything that was unfit for him in a matter of £7 10s. And so this matter ended. |

Then was the 18th and last Observation [*alleging the Board had failed to account for certain specified prize vessels*] called for and read, and my Lord Brereton and Thomson giving place, Mr Gregory[37] advanced to their station, and in proof of the Observation tendered a list of particular ships and goods charged on and not owned by us. | I then | read several parts of my reply to their list. In my doing whereof, Mr Gregory moved that my pains might be spared in reading those particulars which were not mentioned in the list now given in, and that I might answer to those and those only. Upon which I took leave to observe, first, the unfairness of their proceedings in being desirous to suppress anything that should discover their being satisfied. | Besides that, I observed that (if I was not mistaken therein) they did now not only suppress the old instances they are satisfied in, but bring upon us new ones by surprise, contrary not only to all fair proceedings, but to our repeated desires by letter of having the instances first sent to us, and my Lord Brereton's and Col. Thomson's repeated promises before His Majesty and this Board that we should have them. Which method of theirs I showed would moreover perpetuate the dispute without any end to be foreseen of it; while answers being given to satisfaction to this day's objection, that satisfaction shall never be owned, but in lieu thereof a new race of objections shall be started, so as I plainly told His Majesty, my work must be to get a son and bring him up only to understand this controversy between Brooke House and us, and that His Majesty too should provide for successors to be instructed on his part in the state of this case, which otherwise would never likely be understood. | At this the King and the whole Board and all bystanders discovered by their murmur a disdainful resentment of these gentlemen's proceedings, and the King and Duke after their being up, took notice of it in like manner publicly at supper as of a matter most enormous and oppressive.

I then in the second place proceeded to assert | that whatever was pretended by these Commissioners and now by Mr Gregory, not one particular in either of these lists are to my best knowledge chargeable on the Office of the Navy by anything that can rightly charge them. | To this Mr Gregory, in a cynical, froward manner, answers that for his part we (viz. the Principal Officers of the Navy) are charged with all these things by the books of the Commissioners for Prizes, presently turning to one of their books and showing therein the 'Office of the Navy', are made debtor to such and such ships and goods. I replied that we were not accountable for the keeping of those books, much less for the wording of it, but that whatever was the meaning of the Commissioners of Prizes, who might perhaps call the under-officers of the Navy by the general name of the 'Office of the Navy', as esteeming them persons acting by and for us and accountable to us, I do affirm that the charge is wholly untrue in reference to us the Principal Officers and Commissioners of the Navy. To which Gregory snappishly answered that what he had reported was upon the entries in the books of the Commissioners of Prizes, and that he did not doubt but that they were able to justify the truth of their books, and this I drove him to repeat several times. | Here my Lord Lauderdale interposed, saying

| that he was confident the goods were not delivered to the Office of the Navy but to the under-officers thereof in the yards. | But that if His Majesty pleased, he and the rest of the Principal Commissioners for Prizes would take this matter into examination and give His Majesty satisfaction therein. Which the King approved of. |

And so this matter and the whole business of these Observations ended with a profession of all satisfaction on His Majesty's part in reference to every particular that I can remember either urged therein or offered upon the debate thereof by the Commissioners of Brooke House.

1. Pepys and his wife had been visiting France and the Netherlands since August; she died on 10 November, the day after Pepys had been defeated in a by-election at Aldeburgh.

2. Will Symons and Pepys had been fellow members of a 'club' of young government clerks under the Commonwealth: *Diary*, I, p. 208 and *passim*; X, p. 406. Brouncker and Coventry, at this time Extra Commissioners of the Navy (i.e. without portfolio), were the two colleagues whom Pepys most respected; Coventry in particular was his exemplar.

3. Appointed 9 November 1669 (*LJ*, XII, pp. 261–2), to examine the report of the Commissioners of Accounts.

4. Joseph Ayloffe of Gray's Inn. Robert Sawyer, Kt 1677, AG 1681–7, had shared a room with Pepys at Magdalen: *Hist. Parl.*, III, pp. 399–403.

5. Sir George Downing, Secretary to the Treasury 1667–71, who had been Pepys's superior in the State's Exchequer: *Hist. Parl.*, II, pp. 224–9.

6. Long was Auditor of Receipt in the Exchequer, although exercising a much larger role in the Treasury; Warwick had been Treasury Secretary during the war, and continued as an ad hoc adviser: S.B. Baxter, *The Development of the Treasury, 1660–1702* (1957), pp. 126–7, 175. *Hist. Parl.*, II, pp. 758–9.

7. Commissioner of the Treasury, and a close colleague of Sir W. Coventry: *Hist. Parl.*, II, pp. 243–7.

8. Lord Keeper: Sir Orlando Bridgeman (another Magdalene man); Secretaries: Lord Arlington and Sir John Trevor. Ormond was Lord Steward and a Privy Councillor.

9. Thomson had been an Admiralty Commissioner during the Commonwealth; the other Brooke House Commissioners were chiefly interested in Treasury business.

10. 19 & 20 Car. II, c. 1, which established the Brooke House Commission and defined its terms of reference.

11. The House of Commons.

12. MS blank; date supplied from BL, Stowe MS 489, f. 250v.
13. The 'General Defence of the Navy Board' (27 November 1669, which rehearses and responds in detail to each of the eighteen 'Observations' of the Brooke House Commissioners), the 'Particular Defence' of Pepys's own conduct (6 January 1670), his letter to the King (8 January), and another of same date to the Duke of York, are printed from PL MSS in *NWB*, pp. 271–333.
14. Sir John Mennes, Comptroller of the Navy (1661–71); Col. Thomas Middleton, Surveyor of the Navy (1667–72).
15. Member of the Brooke House Commission; as Lord Mayor of London 1668–9 he was much concerned with rebuilding the City after the Fire; connected to Pepys by marriage: *Diary*, X, p. 460. *NWB*, p. xxvii, n. 5. *Hist. Parl. 1690–1715*, V, pp. 708–9.
16. The Board's main contract with Warren on 10 September 1663 had been for £3,000 worth of masts from Gothenburg, Norway and New England; Pepys had handled the negotiation, outmanoeuvring the then Surveyor (Sir William Batten) who favoured the counter-bid by William Wood. Warren's accounts were not settled until 1675: *CSPD 1663–4*, p. 270. *NWB*, pp. 9–12, 79–81, 148–54, 193. *Diary*, IV, pp. 303–4. HMC, *Lindsey*, pp. 116–54. B. Pool, *Navy Board Contracts 1660–1832* (1966), pp. 26–8.
17. This was for purchases made under commission from the King and Duke (i.e. not by contract with the Navy Board): *NWB*, pp. 174–6.
18. Pepys produced in evidence the Board's invitation to tender, sent to Wood, Warren and Capt. John Taylor on 26 July 1664: *NWB*, p. 311.
19. Of 16 August 1664: HMC, *Lindsey*, p. 147.
20. The execution at Tyburn of Claude Duval, the Dick Turpin of his day, attracted great interest.
21. Previously (*NWB*, p. 368 n. 1) understood to mean the parliamentary rule before Oliver Cromwell's protectorate, Thomson being an Admiralty Commissioner 1652–3; but this reference is more likely to be the period between Richard Cromwell's fall and the King's return (1659–60), when Thomson was again at the Admiralty: A.C. Dewar, 'The naval administration of the Interregnum, 1641–59', *MM*, XII (1926), pp. 427, 429–30.
22. The small church of St Pancras in Cheapside (destroyed in the Fire and not replaced).
23. Two years earlier Pepys had heard Brereton play the organ as an after-dinner entertainment at Carteret's house: *Diary*, IX, p. 11.
24. Sir Heneage Finch, later 1st Earl of Nottingham, at this time Solicitor-General.
25. The Navy Treasurer took 3d in the £ commission on all moneys he received from the Exchequer. Pepys noted a precedent from 1566: PL 2874, p. 367. He had acquired from John Evelyn a collection of account books of Benjamin Gonson, Navy Treasurer 1549–77 (an ancestor of Evelyn's wife): *Diary*, VI,

pp. 307–8 & n. 1.

26. The Duke of York's General Instructions to the Navy Board (1662), to which Pepys repeatedly refers; printed in 1717 as *The Œconomy of His Majesty's Navy Office.*

27. The Dutch raid on the ships laid up in the Medway, 1667.

28. The Dutch Navy was controlled by five interlocking Admiralty colleges, reflecting the federal structure of the state. Inefficiency certainly resulted, though offset during the 1664–7 war by the energetic central direction of Johan de Witt: J.R. Bruijn, *The Dutch Navy of the Seventeenth and Eighteenth Centuries* (Columbia, SC, 1993), pp. 5–12, 216–17.

29. The King knew well enough what his own expenditure had been; the yield from parliamentary votes has been calculated at £5,367,000; to this should be added £779,134 which he spent from his other revenues. But Charles seemingly much exaggerated the Dutch war expenditure, which has been reckoned about £2 million: Chandaman, *Revenue*, p. 211. J.R. Jones, *The Anglo-Dutch Wars of the Seventeenth Century* (1996), pp. 93–5. *NWB*, pp. 338 & n. 1, 401 n. 1. It is just possible that here 'late war' refers to the First War and the calculation includes losses to the Dutch merchant fleet.

30. Pay vouchers given to discharged seamen: see Introduction above, p. 2.

31. Jack Fenn, Paymaster of the Navy 1660. 8: *Diary*, X, p. 129.

32. Prince Rupert and the Duke of Albemarle, joint-commanders of the fleet in 1666.

33. The Navy Victualler.

34. Henry Slingsby, Master of the Mint and Trade Commissioner; another of this name was about to enter Court service (*Hist. Parl.*, III, pp. 439–40), but Pepys's informant is more likely to have been the senior man; in *NWB* this entry is wrongly indexed to Sir Guilford Slingsby (d. 1661).

35. John Gregory, who was to speak for the Commissioners on the 18th and final Observation.

36. Anthony Stephens, a clerk in the Navy Treasury. Pepys duly demanded an explanation from him (*Further Corr.*, pp. 263–4, where the seaman is named as John Capps, and the sum as £9 7s). Nothing more is known of the matter.

37. John Gregory was a former Exchequer official now working for the Undersecretary of State, Joseph Williamson: *NWB*, p. xxvii & n. 6.

TWO

The King's Bench Journal
20 May 1679–30 June 1680

Three years after the Brooke House proceedings, with England again at war with the Netherlands, Pepys's career moved forward. When the Test Act obliged the Duke of York, as a Roman Catholic, to resign as Lord High Admiral, the King put the office into commission and installed Pepys as Admiralty Secretary. Also in 1673 Pepys secured the seat in Parliament he had long coveted, which enabled him to promote the Admiralty's interest more effectively. His most notable achievement in these years was to secure funding for thirty new warships in 1677, when the French had replaced the Dutch as the potential maritime enemy. Pepys did not, however, find the House of Commons altogether welcoming, as has often been the case with those who arrive there with ready-made reputations. Pepys found his very election challenged by opponents of the Court, who correctly suspected that he would be an agent for the Duke of York's continuing influence in naval affairs. By extension he could be targeted as a crypto-Catholic, all the more plausibly because of his open interest in Catholic art and music. The issue was not brought to a head in 1673, and Pepys kept his seat. However, those who had made trouble for him knew that the same mud could be thrown again whenever they chose, and they would wait their time. Meanwhile Pepys contrived to make a good many new enemies with his ponderous and condescending manner. The finely-structured periods in which he had addressed the Brooke House Commission were redeployed against his fellow MPs. Quite a few of them understandably objected to Pepys's oratory in itself, irrespective of content. Rather more were worried about Catholic influence in the Navy, and concerned to monitor the increased spending to which Pepys had persuaded them.

The Opposition's chance came in 1678 when the Popish Plot erupted, a combination of authentic concern about the King's pro-French policy and bogus rumours about threats *against* the King. Pepys became personally involved when his clerk, Samuel Atkins, was accused as an accessory to the murder of the London magistrate Sir Edmund Berry Godfrey. Atkins was palpably innocent, and Pepys competently marshalled evidence to prove it when Atkins stood trial at King's Bench in February 1679. This was only a temporary respite; indeed the affair may have been no more than a rehearsal for the assault on Pepys himself. In truth even he was a relatively minor figure on the Opposition's hit-list. Pepys believed that he had long been marked down by the most masterful of the agitators, the Earl of Shaftesbury, and this interpretation has generally been accepted. Shaftesbury was certainly behind the attempt to exclude Pepys from the Commons in 1673, though Shaftesbury's biographer thinks his man was only toying with him: 'Had he really wished to ruin Pepys he could easily have done so.' It is further suggested that the Duke of Buckingham rather than Shaftesbury was behind the renewed attack on Pepys in 1679, while conceding that Shaftesbury helped to procure 'evidence' to be presented to Parliament.[1]

Attempting to run with the storm, Charles appointed Opposition leaders to a new ministry in April 1679 and to a new Admiralty Commission the following month. Pepys tried to hold on to his post, or even to be promoted to the Commission itself, but this was wholly unrealistic. Following the government reshuffle, the Commons had appointed a new Committee for Naval Miscarriages, which was filled with MPs already hostile to Pepys. Its chairman, William Harbord, was particularly anxious to see Pepys removed because he had some hopes of taking his job. Harbord's men were fed with a rag-bag of allegations, ranging from backstairs gossip about closet popery to circumstantial charges of piracy and espionage. The latter also involved the shipwright Sir Anthony Deane, a long-standing ally of Pepys and himself a Navy Commissioner.[2]

On 20 May the Miscarriages Committee reported to the Commons, and witnesses were produced at the bar of the House to read the depositions they had already sworn before the committee. First of all it was alleged that during the Third Dutch War Deane had fitted out a privateer, the *Hunter*, from the King's stores at Portsmouth, where he was then Resident Commissioner. Pepys had arranged for her Captain, Samuel Moon, to receive the standard commission of reprisal to seize Dutch ships and goods in notional compensation for injuries suffered by the English. Moon was then instructed to sail to Calais or Dunkirk and to obtain a similar commission from the French King. Although England and France were at that time allies against the Dutch, Moon persuaded himself that his instructions were improper, and resigned his command. Being nevertheless in Dunkirk on some other occasion, he had seen the *Hunter*, now commanded by Thomas Swayne, bring in as prize the *Catherine of London*. Moon also had claimed that Pepys's brother-in-law, Balthasar St Michel (himself a shareholder in the *Hunter*) took a message from the French Ambassador in London to his home government, urging that the *Catherine* be retained as prize by the French Admiralty court, despite counter-protests by the English government that she was not an enemy vessel. Moon further alleged that Deane had him clapped in irons and imprisoned, and those owning and trading in the *Catherine* claimed damages of £5,000. Deane was certainly and legitimately a shareholder in the privateer; he was not entitled to fit her out from dockyard stores, but that was a minor issue. The piratical seizure of a friendly ship was not denied, but Deane would blame this on the Captain, and Pepys declined any connection with the business.

The second charge was that Pepys and Deane had conspired in the making of various maps, plans of ships, ship models, and papers concerning the state of the Royal Navy and English maritime defences; all of which had in 1675 been handed over by Deane to the Secretary of the French Admiralty, the Marquis de Seignelay, in order to assist the Papistical Plot for invading England and overthrowing the Protestant religion. Making this announcement to the House of Commons was the man whom Pepys came to recognise as the key informer against him, John Scott. It was the first time they had come face to face, and Pepys had yet to piece together the colourful story of Scott's life, from shady beginnings in New England to the underworld of London and Paris in the 1670s. Scott has acquired some defenders, who see him as an early model of the pioneering spirit; the considered view is that 'he remains a ne'er-do-well and villain of the first order'.[3] Unwittingly, Pepys had already been on his trail after the Godfrey murder, when Scott escaped to France in disguise. Scott was already working for the Opposition leaders who were running the Plot, and there is no reason to suppose he held any personal grudge against Pepys. He was simply acting on directions from his controllers.

It was a different matter with the other witness produced by Harbord on 20 May. This was John James, Pepys's former butler, who had been sacked after being found in bed with the housekeeper. In view of the relentless adulteries which punctuated Pepys's own younger days, it seems surprising and disagreeable that he should have reacted so severely to his butler's lesser indiscretion. James was prompted to a similarly excessive but poetic revenge. His tryst had been discovered by Pepys's household musician Cesare Morelli. James claimed that it was he who had discovered Pepys and Morelli up to no good in the middle of the night, singing psalms and talking popery. Morelli had a room full of crucifixes, daggers, a *trap-door*, and other treasonable gear, and was demonstrably a Jesuit. Fanciful though this mostly was, Pepys's aesthetic tastes aroused legitimate suspicions; men were being sent to the gallows for less. So although the popery appears as no more than an embellishment to the allegations presented in the Commons, Pepys knew that it would be more difficult to rebut than the specific charges about ships and maps.

After witnesses had been heard on 20 May, Deane and Pepys were committed to the custody of the Serjeant-at-Arms, the policeman of the House. Two days later the Committee of Miscarriages presented a summary of the depositions, at which point Deane and Pepys were sent to the Tower. The second of the 'later diaries' opens with a bare record of these parliamentary proceedings. It then describes in detail the appearances made by Pepys and Deane in the court of King's Bench, where for over a year they sought to have their cases tried, or else to be discharged. Since no trial in fact resulted, the journal is a little lacking in drama. What impresses, as ever, is Pepys's ability to recall a mass of argument and to report it coherently. He would certainly have made shorthand notes during the hearings, and may have worked these up from time to time; but it is likely that the whole journal was composed as a piece, after the final hearing it records. It now forms one of the opening entries in the two-volume 'Book of Mornamont', a collection of documents relating to the accusations against Pepys and his evidence in defence.[4]

While Pepys was still a prisoner he began to compile this dossier. Once he and Deane were released on bail (9 July), the process could be accelerated; indeed it became his principal occupation for the next twelve months. The journal shows something of this activity. Pepys had lost his official residence at the Admiralty, and was lodging with his former Clerk, William Hewer, at York Buildings off the Strand. Here we find him late on the night of 26 January writing to Brussels, where his agent James Puckle had made contact with an army officer whose name Pepys thought to be Coleson. This man (actually Collinson) could testify that Scott was a maker of maps, and Pepys needed to show that it was Scott, not Deane, who had provided the French Admiralty with English naval charts. So he wanted Puckle and Collinson to come to London in time for the expected trial. The next diary, 'Proceedings with James and Harris', running simultaneously with the King's Bench Journal, shows in much more detail how Pepys went about collecting evidence and (in the case of James) trying to get a prosecution witness to change his story.

The process was complex, expensive, and uncertain. Pepys had to employ agents in France and the Netherlands, and to pay the travel and accommodation expenses of those witnesses he did manage to collect. Much of the detective work was done by St Michel – hitherto a comic turn, but now developing as a competent lieutenant.[5] There was no certainty when the trial might be, and those who were brought over from the Continent had to be sent home again when they could not be used. Even if they could be found again, Pepys was warned that the testimony of Catholics and foreigners would count for nothing with an English jury in the current public mood.

Pepys never had sight of a juror, and his army of witnesses hovers off-stage. The judges and the law officers are the dramatis personae here, and Pepys gives some instructive portraits of them. Presiding over all was Lord Chief Justice Sir William Scroggs, a man whose unsavoury reputation seems so in keeping with his awful name. His bullying and sarcastic manner is eclipsed in the public mind only by that of his subsequent successor Sir George Jeffreys. Jeffreys at least was a handsome figure, whereas Scroggs looked as nasty as he sounds. He had already conducted several of the prominent Popish Plot trials, and these were continuing. Pepys followed them closely, and had every reason to suppose that he would soon be among the Lord Chief Justice's victims. So it is a little surprising to find Scroggs portrayed as a reasonable man, even a figure of some dignity. The reason, of course, is that he gives Pepys a modest amount of encouragement. He allows Deane and Pepys bail, as 'the right of Englishmen', and repeatedly asks the Attorney-General to produce his witnesses and allow a trial to proceed. Pepys overhears him criticising the prosecution to his fellow judges ('They . . . would fox us, I think, with informations'). He later expresses his indignation in open court, refusing to admit in evidence a document which the prosecution produced without proper notice. Above all he allowed that the committal of Pepys and Deane came within the construction of the statute of Habeas Corpus, and that they were entitled to trial or discharge under its terms.

In this Scroggs was supported by Jones, J., while Dolben, J. and Pemberton, J. argued that Pepys and Deane were committed without treason or felony expressed, and were therefore outside the protection of the statute. This difference of opinion reflected the political complexion of the bench. Sir Francis Pemberton was overzealous in supporting the Plot, and was dismissed from the Bench in February 1680 because he did not curb his enthusiasm when the government wanted him to do so.[6] Sir William Dolben would lose his place in 1683, supposedly because he opposed the attack on the City's charter by writ of *quo warranto*. He was duly reinstated after the Revolution. Sir Thomas Jones was a convert to the Court in the early years of Charles II's reign, and was consistent in support of the King's policies. In particular he promoted the *quo warranto* proceedings to which Dolben had objected, and was rewarded with elevation to the Chief Justiceship of Common Pleas.[7] Pemberton is particularly disliked by Pepys for 'continued unkindness'; his brother Jones, on the other hand, seems to be more sympathetic and is treated accordingly.

The principal villains were the successive Attorneys-General, Sir William Jones and Sir Creswell Levinz. Jones was Buckingham's protégé, and generally associated with the Opposition. He continued to lead for the Crown in the Popish Plot trials until October 1679; indeed the journal provides some detail as to the circumstances of his resignation. As a back-bench MP he became active in the attempts to exclude the Duke of York from the succession.[8] Naturally, Pepys disliked him a great deal, and he retails with relish every instance of the Attorney's embarrassment in court. We have a rather ampler picture of Mr Attorney Levinz being visited at his Inn by Pepys, Deane, and Pepys's solicitor John Hayes. Levinz almost casually points out that the crimes against them would be 'very great and capital'. Pepys can have needed no reminding. Confident though he was of his own innocence and his ability to prove it, he knew that a guilty verdict was still possible, and that his best hope might be that the King would commute the sentence to beheading. This prospect was not much improved by Levinz telling him, with much regret, that bringing witnesses from France would be a waste of money.

The prosecution's problem was that they had only a single witness to the capital charge.[9] The embezzling of stores for the *Hunter* was a misdemeanour matter for the Hampshire assizes at Winchester, where it would only involve Deane. The popery allegations against Pepys were not solid enough to support a case. The only treason was the passing of naval secrets to the French, and for that only Scott's testimony could be produced. Two witnesses were necessary in a treason prosecution, and it was on the promise of being about to produce a second that the Attorneys persuaded the court to keep Pepys and Deane remanded on bail. It was not even necessary to have two witnesses to the same overt act; two such acts witnessed by separate individuals would satisfy the law. The Restoration judges took a broad view, and might interpret more or less any breach of law as a denial of the King's authority – and therefore high treason.[10] The odds were stacked against the defendant in a treason trial, who was not allowed counsel, and was not shown the indictment until the proceedings began. A second witness was nevertheless essential, and in this case the Law Officers could neither find one nor build one.[11] Pepys's energetic gathering of defence evidence undoubtedly spiked the prosecution's guns, but in the end he survived because of the law not in spite of it.

The text is here printed for the first time from the sole manuscript copy, PL 2881, pp. 45–77.

1. Haley, *Shaftesbury*, pp. 363–4, 520–1 & n. 1.
2. Deane had instructed Pepys in his early days at the Navy Office, and was a principal agent in the 1677 shipbuilding programme; he had been Navy Commissioner at Portsmouth 1672–5, and since then Comptroller of Victualling Accounts: *ODNB*. *Hist. Parl.*, II, pp. 200–1. Collinge, p. 96. *Diary*, X, p. 87. A.W. Johns, 'Sir Anthony Deane', *MM*, XI (1925), pp. 164–93.
3. Scott's career as reconstructed by Pepys is given in Bryant, *YP*, pp. 203–9. A. Marshall, *Intelligence and Espionage in the Reign of Charles II, 1660–1685* (Cambridge, 1994), pp. 223–43; quotation from p. 224, commenting on W.C. Abbott, *Colonel John Scott of Long Island, 1634–1696* (1918), L.T. Mowrer, *The Indomitable John Scott: Citizen of Long Island 1632–1704* (New York, 1960), and other accounts.
4. PL 2881–2 ('Mornamont' was Scott's imaginary castle). Many of the original papers from which the Mornamont MS was compiled survive in Bodl. MSS Rawlinson.
5. Many letters to St Michel are printed in Heath, pp. 64x155, beginning when Pepys was still in the Tower. Cf. *Diary*, X, pp. 375–6.
6. G.W. Keeton, *Lord Chancellor Jeffreys and the Stuart Cause* (1965), p. 110. Pemberton was nevertheless recalled to succeed Scroggs as LCJ in 1681.
7. *Hist. Parl.*, II, pp. 665–6.
8. *Ibid.*, II, pp. 666–8.
9. Treason was defined by a statute of 1661 (13 Car. II st. 1. c. 1), recapitulating previous legislation.
10. D. Ogg, *England in the Reign of Charles II* (Oxford, 1934), I, pp. 197–8; II, pp. 512–14.
11. Professor Haley (*Shaftesbury*, p. 521 n. 1) absolves his subject from failure to bring Pepys to trial, but it seems unreasonable to blame the Law Officers instead.

A Journal of the Principal Passages Relating to the Commitment of Sir Anthony Deane and Mr Pepys, and the Proceedings Thereon.

Easter term. May 20th, Tuesday. Sir Anthony Deane and Mr Pepys were committed by the House of Commons to their Serjeant-at-Arms.

May 22th, Thursday. Ditto, to the Tower.[1]

May 31th, Saturday. Brought by *habeas corpus* to the King's Bench, where we desired our discharge, no cause being assigned in the warrant for our commitment, and the Parliament that committed us being prorogued;[2] upon which Mr Attorney-General[3] being called upon, and being found to be sick, Mr Solicitor-General[4] informed the court that Mr Attorney-General had by his servant Mr Clare desired him to let the court know that he had as yet received no information against Sir Anthony Deane and Mr Pepys, and therefore left it to the court to determine concerning them as they should think fit. Upon which the court being at some stand, Mr Justice Pemberton[5] urged that we had been committed by the Parliament, as appeared by the Lieutenant of the Tower's return, and for matters said to be of the most dangerous importance, and that therefore it would not be fit (at this time too) for the court to discharge us till they understood the case more particularly from Mr Attorney-General, who was ordered to be sent to that he might demand information concerning it from Mr Harbord,[6] to whom Mr Williams the lawyer (a Member of the House at the Bar)[7] told the court that the House had committed it. And thereupon a rule was made for the Lieutenant of the Tower's bringing us thither again on Monday.

June 2d, Monday, being the last day of the term. We were brought again to the court, where Mr Attorney-General appearing, Mr Harbord acquainted the court with his having the charge from the House of Commons of having the informations brought in against us by Col. Scott[8] (who was then in court) to Mr Attorney-General; upon which Scott's information now delivered in upon oath was read and by him owned, with the like upon oath from Capt. Moon[9] (as I remember) and James.[10] After which our counsel and we moving for bail, Mr Attorney-General confessed that though he had two witnesses for what related to the charge of piracy and felony against Sir Anthony Deane, he had but one for the other charge of correspondence with France, wherein Mr Pepys as well as Sir Anthony Deane was concerned; but that nevertheless though one witness were not enough to found any indictment upon in the case of treason (such as this would certainly be if proved) yet it was enough for commitment, and therefore insisted upon it on behalf of the King that we should stand committed without bail until next term, urging that such a commitment could not be thought very grievous to us, the vacation being not three weeks long. To which the court appearing inclined, we pressed for our speedy trial. To which Mr Attorney-General replied, that for Sir Anthony Deane's single charge of felony it must be tried in the county in which it was committed, and undertook that it should so be at the next assizes at Winchester;[11] and that for the other wherein we were both concerned, he would endeavour to get other evidence (this was his very words, and observed so to be by Mr Wright[12] and Mr Hayes,[13] as well as myself and others) in order to its being tried the next term. Upon which we were ordered to be brought to the court again by the Lieutenant of the Tower the first day of next term.

June 20th, Friday, the first day of Trinity term. We were by rule of court brought thither again this day, where we prayed our trial. To which Mr Attorney-General answering that he was not yet ready for either, and we being told by the court that we should be tried as soon as the King's counsel were ready, we were in consideration of the warrant expressing no cause for our commitment discharged from the Tower and committed to the King's Bench[14] upon the affidavits formerly read in court from the Attorney-General.

Memorandum, that one day this term[15] Mr Attorney-General moved the court that Mr Pepys's being seen the day before, being Sunday, at Whitehall might be interpreted an escape, though by the express warrant of His Majesty by my Lord Sunderland, Secretary of State, to the Marshal of the Court to bring him to the King, which warrant was shown to the court by the Marshal for his justification.

July 9th, Wednesday, the last day of the term. We being brought by rule to the court, Mr Attorney-General owned that he had not yet any further evidence than what he had the last term, (viz.) Col. Scott's in the matter of his information against us; but hoped (that was his words) he should have another evidence in four or five days, and therefore insisted upon it that we ought not to be bailed, especially since he had now two new affidavits, which though they touched not the very matter whereof we stand accused, yet they show something that implied guilt by our endeavouring to suppress evidence, and then reads an affidavit of Harris's wife[16] touching one that enquired at her house for James as coming from Sir Richard Mason's,[17] but only pretendedly; who afterwards meeting with James is said to have offered him encouragement to forbear to pursue Mr Pepys.

Then was the other read of one Hill,[18] a founder in Houndsditch over against (as I think) Devonshire House, at whose house Scott lay in April 1677, and Scott sent him over the way to one that lived there, Gladman,[19] a tobacconist, to enquire what passed between him and a certain person who Scott said had dogged him from Covent Garden thither, and he was afterwards declared by that Gladman (I think) to be Conyers the priest[20] or a brother of his, and that his business (as he had discovered in taking a pipe of tobacco with him) was to bring about the making of Col. Scott friends with Mr Pepys.

To the former little was said more than whether the party that came on the message could be produced, and that there was nothing that James had said that I needed to trouble myself with to get suppressed.

To the latter I offered to put the issue of the whole cause upon its being proved by good witnesses that I ever conversed with or knew Conyers, or had acquaintance with any one Romish priest. I also, having a sight given me of the affidavit, took notice to the court that though it bore date but this day, yet this thing happened above two years since; and demanding the reason of it, Scott answered (as formerly he did open it in Parliament) that during the lives of Pellissary[21] and La Piogerie[22] he was under secrecy, and so was not at liberty to declare it. Upon which my Lord Chief Justice observed (with some remark) by way of question to Scott in these words: 'Why, are they both dead, then?' To which Scott answered yes.

Note here for future use that it may be fit to enquire what other dealings there have ever been between Scott and me, that I should desire to have Scott at peace with me when I could not know what had passed of the matter whereof I am accused, he having not then been at liberty to discover it.

Another, and the main reason was that the Duke was then in power,[23] who was his greatest enemy, and Mr Pepys known to be the Duke's greatest favourite and confidant, and that therefore there was no justice to be expected against him while the Duke was upon the place. Which he had no sooner said [but]* Mr Attorney-General added: 'And this, my Lord, will be allowed (I doubt not) for a good reason', or words to that effect. But it met with no such approbation from the court, my Lord Chief Justice putting them in mind that the only thing now under debate was whether bail or no bail, which Mr A.G. continued to withstand, alleging that the matter whereof we stood accused was of great moment, and being seconded with these affidavits, bail ought not to be granted, insisting upon Scott's evidence. Which being called upon from him to give a fresh account of, he insisted upon the letter he saw under my hand, which being asked, he said he knew to be mine by many things that he has since seen signed by me. Which my Lord Chief Justice took notice of, and the court (viz.) of his not knowing my hand before he saw the letter, which he permitted to pass without any objection or reply to, as being plainly surprised therewith, and suffered that discourse to go on upon the remarkableness of my hand, that it might be easily remembered. Upon which my Lord Chief Justice desiring it, I wrote my hand in court, and it was thought by them to be a remarkable hand. Though I could (but forbear it till hereafter) have shown the facility of its counterfeiting by several of my clerks, and contented myself with affirming that it had been often counterfeited abroad upon passes, and several instances sent over thereof, and that it was not impossible but Mr Scott might hereafter appear concerned therein.[24]

But here I taking occasion to note again to the court that according to Scott's own pretence his acquaintance with my hand has wholly arisen since his meeting with this letter at Paris in August 1675, and that he had owned also somewhere in his discourse this day that he had never seen my face till he saw me in the House of Commons when he came to charge me there. He had by this time reflected upon this matter and the consequence of it, and thereupon told the court they were mistaken in thinking he had said that he had never seen my hand before he saw that letter, for he had never said any such thing. Upon which the court universally, and particularly my Lord Chief Justice and Judge Dolben,[25] declared their having taken him to [? have]* plainly said it, which I also urging as a thing most true, and desiring nevertheless that since he would now have it otherwise, he should declare where and on what occasion he had before seen my hand. He answered that Capt. La Piogerie, who he said was Major of the Fleet under D'Estree[26] in our Channel, had formerly shown him twenty orders relating to the service of the war delivered to him signed by me. Upon which I presently observing to the court the impossibility of this, he having in the opening of this matter this day to the court declared that when he saw this letter of mine at Paris in August 1675, La Piogerie was then at Rochefort looking after his ship, and came not from thence to Paris till the January following, and consequently could not show him these orders before he saw this letter. Upon which the court was surprised with the convincingness of this observation, and Scott himself strucken mute with it, making no reply to it, not saying anything afterwards, but soon withdrew with shame out of the court. Mr A.G. also telling the court that this matter was handed to him from the Parliament, and that he had done his part in showing his reasons against the accepting of bail; he said that for his part he would leave it with the court to do what they saw fit in it, and so withdrew out of the court with appearance of some disorder.

Memorandum, that insisting at one time upon my right, in case they did not think it my right to have the benefit of bail, my Lord

Chief Justice did say with a good deal of openness and resolution that we were Englishmen, and God forbid we should not have the right of Englishmen. To which I adding that as I was an Englishman, so I had the honour of serving my country as a commoner in Parliament,[27] Mr A.G. replied that if Mr Pepys insisted upon any privilege as a Member of Parliament, he would undertake to answer for any breach of that privilege. Whereunto I answered that I insisted upon no privilege, but urged that particular only as a more signal instance of my being an Englishman, and in justification of my demanding my right as such, but with all submission to the court, offering to have my liberty limited to what distance they pleased from the town, so as I might not pass this hot and long vacation under confinement, and to be remanded to prison in case any additional evidence should come in, and to give in the mean time bail to whatever value the court pleased. Upon which, though Mr Justice Pemberton had during the debate let fall several expressions in our disfavour, yet the judges did unanimously assent to the allowing of my bail, declaring that my case was very different from Sir Anthony Deane's, Scott having given no positive evidence against me, but had against Sir Anthony Deane in swearing that he actually saw him at Mons. Pellissary's. And so demanding four sureties at £5,000 apiece, besides my own in £10,000, I presently gave and they accepted that bail. As they also afterwards did (beyond my hopes) of Sir Anthony Deane, upon their considering Sir Anthony Deane's earnest motion the last term, and Mr A.G.'s express promise of having his trial for the felony at Winchester the next assizes, which Sir A.D. did now again insist upon with him, while Mr Attorney-General declared it could not be, he not being yet ready for it. The like we both of us did in demanding and pressing for our trial in our joint cause before Mr A.G.'s going out of the court, he in the like manner declaring that he had not yet any more evidence and so was not yet ready for us.

Memorandum, that as soon as Mr Attorney-General's back was turned out of the court, I overheard my Lord Chief Justice say (and the like did Mr Hayes) that let the cause come from whence it would, he would see right done to every man; and turning to his brethren, said with some indignation: 'They think to impose any story upon us, and would fox us, I think, with informations; for my part I am ashamed of it' — or words of that import.

Also, that I moving for copies of the affidavits read this day (if it stood with the method of the court), Mr Attorney-General told Mr Hayter[28] that they should be given me, but seems to have forbidden it afterwards, the being denied to Mr Hayes.

Memorandum, that Mr Attorney-General not being satisfied with my pleading this 9th of July for bail, could not forbear showing his dissatisfaction with it in these words, that my eloquence and rhetoric would be more seasonable when I come to my trial. Moreover, that I asserting my Protestancy and my placing my greatest glory and felicity in being so, Scott said that as much a Protestant as I would be thought to be, he had seen a whole trunk-full of crucifixes, *Agnus Dei*,[29] &c., put up at Mons. Du Moulin's[30] at Dieppe or Calais and directed to Mr Breames at Dover,[31] who afterwards told him that they were sent to me. Upon which I offered to put my whole cause and life upon that issue, in case any such thing could be proved.

Add that Scott pretending that he had been solicited very often by several persons to be friends with Mr Pepys, and being asked who, he answered: 'By twenty'; and being urged to name some, he said that he could not presently remember any but one, and that was Lewis my clerk,[32] saying that he came to him once in a coffee-house and remembered his master's service to him, and told him that his master had a desire of friendship with him, or words to that effect.

Memorandum, that together with the other two affidavits mentioned in the beginning of this day's work, there was a third read of Scott's own, touching some words that lately should have passed between him and Col. Roper in the Tower,[33] alleging that Roper quarrelled him and threatened him in very high manner for his accusing of Mr Pepys, adding words to this effect, that Papists were not yet brought so low as to (something or other which I have forgotten) but they were — words of very ill sound, and were improved with the other affidavits by Mr Attorney-General against me to confirm my being a Papist and concerned in the matter I am accused of by the plotters' interesting themselves for me. Upon reading of which affidavit of Scott's and his owning it in court, Mr Roper (who was attending the court in the same time in the Hall upon the score of bail for himself) was called, and by and by came into the court. But the court being engaged in some other points relating to my business, nothing was asked of him, nor was I desirous unnecessarily to have Mr Roper engaged in any discourse that might make him look as a person concerned in my defence; and thereupon he happening to stand very near me, I prevented his addressing himself to the court about it, and so that matter went off, he avowing to me in private that the whole thing alleged by Scott as to what appeared blameable in him was entirely false, and he would not give way that I or any other gentleman in my condition should suffer injury upon his account. And so we departed the court at liberty with our bail, viz. Sir Richard Dutton, Mr James Houblon, Sir Thomas Beckford and Mr Pallavicini for me, with the two last and two Mr Griffiths, merchants, for Sir Antho. Deane, and so continued all the Long Vacation.[34]

Towards the end whereof we did by our solicitor Mr Hayes put Mr A.G. in mind of our trial the next term, and intimate to him our preparing ourselves for it by desiring of him the copies of the affidavits which he promised us; but now he said that he was going out of his place, and that we must now apply ourselves no more to him but to his successor, which we directed Mr Hayes and he did do, as soon as ever Sir Creswell Levinz was declared Attorney-General, which was (I think) the first or second day of the term, whose answer was that he would give us all the furtherance in our trial he could so soon as he should receive the papers relating to our cause from his predecessor.[35]

October 23, Thursday, the first day of Michaelmas term. We appeared in court, had our appearance entered, and repeating our desire of trial but without any answer from the court, the new Attorney-General not appearing there this day, so we departed with directions only to appear there again the last day of the term.[36]

Towards the latter end of this term we did several times by Mr Hayes and once got the King himself in the Council Chamber by the means of Sir Robert Southwell[37] to speak to the Attorney-General to bring our business to a trial, that we might either be tried or discharged at the end thereof; but all in vain, Scott having never appeared to him and Mr Harbord having returned answer to His Majesty by Mr Clare,[38] as Mr Attorney-General did afterwards inform Mr Hayes, that the Parliament being dissolved that gave him the care of this work, he would have no more to do with it, or to that effect.[39]

And it is also worth remembering what account Sir Thomas Clarges[40] did some time before by letter give Sir A.D. of the late Attorney-General's answer to my Lord Clarendon[41] touching our business, namely that it was nothing but clamour, and that if he had not seen it to be so he would never have given way to our being bailed.

November 28th, Friday, the last day of term. We appeared again in court, where both our counsels and I myself moved for our discharge, and that failing, pressed for our trial, which my Lord Chief Justice answered by saying that the court could do nothing in it, but that we must apply ourselves to Mr A.G. for it. Upon which one of our counsels moving that our own bail alone might be taken without continuing the others, my Lord Chief Justice answered that he was sure that our bail would not think it much to continue bound for us, and so we went away out of the court without their calling upon our bail to enter into any fresh recognizance, but suffering us and them to remain in the same condition we were in before, to the rendering it disputable with us whether our bail continues bound for us or no.

Memorandum, that fourteen days before the next term, (viz.) upon Friday the 9th of January, Sir Anthony Deane, myself and Mr Hayes went to Mr A.G. Levinz at his chamber in Gray's Inn to let him know that we did design by our counsel to move the first day of the term for our discharge, we having according to the Act demanded our trial the first and the last day of every term since our being accused. Whereto he answered that he was very well satisfied we should do so, only seemed not to have known that we had moved for our trial the first day of the last term; and in mixed discourse told us that our crime, if proved, would be judged very great and capital, and that Mr Harbord had since the last term told him that he had now another witness, but he had to this day heard nothing from him since, nor ever anything at all from Scott.[42] And when I intimated to him our great charge in fetching witnesses from France and elsewhere abroad, he presently told us with an appearance of regret on our behalf from the present malignity of the age, which begot a great many other evils, that he feared whatever witnesses were brought out of France would at this time have very little credit given them; and so, after a great deal of other like discourse and promises of all just and fair proceedings on his side, we parted.

January 23, Friday, the first day of Hilary term. A brief of our case having been prepared and delivered to each of our counsel, (viz.) Mr Holt, Mr Saunders, Mr Pollexfen and Mr Scroggs,[43] the court was moved for our being tried or discharged this term according to the Act, as having moved for our trials every time of our attending the court since our being brought first thither. To which Mr Attorney-General raised a question and was seconded therein by Mr Justice Pemberton whether, having been committed before the first of June by the Parliament, we could come within the Act. To which it was replied, and by recurring to the rules of court, it appeared that commitment as being found illegal by reason of its being *sine causâ* was made void, and we committed *de novo* by the court upon the 20th of June. That being done, my Lord Chief Justice &c. demanded of Mr Attorney-General how he was prepared to proceed against us, with words importing that we might expect to be tried or discharged this term. Upon which Mr Attorney-General desired leave (on his own behalf by preventing the world's expecting more from him in this cause than it would bear) to open to the court that he had no more evidence than Scott's in the business, which in itself, if fully proved, would be high treason, (viz.) of communicating maps and charts of our coasts, drafts of ships and the state of our fortifications to the French; but upon that evidence he could not draw up an indictment as for a crime capital. And as to the other business of the stores, which would be felony if charged upon him within a year, would be only a misdemeanour to be tried within the county. After which I took leave to observe that we made it more our business to solicit for our trial than discharge; that we had been now near a year in the hand of the court, this being the fourth term; that our adversary had laid the scene of our charge in France, and that to disprove his evidence we were driven to the charge of sending for witnesses from France, Flanders and Holland, some of whom we have had here at our expense several months, others now coming over and others, that have been here and returned, to be sent for a second time – all which being matters of great charge to us, without hopes of any amends for it; and calling for time for sending for those witnesses, I prayed the court we might have present notice whether we were to expect a trial or no, and when. Upon which at my Lord Chief Justice's desire, telling us that we should have all fitting justice, and we replied that we asked no more, Mr Attorney-General did promise to give the court an account on Tuesday next what it was that from the evidence he had he should find himself prepared to do in our prosecution. And so direction being given that our demand of trial this day should be entered, we were dismissed.

Memorandum, that after ending what I had to say, Sir Anthony Deane took notice of his having not obtained the trial so long since promised him at Winchester upon the felony, and that whereas the Lords of the Admiralty had thought fit very newly to put an additional trust upon him of being Comptroller of His Majesty's Naval Stores, he was so far from thinking himself fit to take an increase of trust upon him that he had chosen to lay down the employment he had under His Majesty rather than hold the same under so great an accusation as this is without opportunity of clearing himself thereof.[44]

Monday January the 26th. About 10 at night, as I was finishing a letter to Mr Puckle pressing him with one Capt. Coleson to repair hither immediately out of Flanders,[45] as being under some late hopes for having a trial this term, Mr Hayes came in to me from Mr Attorney-General with an answer to our message I had this day sent him by Mr Hayes to know whether I might hope for a trial this term or not, in order to my making use of this post for the sending for these witnesses, as being impossible for them to be here time enough unless I sent for them this post. To which he answered by Mr Hayes that it would be in vain for us to put ourselves to the charge of sending for any witnesses from abroad now, for that he is sure it was impossible for us to have any trial this term, nor could foresee whether we should ever have any or not, letting me also know that he should be ready tomorrow to give the court a perfect account of the state of our affair in case we should, by a motion, give him occasion for it, adding in discourse to Mr Hayes that Mr Harbord lately told him that his witnesses had declared to him that they would not give evidence in our case but while a Parliament is sitting.

Tuesday January the 27th. Sir A.D. and myself being in court with Mr Hayes and W.H. [*William Hewer*] we did by our counsel Mr Scroggs move that we might have the judgment of the court in this single point, whether we came within the late act of HABEAS CORPUS in order to our being accordingly tried or discharged this term, to which Mr Attorney-General opposed the consideration of being but under one continued imprisonment, though by divers authorities, first of the House of Commons, then of this court. But that was soon removed by recollecting the rules of the court stated and produced this day by Mr Astrey, Clerk of the Crown. But then it was observed by Judge Pemberton that now the case stood thus, that though we should be allowed to come within the Act, yet we had forfeited it by neglecting to demand our trial the first day of Michaelmas term, which was the first term after our last commitment, and [*which*] was upon the 20th of June last. Whereunto it was avowed by our counsel as well as we that we did that very day demand our trial, though we did not demand its being recorded as it is now, the letter of the Act not requiring it. Whereupon Mr Justice Jones[46] declared that in his opinion we were within the Act of Parliament and ought to be tried or discharged. But Mr Justices Dolben and Pemberton said they did not see how we could come within that Act, for that extended only to such persons as were committed for treason or felony plainly expressed in the warrant of commitment; but there was no warrant of commitment at all in this case, but only a rule of court, this Act seeming to them to have been calculated by the Parliament for relieving the subject against any extrajudicial commitments from the Council Board or suchlike, and not the ordinary commitments of this court, where it is done without warrant. To which my Lord Chief Justice answered that, though this Act might more particularly aim at such extrajudicial commitments, yet he doubted not but it had also regard to the securing the persons of the subjects against any commitments for a time indefinite, and that therefore we might expect (though committed by this court without warrant) the same relief as if we had been committed with it, especially since by the course of the court no man without extraordinary cause is denied being brought to his trial within two terms after he demands it.[47]

After which my Lord Chief Justice demanded of Mr Attorney-General an account how and when he designed to proceed to our trial. To which he answered that as to the business of the stores, Sir A.D. might expect an information to be exhibited against him as a misdemeanour at the next assizes at Winchester. But as for the treason wherein Sir A.D. and Mr P. were both concerned, he had no evidence but Scott's, and therefore could not tell how to proceed at all in that matter, either at this day or any other, there being also nobody bound to prosecute but only Moon in the case of the stores; and thereupon desired Mr Harbord, who was then (upon his summons) in court, to give the court an account how the business stood in reference to witnesses, he having not to this day seen one of them. To which Mr Harbord answered that he bore no ill will to either of us, but that what he had done was in obedience to the commands of the Parliament, as being chairman of the committee to whom the matter of the Navy was referred, and that having delivered over the papers belonging to it to the Attorney-General, he had no more to concern himself in it. Upon which my Lord Chief Justice asking Mr Attorney-General what he had heard concerning the witnesses – whether he had sent to them, whether they were ready to give in their testimony in the matter. Whereto Mr Attorney-General replied that he knew not nor could learn anything of them, nor knew where they lived, nor any evidence yet before him but what he had in paper of the first affidavits, but desired his Lordship to take satisfaction therein now from Mr Harbord, who he had desired to be here to that purpose. Which being asked of him by my Lord Chief Justice, Mr Harbord answered that since it was required of him he would tell them the plain truth, which was that where any of the witnesses lived he knew not, but that he had lately spoken with three or four of them concerning their proceedings in this business, and had received from them this answer, that they were resolved not to give any evidence therein but when the Parliament should be sitting. Upon which a general silence remaining in the court for some time, and my Lord Chief Justice and the rest of the Judges conferring privately together upon the bench, my Lord at last applied himself to Mr Attorney-General and said: 'Mr Attorney-General, my brothers and I are of opinion and do direct that you do come prepared the last day of this term to tell the court how you mean to proceed against these gentlemen the next term, whether by a trial or not, and if not, to show us a very good reason, I say a very full reason, why not, that so these gentlemen may be tried or discharged the next term. I do not say this' (says he) 'as any rule or resolution of the court, but as an intimation of the opinion of the court, that these gentlemen should not be kept in this condition under bail and with the imputation of treason upon them (which was very grievous indefinitely)'.

Memorandum, that this last expression arose from something that I took leave to say in court in reply to Mr Justice Pemberton, who among many other instances of his continued unkindness to our cause, had said to our counsel, and particularly Mr Saunders, by way of reflection: 'We know what you would be at, you would put us upon difficulties by pressing for a discharge'. To which I say I took liberty of desiring leave to remove that mistake by appealing to the court whether we ever moved for discharge till this day, though this is the fourth term since our commitment, and that we never failed at any one of our appearances here to press for a trial, and had it promised us three terms ago, and that our demanding it now is only upon condition of our not being able to obtain a trial, which we desired more than our discharge, by how much our reputations are more valuable to us than our liberties, and therefore prayed the court before all things to find some expedient for our having opportunity of clearing ourselves by a trial; but if that cannot be had, that we might not be kept in bonds without knowing when we should be quit of them, which my Lord Chief Justice said to Mr Attorney-General was very reasonably and very modestly demanded, and therefore pressed him as he did before.

Memorandum also, that I taking notice to the court of that gentleman, naming Mr Harbord, his mentioning us at this time with so much temper, I told the court that, notwithstanding all the hardships we had suffered, I did nevertheless believe that the vehemence with which he had prosecuted us in the House of Commons had arisen from his being then of a belief that the evidences he then went upon had been good, though yet they have not been proved so, nor, I was sure, ever could. To which he in short replied that, as the evidences were then given, he still owns that he could not think us persons fit to be continued in so great a trust in the government as we then were in.

Memorandum also, that Mr Justice Jones in particular did expressly declare this day that he did very well remember that Mr Attorney-General Jones did promise Sir A.D. his trial at the assizes, and that we had from term to term demanded our trial, as was asserted by ourselves and by our counsel, and particularly by Mr Saunders and Mr Scroggs.

February the 11th, Wednesday. His Majesty being pleased this day at my desire to speak to Mr Attorney-General in the Council Chamber to do his just endeavours tomorrow, being the last day of the term, to bring our business to an issue (this being the fourth term since our commitment) either by discharging us or securing us of a trial the next term, which is all we desire, he answered the King (as His Majesty was pleased afterwards to tell me) that at 6 a-clock this evening he had not received any further evidence, nor had he anything to this day from Scott or any other witness, nor from Mr Harbord, since his last being in the court the beginning of this term. The King was likewise graciously pleased to signify his desire to the same purpose lately to my Lord Chief Justice, and to direct Col. Phillips of his Bedchamber[48] to do the same from him tomorrow morning to Mr Justice Dolben before he goes to the Hall, but without the least intimation of any partiality to be desired from them, but only bringing our cause to some issue.

Memorandum, that the King told me that he would send also by Mr Chiffinch[49] to Sir Thomas Meres[50] to come to him betimes tomorrow morning before His Majesty's setting forth for Windsor, in order to his speaking also to his brother Dolben. *Q.* Whether he did or no.

February 12, Thursday, the last day of the term. We attending the court, and my Lady Powis and Sir Robert Peyton being first bailed,[51] our counsel moved for our being called into court; which being done, my Lord Chief Justice demanded of our counsel what they moved for. Who answering that we might be discharged, my Lord C.J. demanded how long we had stood committed, and being answered four terms, his Lordship applied himself to Mr Attorney-General, saying: 'Mr Attorney-General, what have you to say to these gentlemen as to the thing they move for?' Who answered that truly he had nothing to say to them more than what he said at the beginning of the term, as having not yet seen any of the witnesses nor heard anything from them that should enable him to proceed against these gentlemen, only this, that last night a paper was brought to him, in a manner very extraordinary and such as he confessed he could not be satisfied with, containing, as it would pretend, extracts of several letters from beyond the seas relating to this business, but not signed by anybody, but brought by one Goodenough,[52] an attorney, as from Col. Scott, with a pretence that Scott had been there himself to accompany him, but not finding him, the Attorney-General, at home, went away. To which Mr Attorney-General adding that he had directed this attorney to bring Scott to the court this morning, the attorney and Scott were called; and the former of them appearing, Mr Attorney-General asked him whether he had brought Scott or no. To which he answered that he had spoke to Scott to attend the court, but his answer was that he would not come. Upon which the whole court expressing great dissatisfaction, and Mr Attorney-General asking whether he should read the paper he had mentioned and which he then produced and put into Mr Hayes his hand, to be by him passed over to the Clerk of the Crown, my Lord Chief Justice, with some indignation, forbad the reading of it, saying that they could take no notice of it, being not owned by anybody. And so it was handed back to Mr Attorney-General, to whom I made an offer of a desire to see it (my design being only to observe whether it was writ by Scott or no, or by whom), but Mr A.G. declined showing it me, and I did not insist upon it. My Lord Chief Justice then applied himself to me and said: 'Why, Mr Pepys, would it be much inconvenient to you to appear again here the next term?' and therein being with a great deal of respect and gentleness seconded by Mr Justices Jones and Dolben (Judge Pemberton not speaking one word good or bad all this day in our business), I replied that it would be very inconvenient, first in regard of the greatness of our bail and the keeping of our friends so much the longer in bonds for us, which we above all things desired they might be eased of; and next, that being now wholly unconcerned in public business, my affairs did call me very earnestly into the country, where I had not of many years been to look after them. To the former of which the court answered they would wholly discharge our bail and take our single obligation for our appearance. To the other, that if the next term were too soon, we should take the first or the last day of the term following. Upon which I asked my Lord's leave to demand what assurance we should have then more than now of being fully discharged. Whereto he replied (with some fresh expressions of respect) that as to any assurance, the court could give us none, but that from their present proceedings we might very well judge what the inclinations of the court would be to do then. Upon which, considering the first treatment the court showed us and the ill constructions and possibly worse success of our pressing the court to do anything in our favour unwillingly, our obtaining one principal point of having our bail discharged, and lastly the credit of that greatened by our declining to insist upon more, what probability we might have had it, I thought advisable, especially being pressed by Sir A.D.'s urging me privately and with repetitions to take it, take it, take it, and then reflecting also that if the Parliament sits in April, as I would not be brought upon the stage in the very beginning of their heats (which would probably be just in the next term, they being prorogued to the middle of April), so I would not be thought to be afraid of being tried while a Parliament is sitting, any more than at any other time, I made answer to the court that we would be contented to be obliged to appear the first day of Trinity term, which is the 12th day of June. Upon which the court seemed very well pleased with our compliance with them therein, discharged us and our bail of our former recognizances, amounting to £60,000, and took fresh from us in one thousand pounds each for our appearance there accordingly the first day of Trinity term. For which thanking the court, we departed.

Memorandum, that enquiring afterwards of Mr Hayes touching the hand in which the forementioned paper is wrote, he tells me that he observed it well (though he had not time to read the contents of it) and knows it to be wrote by the hand of Goodenough the attorney, from whom he has some expectation of getting a copy of it.

Pepys's first-person narrative ends here. There follows (pp. 78–83) A brief of the case of Sir Anthony Deane and Mr Pepys stated for their counsel,53 which summarises the proceedings hitherto recounted, and (p. 82) extends to their conclusion:

June 7th 1680, Monday. Notice was given Mr Attorney-General by their attorney that they would move the first day of Trinity term for their discharge.

Trinity term 1680. June 11th, Friday, the first day of the term. They appeared and were prevented in their intended motion for their discharge by my Lord Chief Justice's telling them that their appearing should be recorded, and that motions for discharge are to be respited to the proper day (viz.) the last day of the term.

June 26th, Saturday. Mr Attorney-General was attended by their attorney, Mr Hayes, to advise him of their designing to move for their discharge the last day of the term, which he appeared very willing they should do.

June 30th, Wednesday. The last day of the term. They appeared in court, and upon their motion for being discharged, the Lord Chief

Justice asked Mr Attorney-General what he had to say against it. Who answering that he had nothing more than what he had told the court formerly, the court, without any more words at all on any side, told them they were discharged, and directed them to depart, which they accordingly forthwith did.[54]

There follows (p. 83) a memorandum about others discharged, or refused discharge, at the same time.

1. *CJ*, IX, pp. 626, 628.
2. Before the Habeas Corpus Amendment Act of 1679 (31 Car. II c. 2) only those imprisoned by specific warrant might sue for the writ of *habeas corpus*, by which they could be brought before the courts. On the writ itself see E. Jenks, 'The story of the *Habeas Corpus*', *Law Quarterly Review*, XVIII (1902), pp. 64–77. For the 1679 statute see W.S. Holdsworth, *A History of English Law* (1922–64), IX, pp. 112–25; *The Stuart Constitution*, ed. J.P. Kenyon (Cambridge, 1966), pp. 424–6, 430–2. Parliament stood prorogued since 27 May, and was dissolved without further assembly.
3. Sir William Jones, AG 1675–9.
4. Heneage Finch, 2nd son of the 1st Earl of Nottingham, and himself cr. Earl of Aylesford 1714: *Hist. Parl.*, II, pp. 322–4.
5. Sir Francis Pemberton, JKB 1679–80, LCJ 1681–2, CJCP January–September 1683: Foss, pp. 507–9.
6. William Harbord (alias Herbert), chairman of the Commons committee for enquiring into the miscarriages of the Navy: *Hist. Parl.*, II, pp. 482–8.
7. William Williams, barrister of Gray's Inn; Speaker 1680–1, SG 1687–9: *Hist. Parl.*, III, pp. 731–5.
8. John Scott, Pepys's principal accuser; his deposition dated 7 June is in PL 2881, pp. 17–20. For his claim to military rank see Ollard, *Pepys*, pp. 248–9.
9. Samuel Moon, former Captain of the *Hunter* sloop; his deposition dated 4 June is in PL 2881, pp. 21–3.
10. John James, formerly Pepys's butler; his deposition to the House of Commons [n.d., but delivered 20 May 1679], is in PL 2882, pp. 1181–5. His evidence is the subject of the next diary.
11. Assize town for Hampshire, the alleged offence having occurred at Portsmouth in that county.
12. Serjeant Robert Wright of Lincoln's Inn, Counsel for the Navy; Kt 1680, JKB 1685–7, LCJ 1687–8: *Hist. Parl.*, III, pp. 766–8.
13. John Hayes, Pepys's solicitor.

14. The King's Bench prison (the Marshalsea in Southwark). An observer reported the prisoners' return there, pending Deane's appearance at the Hampshire assizes and Pepys's trial at the end of the current term: *CSPD 1679–80*, p. 185 (John Speke to his brother, 21 June).

15. This was on 30 June: Sunderland's warrant to the Marshal of King's Bench required Pepys to be brought to the King at Whitehall on the afternoon of 29 June, which was Sunday: *CSPD 1679–80*, p. 190.

16. Mary, wife of the Admiralty porter Alexander Harris; her deposition dated 8 July is in PL 2881, pp. 29–30.

17. James had come to Pepys's employment by Mason's recommendation: *ibid.*, p. 265.

18. George Hill; his deposition dated 3 July: *ibid.*, pp. 33–4.

19. John Gladman; his deposition dated 8 July: *ibid.*, pp. 35–6.

20. George Conyers, SJ, whom Hill named in connection with the betrayal of naval secrets; but since (according to Titus Oates) Conyers was to be the actual assassin of the King, this conveniently linked Pepys to the centre of the Plot: cf. Kenyon, *Popish Plot*, pp. 64–5.

21. Georges de Pellissary, *seigneur* de la Vourdasière, late Treasurer-General of the French Navy; for his contacts with Scott see PL 2881, pp. 237–40, 515–17.

22. Louis Heroüard, *sieur* de La Piogerie, late *Major de la Marine*: PL 2881, pp. 515–17. Heath, p. 68 n. 3.

23. Before the Duke of York resigned public office following the passage of the Test Act in 1673.

24. Pepys's handwriting is certainly distinctive (and uncharacteristic of an otherwise obsessively tidy man).

25. Sir William Dolben, JKB 1678–83, 1689–94: Foss, p. 224.

26. Jean, *comte* d'Estrées, Vice-Admiral of France; commanding the white squadron in the combined Anglo-French fleet of the Third Dutch War.

27. Pepys entered the Commons as MP for Castle Rising in 1673; in 1679 he was sitting for Harwich.

28. Thomas Hayter: see below, p. 105 n. 11.

29. Any image of Christ as the paschal lamb; specifically one cut in wax and blessed by the Pope.

30. A Mlle des Moulins was one of Pepys's French sources, but this possibly refers to Pierre Du Moulin, a Huguenot employed by Willem III as a propagandist and secret agent: Heath, p. 98 and *passim*. K.H.D. Haley, *William of Orange and the English Opposition, 1672–4* (Oxford, 1953).

31. Walter Breames, Kent JP: *Calendar of Assize Records, Kent Indictments, Charles II, 1676–1688*, ed. J.S. Cockburn (1997), p. 88.

32. Phelix Donluis alias Lewis: Sainty, p. 137 (recorded by surname only).

33. William Roper; Scott's deposition dated 8 July, and Roper's response dated 11 February 1680, are in PL 2881, pp. 25–8.

34. Houblon, a Huguenot merchant, and Peter Pallavicini were among Pepys's oldest friends. Beckford sold slops (clothes) to the Navy. The granting of bail was derided in a ballad distributed by the Opposition (quoted Bryant, *YP*, pp. 276–7).

35. Jones gave health and family reasons for his resignation, but was also said to be weary of the Popish Plot prosecutions; he was later a prominent exclusionist: *Hist. Parl.*, II, pp. 666–9. Levinz was KC 1678, JCP 1680–6: Foss, p. 406.

36. Harbord was also absent. Pepys was encouraged to think that if the prosecution continued silent, he should be automatically discharged: Howarth, p. 89.

37. Clerk of the Privy Council; a friend of Pepys since the 1660s: see *Diary*, X, p 401.

38. The Attorney's servant.

39. Parliament had been dissolved on 12 July.

40. MP and member of the committee to enquire into the Popish Plot, in which he was a firm believer: *Hist. Parl.*, II, pp. 74–81.

41. Henry Hyde, who succeeded his father (the former Lord Chancellor) in 1674.

42. Pepys told the Duke of York (6 January) about Harbord's dealings with Levinz: Howarth, pp. 90–1.

43. John Holt, barrister of Gray's Inn, Kt 1686, LCJ 1689; Edmund Saunders, LCJ and Kt 1683; Henry Pollexfen, bencher of the Inner Temple, AG 1689, CJCP 1689–91;Wiliam Scroggs, son of the LCJ, followed his father as barrister and (1681) bencher of Gray's Inn; Kt 1681: *ODNB* (Scroggs). *Hist. Parl.*, II, p. 572 (Holt); III, pp. 259–61 (Pollexfen). Foss, pp. 585–7 (Saunders).

44. In fact Deane was appointed Comptroller of Storekeepers' Accounts on 30 April 1680, but resigned from this (and so from the Navy Board) on 29 July, claiming (by letter of 27 July) that he had only then obtained the King's permission for 'retirement': Collinge, p. 96; PLB 52.

45. James Puckle had supplied Pepys with information about Scott's frauds; he had written from Brussels on 24 January, and wrote again from Bruges on 9 February. 'Coleson' was Capt. Robert Collinson, who had supplied information about Scott's manufacture of maps (27 June 1679): PL 2882, pp. 709–11, 835–7 (cf. pp. 819–33).

46. Sir Thomas Jones, JKB 1676–83, CJCP 1683–6: *Hist. Parl.*, II, pp. 665–6.

47. 31 Car. II, c. 2 (*Statutes of the Realm*, V, pp. 935–8). Clause 3 ruled that one who *willingly neglected by the space of two whole terms after his imprisonment* to request a writ of *habeas corpus* should not have it granted in vacation time. Clause 6 allowed that if those committed for high treason or felony *plainly expressed in the warrant of commitment* were not indicted in the term following confinement, the court might discharge them upon bail.

48. Robert Phillips, Groom of the Bedchamber 1661–85: Sainty and Bucholz, I, p. 153.

49. William Chiffinch, Page of the Bedchamber 1666–88, Charles II's most trusted close attendant: *ibid.*, I, p. 86.

50. MP and member of the committee to enquire into the Popish Plot; Commissioner of the Admiralty 1679–84: *Hist. Parl.*, III, pp. 48–59. In 1674 he had shown some sympathy towards Pepys over the accusations then made of his owning Catholic artefacts: Grey, *Debates*, II, p. 430.

51. The Countess of Powis and Peyton had been implicated in a sub-plot known as the 'meal-tub conspiracy': Kenyon, *Popish Plot*, pp. 189, 190, 199. Cf. *Mr Tho. Dangerfield's second narrative . . . against the Lady Powis* (1680) and *A true narrative of the Popish-plot . . . with . . . transactions of Sir Robert Peyton* (1680), in Pepys's collection of 'Narratives and Tryals': PL 2251(10, 12).

52. Richard Goodenough, a republican, among the accused in *The tryal . . . For the riot at Guild-hall, on Midsommer-day, 1682* (1683): PL 2252(32). Later involved in the Rye House and Monmouth conspiracies: *ODNB*.

53. Two incomplete drafts of 'A brief of the case' survive in Bodl. MS Rawlinson A. 173, ff. 83–99, along with the writs for appearance in court and other materials from which the longer journal must have been compiled.

54. As reported in *London Gazette*, no. 1525 (28 June–1 July).

THREE

Proceedings with James and Harris
24 January–10 April 1680

he scene shifts from the large magnificence of Westminster Hall to a
modest house, still within sound of the Abbey bell. Here John James,
Pepys's sometime butler and latterly his accuser, is dying of tuberculosis in
the bed he must still share with his widowed mother and his unmarried
sister. The following diary tells how Pepys secured from the dying man a
retraction of what he had told the House of Commons. James is therefore
the central character, and an unattractive one. He is revealed as an
unprincipled rogue, ready to sell himself first to one side then to the other.
Only in his last days does he show some courage. The best said of his life
before then is his mother's proud assertion that he was a good butler.

Perhaps he found it a dull business after his early adventures. James had
served during the Second Dutch War, and continued in the Navy thereafter.
In February 1670 his ship the *Sapphire* had joined Sir Thomas Allin's
squadron in the Mediterranean. Three months later, outward bound from
Messina, she encountered four vessels which were thought to be Algerine
corsairs. Rather than stand and fight, the *Sapphire*'s Captain ran his ship
aground off Cape Pessaro, where she broke up. Early reports suggested that
the officers and crew connived in this cowardly act, and then sold what
they could of the ship and her ordnance to the locals. A different story
emerged when the Captain and Lieutenant were court-martialled on their
return to England. The decision to run from what in fact were friendly
ships had been theirs alone, and had been contested by the master and the
crew ('God blesse you, Master, let us fight them' was their cry). So the
Captain and Lieutenant were executed. Meanwhile some of the crew had
been kidnapped by real pirates, though others were reported safe in July.[1]

James made his escape, and on his return was found work by Sir William
Coventry. Presumably he also then served Sir Richard Mason, Clerk
Comptroller of the Greencloth, by whom he was directly recommended to
Pepys. His naval record, especially as one of the *Sapphire*'s men, must have

impressed these successive employers. And there is no reason to suppose that he did not competently exchange the cutlass for the corkscrew. But then, as Pepys told the Commons, it was 'his ill luck to fall into an amour with my house-keeper'. We might think his luck actually ran out because the musician Morelli was prowling about the house at 3 o'clock on a Sunday morning. James was summarily dismissed, and Pepys suspected that he returned to the house to pilfer some loose cash. James subsequently denounced Pepys and Morelli to the House of Commons as popish suspects.[2]

A month after Pepys had been arrested James received a testimonial from the Duke of Buckingham, recommending him for the post of storekeeper at Woolwich dockyard. Buckingham calls James his servant, and seems to have fed him, though this did not necessarily mean he was permanently employed in his household. James was certainly on the party payroll, because he was soon making weekly withdrawals at a Fleet Street bank on the account of the MP William Harbord. It was Harbord, as chairman of the committee investigating the Navy, who had directed the attack on Pepys.

Harbord himself features prominently and unappealingly in the diary. In public he protested his reluctance to bring an accusation against Pepys ('a man I have lived well withal'). They were certainly well acquainted, but had never been friends. Harbord's younger brother Charles had been much favoured by Pepys's own former patron, Lord Sandwich. Pepys thought him lazy, and prevented his appointment to a post in the Tangier administration. Pepys and the Harbord family were briefly united in mourning when Sandwich and Charles Harbord died together at Sole Bay (1672). William Harbord became one of Pepys's most frequent parliamentary critics during the 1670s, and his appointment to chair the 1679 committee followed naturally from that. Writing to the Duke of York from the Tower on 9 June, Pepys had blamed his troubles squarely on Harbord.[3]

James boasted that he enjoyed the patronage of Buckingham and the other great Whigs whose interest Harbord and his committee served. By the end of the year, as the Plot began to fade without Pepys being brought to trial, James found that his grand friends lost interest in him, and his allowance was stopped. So he turned against his recent paymasters, and began to regret that he had testified against Pepys for their benefit. This much he confided to one of Pepys's Admiralty clerks, Phelix Donluis, who early in the New Year made a formal statement of what James had said to him, expletives not deleted.[4]

Pepys must therefore have been expecting some approach from James, and when shortly afterwards he was told by intermediaries that a third party wanted to help him in some mysterious way, he soon suspected that James was behind it. He was reluctant to see him, not least because the middlemen, John and Alexander Harris, were themselves uncongenial. John had been Admiralty porter until (as explained here) Pepys dismissed him for some unstated offence. Alexander was still employed as head messenger at the Admiralty, though clearly at odds with Pepys over his remuneration. The brothers began by rehearsing their own grievances before revealing the main purpose of their call, which was to arrange a meeting between Pepys and James.

The diary which Pepys now begins is dedicated to this specific business between himself, James and the Harris brothers, and concludes with James's death. It again forms part of the Mornamont volumes. That compendium and the contributing MSS in the Rawlinson collection contain material for several such individual episodes, as Pepys amassed evidence from a wide range of sources. Only the James matter is set out in the form of a diary, which demonstrates the importance which Pepys attached to it.[5] Its scope is therefore even more limited than the King's Bench Journal. Yet it does diverge just a little from the business in hand, and contains some social details which recall in a modest way the enthusiasms of the great Diary. Pepys bustles about London and Westminster much as he did in the 1660s, dealing with his bookseller and stationer, walking in the pleasure gardens, and attending the theatre. He twice mentions the plays he saw: Etherege's *She Would if she Could*, an old favourite, and Thomas Otway's *The Orphan*, which was new. This diary is establishing evidence for both productions. He was often in the company of his friends the Houblon family, and had a little group of female devotees. Just once he tells us what he had for dinner, and twice he uses the phrase by which the great Diary is most often mimicked: 'And so to bed'. More significantly he was keeping up contacts with old friends: James Pearse the surgeon and the Cromwellian courtier Edward Rolt, and big City men such as Sir Robert Vyner and Sir John Banks. He also went freely to St James's Palace to pay his respects at the coming and going of the King and his brother. All this, it should be remembered, was while he was on bail, with a treason trial looming among his future engagements.

Pepys may have added the ancillary details to this diary casually, instinctively reverting to a habit once so familiar. More probably he wanted corroboration of times and places. In the process he has enhanced the interest of the piece without disturbing the coherence of the main narrative. That remains a little complicated, and may be summarised as follows.

Pepys meets James on 27 January, stipulating that Will Hewer should be present. At this first interview very little of substance emerges. James seems uncertain what stance to take. He admits the sexual misconduct which led to his dismissal, but denies the charge of subsequent burglary, and complains that Pepys did not give him a reference. He says that he was suborned to make the popery allegation in the Commons. In the process he makes a nice distinction between his readiness to lie to Parliament, and his abhorrence of formal perjury. At the same time he boasts of having organised the piracy charge against Pepys and Deane. Coming at last to his point, he claims that Scott and others are about to launch new and more damning charges. In return for revealing their plans he asks that the Harrises be paid the arrears they claimed, and that he himself should be given employment in the Navy. Even more grandly (as is later recalled), he says it is in his power to make Pepys of greater consideration in the world than ever before. In the face of all this Pepys is understandably wary. He explains that he can promise no material rewards, but would be glad for any information which James might pass to him.

This was a poor start for James, and Harris reported (30 January) that he was dithering all the more between contrition and bravado. Pepys stood firm, and again said that while he would welcome news of his enemies' intentions, he would not put himself in anyone's debt for that sake. When James himself appeared again (6 February) he began by asking coyly if it was in order for a parliamentary committee to meet in private session at a Fenchurch Street tavern. Here Harbord and others had colluded with the merchants involved in the *Hunter* to bring the piracy charge; James is now just informing, no longer claiming to have originated the business. He then asks yet more innocently if it is usual for MPs to pay witnesses. He admits receiving money at various times from Harbord and his agent Col. Mansell, but denies that regular sums had been paid to him at Harbord's bank. Although qualified, this was solid evidence, and James had helpfully kept the details in his pocket-book.

The next Pepys heard (25 February) was that James was gravely ill, and wanted a complete reconciliation before he died. James also offered to make a further and more substantial revelation to Hewer. Hewer was away, and several other names had to be canvassed. James rejected Pepys's other nominees because he decided a lawyer was needed; the lawyer Pepys found said it should be a JP, and the JP proposed was rejected by Harris as being too close with the Whigs. Pepys eventually engaged his old friend Thomas Povey, who took a deposition from James on 2 March. This (although

Pepys does not say so at the time) contained the vital information about receiving payments from Harbord.

Pepys now had some reason to be grateful to James, and responded by making arrangements for him to receive the sacrament. James had thought to ask the nearest clergyman, but Pepys (always going for the best) called in Westminster Abbey in the person of Canon Adam Littleton. He ministered to James on 6 March; Pepys notes that James's mother also communicated, though a Dissenter. James himself may well have been of the same religion.

For the next few days Pepys has other preoccupations. He does, however learn an additional and alarming story about a scheme to kidnap Hewer (8 March). Hewer visits James the following day with a second charitable gift from Pepys; James admits to him, with evident embarrassment, that he was privy to the proposed kidnapping. Meanwhile the news of James's confession had reached and infuriated Harbord (10 March). He was of course most concerned by the allegation that he had bribed James to testify against Pepys. He made the extraordinary proposal that all interested parties should hold a conference at James's bedside. All this was reported by Harris to Hewer, and by him (early on 11 March) to Pepys.

The proceedings in James's house on the morning of 11 March are the centrepiece of the diary. Harbord was massively attended by two divines, two JPs, two MPs, a clerk, and 'others'. With Pepys were his usual minders: Hewer, Povey, and his solicitor, Hayes. James still asserted the truth of his deposition to Povey, but was persuaded to sign another paper (which Harbord had ready) withdrawing the allegation of bribery, and saying that the moneys he had from Harbord were simple charity. Though Pepys cannot have believed this for a minute, he recognised the *quid pro quo*. Harbord generously said he did not contest James's withdrawal of the popery accusation. So Pepys was cleared of that, and Harbord himself was cleared of bribery; James had made his peace with both of them. Harbord suggested he and Pepys should each give James two guineas, which they did (or rather borrowed from Povey for the purpose).

This was not the end of it, because Harbord and others went to James again, angrily demanding that he sign another document, alleging that Alexander Harris had bribed him to go to Pepys (14 March). James, to his credit, refused to be intimidated. Pepys was annoyed by a newspaper article which referred to James's informal first deposition as an affidavit (17 March). Hewer visited James (19 March) and they agreed the text of a correction for the paper. On the following morning James died. The same day his mother brought Pepys the crucial pocket-book. A week later Pepys has the mother and her daughter to dinner; Mrs James says what she can in her son's defence, and gives Pepys some further useful information. She comes back (7 April) asking for money. Pepys takes time to consider; he has already been charitable, and must have feared repeated appeals. There might also be counter-allegations of bribery. But it was Easter Eve, so he paid up, remembering to ask for a false receipt.

Such were Pepys's proceedings with James and Harris. Like all the Mornamont papers it was wasted effort in the sense that Pepys never needed to produce the evidence so laboriously collected. That was not realised when Pepys closed this little diary. Reference back to the King's Bench Journal will place the piece in its larger context; Pepys was still not out of trouble.

The text, which has not been published in full before, is taken from the only copy, PL 2882, pp. 1189–1235. Some sections are little more than jottings, incorporated raw into the text as they came to hand (10, 11 March). Pepys is also sometimes referred to in the third person (as 'S.P.'). This was not his normal practice, except where he uses his initials along with others to indicate those present at a meeting, or the signatories to some other document.[6] The sections using 'S.P.' may reflect some intermediate process in composition among Pepys and his clerks. Or perhaps he was simply influenced by the great quantity of initials already on the page. Although the surviving MS is not in Pepys's hand, it was undoubtedly written up at his direction. But he evidently did not trouble to go through it and enforce a uniform style. Had he done so he might well have edited out the ladies and the lobster pie; so we must be grateful that on this occasion he left us an unfinished article.

1. PL 2882, p. 1273 (Buckingham to Sir Thomas Lee and Edward Vaughan, 30 June 1679). *CSPD 1670*, pp. 83, 189, 222, 285, 331, 396. W. Laird Clowes, *The Royal Navy: A History from the earliest times to 1900* (1897–1903), II, pp. 439–40 (wrongly placing the incident in 1671). Davies, *Gentlemen and Tarpaulins*, p. 101 (citing court martial of the officers of the *Sapphire* [Capt. John Pearce and Lt Andrew Logan], PRO, HCA 1/9, f. 155).

2. James's dismissal must have been after early 1675 when Morelli joined Pepys's household (Bryant, *YP*, p. 139), but was probably much more recent. If so, this would also apply to James's claimed attendance on the Prince of Orange, perhaps on Buckingham's behalf.

3. Grey, *Debates*, VII, p. 304. *Priv. Corr.*, I, pp. 10–11. *Diary*, IX, pp. 374 & n. 2, 418–19, 422; X, pp. 167–8. Bryant, *YP*, pp. 77, 165, 195. *Hist. Parl.*, II, pp. 482–8.

4. PL 2882, pp. 1237–44 (deposition of P. Donluis, 12 January 1680).
5. The 'Mornamont' MSS also contain a diary by one of Pepys's informants, John Joyne: cf. below, pp. 106–7 n. 29.
6. Surviving drafts for the personal Diary use some initials, but are written in the first person: *Diary*, IX, pp. 224–43.

JOURNAL OF MR PEPYS'S PROCEEDINGS WITH JAMES AND HARRIS.

A Journal commencing upon Saturday the 24th of January 1679/80, containing an account of all passages relating to the information given me by Harris and James.

Saturday January the 24th. Sir A.D. [*Anthony Deane*] having two or three times of late told me that John Harris (after his not succeeding with me in his frequent applications for my favour in getting him paid the arrear of wages due to him from the King as porter at Derby House,[1] I having put a brand upon him as discharged for misdemeanour) had been at his house to solicit him for his reconciling of me, professing his innocence and offering from his brother Alexander a readiness of his also to write upon him, which both the brothers had a day or two before together done, Sir A.D. being abroad, and signified the same to him by a note left to that purpose (which Sir A.D. keeps), and afterwards came again, he being within, where Alexander Harris did expressly tell Sir A.D. (Belbin his clerk[2] being in the room writing, and hearing it) that he could discover that that would do him and me more good than anybody else could, and that if he would bring about a good understanding between me and him, that he might have right done from the King in what was due to him, he would do us this justice, owning that he had several times let fall words to this effect to Thomas Beckwith and Marratt the porter,[3] to the intent and with an expectation that they should and would give me notice of it, and I thereupon be moved to give him opportunity to come to me. I say this having happened beforehand, as introductory to what follows, and I coming home late, I found Sir A.D. there, who telling me that both the Harrises had been here to speak with me and had left notice to be sent to at Derby House when I came in, Sir A.D. sent

72

1. Copy of a portrait medallion of Pepys, displayed in the Pepys Library. The original, carved on ivory by Jean Cavalier, 1688, is in the possession of the Clothworkers' Company, Pepys's livery. *(The Master and Fellows of Magdalene College, Cambridge)*

2. Charles II. Mezzotint by Richard Tompson, inserted by Pepys in his copy of Titus Oates, *A True Narrative of the Horrid Plot and Conspiracy of the Popish Party* (1679) [PL 2249(1)]. The original has been accidentally reversed (as evident from the position of the Garter insignia, though the lettering on the garter itself reads correctly); as a result the King appears with a shifty expression. In this reproduction the image is turned, and the King recovers his normal composure. *(Pepys Library)*

3. James II. The only English monarch to have commanded a modern fleet action. Engraving by Pieter van der Banck, 1685, after Sir Godfrey Kneller, in Pepys's collection [PL 2978, pp. 110–11]. *(Pepys Library)*

4. Sir Thomas Jones. One of the Justices of King's Bench before whom Pepys appeared in 1679–80. Engraving from life, 1685 (as Chief Justice of Common Pleas), by Robert White, in Pepys's collection [PL 2980, p. 164b]. *(Pepys Library)*

5. Sir Richard Haddock. Shipwright and Navy Commissioner. Mezzotint by William Faithorne, jun., after Johann Baptist Closterman, in Pepys's collection [PL 2979, p. 234b]. *(Pepys Library)*

6. Sir Anthony Deane. Shipwright and Navy Commissioner. One of Pepys's closest colleagues. Pen and ink drawing, ? after Kneller, in Pepys's collection [PL 2979, p. 127b]. (Pepys Library)

7. Lawrence Hyde, 1st Earl of Rochester. Son of Lord Chancellor Clarendon, and himself Lord Treasurer to Charles II and James II. He arranged the funding of the 1686 Special Commission. Mezzotint by Isaak Beckett after Kneller, in Pepys's collection [PL 2979, p. 37b]. (Pepys Library)

8. Thomas Ken, Bishop of Bath and Wells. Senior chaplain at Tangier. Engraving (as one of the Seven Bishops, 1688) by John Drapentier (? Drapentière), in Pepys's collection [PL 2980, p. 300]. *(Pepys Library)*

9. George Legge, 1st Baron Dartmouth. Commanded the expedition to evacuate Tangier 1683–4. Portrait by an unknown artist. *(National Portrait Gallery)*

10. The *Britannia*. The only 1st-rate of the 1677 programme, built at Chatham by Sir Phineas Pett and launched in 1682. She was notoriously unstable (Fox, *Great Ships*, pp. 169–70, 174). Pen and ink drawing by Willem van de Velde the Elder, c. 1685. *(National Maritime Museum)*

11. The *Grafton*. One of the 3rd-rates of the 1677 programme, built at Woolwich by Thomas Shish and launched in 1679. The ship in which Pepys sailed to Tangier in 1683 (Fox, *Great Ships*, p. 175). Pen and ink drawing by Willem van de Velde the Younger, *c.* 1685. *(National Maritime Museum)*

his boy thither from himself, only to tell A.H. that I was come home. Upon which A.H. and his brother came, and I alone spoke with A.H. apart in the great parlour below. Where, after my asking him his intention in what Sir Anth. Deane had told me of his inclination to speak with me, he begun with taking notice of the long unkindness that he had observed he had fallen under from me, my showing him no countenance, my giving way to his being pinched in the profits of his place (by which I found he meant the twelve-pence for every pass, which was complained of in Parliament among other charges to be exacted for his particular upon every pass), my making no provision for the payment of what was due to him from the King upon his accounts in my hands, nor so much as what might enable him to satisfy the money he had borrowed of me. To which I answered that the first and only thing I took ill of him was the untruth that he told the Lords of the Committee[4] touching words of mine* upon the business of Atkins.[5] Whereto he replied that others of my servants, naming Thomas Beckwith, had been with the Lords before he was, and he believed had said things as little to my advantage as he. For the other particulars I shortly and calmly told him that he had no reason to expect kindness from me, and that for doing of him wrong I never did nor nothing should provoke me to do it towards him or any man. After which he told me that I had received a great deal of wrong and that he had a great deal of inward trouble for it, and that more was yet designed to be done me, and also Sir A.D. and Mr Hewer; speaking concerning the last, that one Mrs Wood had declared to him that great sums of money had passed her hand relating to him, which she would declare when the Parliament sat, which I told him was a foolery. He went on to tell me that he was determined with himself to do us for the future all the right he can, with an expectation that he and his brother should have the benefit of my kindness towards the obtaining of their satisfaction, but without making any other express condition with me for this service than this, viz. that forasmuch as he was not able to perform this service to us without one person more, he would oblige me to promise upon my honour to forgive one man whoever he was that he should name, whatever wrong he had done me, he declaring with great earnestness and some observation that he would himself perish rather than expose this person to any inconvenience by bringing him to do me this good office. At which, being under some surprise for fear it should be [*John*] James, and expressly telling him that I should be sorry it should prove him, and he thereupon peremptorily replying that it was one he could do nothing without, nor would name him till I have given him the promise he asked, I did tell him that out of my reliance of having the benefit of the justice he told me this man could and would do me, I would and did promise him it, and would make my promise good. With which he being satisfied, he told me that within two or three days he would bring the person to me, without at present naming him, adding that he hoped that I would be so kind to him as to assist him in getting so much right done him, at least as might enable him to clear his debt to me, that he might be discharged of that (whatever became of the rest) that was due to him from the King, and that I would do the like in assisting his brother in getting his arrears paid, which I answered by saying that they were not to expect any promise from a man in my circumstances but what was to be done by me as a man of justice they might look for; and so we parted.

Tuesday January the 27th. Coming home at night after I had carried my cousin Wynne Houblon[6] home from a play ('She would if she could'),[7] W.H. told me that A.H. had been here to speak with me, and said that he had the person near hand whom he was to bring along with him, and that he would go to a coffee-house hard by; and accordingly he by and by did come again and brought James along with him; but before I would speak with the latter I sent for A.H. alone into the little parlour to me and told him that I should be loath to speak with James without somebody else with me, and prayed him to tell James so, and know whether he would be contented that Mr Hewer or anybody else should be witness of what passed between us. Which A.H. doing by stepping out to James, he returned and told me that he was very willing Mr Hewer should be by. And accordingly W.H. and I with A.H. and James being together in the little parlour, I begun with observing to James what had passed lately between A.H. and me. To which J. replied with beginning (as A.H. at first did) with a repetition of the injury I had done him saying that the only fault for which I put him away (meaning as I suppose about my woman) was indeed true, but a slight thing not worth naming, and that therefore it was the more hard that I should deny him a certificate of my having discharged him my service, and should accuse him in the House of Commons with robbing my house the last time,[8] when he could make it appear that he was at that time waiting upon the Prince of Orange in Holland, and appealed to Sir Stephen Fox and Sir Richard Mason for the truth thereof.[9] That I did not unjustly accuse him and get a warrant for the committing him for the money that was said to be stolen out of my clerk's desk in the Office, which he said wholly a flam [*fabrication*], he not believing that any money was then stolen by [*because of*] the gold that was left in the desk,[10] but a device of some of my own clerks who he believed in his conscience had the money, affirming that he had never been in Derby House from the time I put him away to that hour (wherein I found him equivocating, he not denying his being in the Porter's Lodge at that time, but would not reckon that to be in the house); adding too, that he had been newly let blood, and so weak as hardly to be able to stir, and therefore unable to execute such a business, and further, that his flying was only to avoid being in prison, for that he was very willing to have come to me privately to satisfy me if I should have given him leave – Harris saying (which I do not remember) that he had often spoken to me to that purpose at that time. He complained too, that I had lately made it my business to bespatter him in my discourse everywhere and to hinder his having any employment by speaking to Sir Thomas Lee and Sir Humphrey Winch against him, as he has been told by some of those Commissioners, and that Mr Hayter and Mr Walbanke had done him ill offices also to his like hindrance.[11] To all which I studiously giving him very sparing answers, and on the other hand taking notice, though gently, of the great wrongs that I had sustained, and much of them he knew were from him, he proceeded and told me that it was more in his power to do me right than in any man's in

England, for that everything that had been done had passed through his hand, he having been the man that first got the merchants together to complain of the piracy,[12] and that it had never been done but for him. That he has been from the beginning employed by our enemies to gather witnesses against us, and particularly into Kent, where he met Norwich my coachman at Gravesend. That he was pressed twenty times by a person of quality to go to give his information against me in Parliament before he did go, and when I observed to him how untrue several things were that he had sworn against me, and particularly that of Monsr Morelli's lying at my country house at Chelsea[13] on Saturday and Sunday nights, I affirming that he never lay there one night, he did most boldly acknowledge (though he said he was sure in general of Morelli's lying out sometimes at night) that he had not much regard to* what he said, but was drawn in to say whatever they had a mind he should say against me; but that whatever it was, he had not sworn it nor had ever taken an oath in his life, for whenever he should swear, he would take care it should be the truth, but for what he only affirmed to the Parliament he was not much concerned, for he had no land to lose and therefore should not be in much pain about the proving of it, for he knew how to go* out of the way if ever he should be called to it. That Mr Garraway was one of the fiercest enemies I have,[14] and that there is more mischief yet brewing against me, but that he could not prevent it all. That he d[id] know Scott and has enough to stop his mouth with, and that he was the next week to meet with Scott and the rest, and particularly the merchants about the *Catherine* to carry on their further design against us. But that if he did this he did expect I should get A.H. his arrears paid, and also his brother's, A.H. having been always truly kind to him and supported him, and that therefore he was bound to return him all the kindness he can, and that he would do so. And that as to himself, he would expect that I should get him preferred to some employment in the Navy. To which* I told him that it was not for me to make nor him to expect promises of that or any other kind from me, especially since I asked nothing of him. But if of his own accord he thinks fit to do me this great justice which he tells me (and

I believe) he is so well able to do, I was very confident he had no reason to doubt my being ready to do him and them all the just offices of kindness I can. To which he telling me that he would leave it with me for three or four days to think on't, and that they would be both ready to come to me, I also telling them on my part that this was a conference arising from themselves, wherein all that we expected or should desire of them was the doing us the justice of helping us to the knowledge of the truth in what related to the unjust proceedings of our adversaries, which they both said, and more particularly James, they could inform us in from the beginning to the end, we parted, W.H. and I being jealous after they were gone of their having villainy enough to make ill use of this their conference with us, and therefore resolved to let them take their course without ever desiring any further communication with them.

Friday January the 30th. Being a day of devotion,[15] A.H. came to us in the morning before church, and in the little parlour told W.H. and me that he came to let us know that he had some further conference with J. since they were here together, whom he finds very unsteady, as being sometimes willing to make good his word in discovering the truth to us, and then at other times backward again, saying to A.H. that he may perhaps get his accounts passed and paid by this discovery, but how should he himself be sure of getting any employment or other consideration when he shall have done the business if he does not secure it beforehand? To which A.H. told us he replied that they could not expect we should in such case as this trust them with promises or rewards beforehand, but that they ought to trust us, and that for his part he should for so much as concerned him. To which James asking him whether he would be obliged to give him some consideration out of his accounts when they should be satisfied, A.H. answered yes, and that he would oblige himself by a bond under his hand to give him £20 out of the money he shall receive thereon. With which A.H. said James appeared very well satisfied, so as we might depend upon their coming to us together very suddenly to give us full information. Upon which I plainly bade* A.H. to take notice that my case was such as needed no indirect ways to support it, and that therefore though it might be very useful to us to get ourselves informed in the unjust proceedings of our enemies, yet we would not put it into his or anybody's power to say we made use of any promises or any other indirect means to compass it; all that we are desirous of knowing being only the truth, and consequently, what in conscience every good man is bound in our case to tell one to another, and therefore as I neither had nor would make no promises, so neither would I be bound to make good or so much as to take notice of any of his.* Whereto he replied that what he had said or should do was not with any such intent or expectation, but only in order to the seeing right done me for the wrong I had received, and so parted; I remembering one expression of James's the other day which I have not set down, viz. speaking touching the disgraces that I had sustained by his means and the rest of my* adversaries, he said he had it in his power to make me amends by rendering me more considerable in the honourable opinion of the world than ever I was yet, by detecting the foul practices of my enemies, and those men of the greatest quality.

February 2d. Monday. Thomas Beckwith came to me in the morning and told me that upon Friday last about noon A.H. and J. being in Derby House together, A.H. his wife came thither with open mouth and fell a-scolding at her husband for keeping company with such a rogue as James, calling him a thousand [*times*] lying forsworn rogue, and this in the hearing of Smith the watchman and one Derby that lives near Derby House. After which J. and A.H. went out together at the Watergate by water. But T.B. could not tell me any particulars that she reproached J. with, but he will send the watchman to me to inform me therein. And at my coming home that Friday night Mr Hewer told me that A.H. had been here that evening and spoke with his mother, but found neither him nor me at home. I remember also that among other things J. did tell me of his being told by two Privy Councillors that the King had said that if he should find any one thing true of one hundred that he had heard touching me and Mr Hewer, we should never see his face more. J. also speaking of his being overpersuaded to give in the testimony he did against me, said that he had great promises made him by people of quality that he should have an employment and be provided for for his services therein.

Wednesday February the 4th. As soon as I came in at night my maid told me that A.H. and J. had been here this evening and spoke with Mrs Anne, Mrs Hewer's kinswoman, to whom they said that they had now been three times here to speak with me and W.H. and could not speak with us, and that if we had a desire to say anything to them, we might send to them. And the same night A.H. sent a letter to W.H. by his brother (which letter I keep by me) to the like effect and to know when they might wait on us.

Thursday February the 5th. Mr Hewer having occasion to be this day at Derby House, A.H. at his coming away took occasion of falling into discourse with him and offering to come to us when we would be at home; they pitched upon tomorrow night for it.

Accordingly, on Friday February 6th at night they both came, and in the inward parlour (a fire being made on purpose there) W.H. and I sat down with them too, where J.J. begun with saying that he was come to give me an account of things relating to myself, and which had passed of late to my great prejudice, and that he would begin with a question or two; of which the first was whether it was a due method of proceeding for a committee of Parliament to adjourn themselves from one day to another, and in the interval that that committee should have private meetings in other places, it having been so in my case: Mr Harbord together with Sir Hugh Bethell with a patch on one eye, and I think Mr Rich and others had private meetings at the Mitre in Fenchurch Street, where the merchants were conferred with and satisfaction promised some of them out of our estates.[16]

That to that purpose our estates were enquired after, and mine not to be found.

His other question was whether it was a due method of proceeding for Parliament men to give money to witnesses, Mr Harbord having declared to him that he had disbursed above forty pounds between Capt. Moon and him, which he owned to have received his share of at several times to about the sum of £12 09s 6d to that day, the greatest part whereof by small sums and uncertain, and in the beginning given him by the hands of Col. Mansell.[17] But afterwards Mr Harbord gave it him himself, the last sum received being the only great one he had, being just three pounds given him by Mr Harbord at his own house on Monday (as I remember) was fortnight the 19th of January – which he remembered so strictly by resorting to a book which he carried in his pocket, wherein he said was entered every particular sum he received and the day he received it on, and other occurrences.

That Col. Mansell first began all the mischiefs that have been done me.

He did not own that he used to receive any money at the goldsmith's in Fleet Street at the Naked Boy,[18] Mr Harbord's goldsmith, but said that that was the place he used to leave and receive letters between Mr Harbord and him.

That Mr Garraway was in particular one of my greatest enemies.

That great matters were designed to be made against Monsr Morelli upon the account of one Mr Neville, who is said to be a priest and now in Newgate, accused by Oates for carrying of letters between foreign parts and us, and to have been familiarly with Morelli at Derby House, as speaking of Spanish and having been, I think, in Portugal, formerly attending at Derby House for satisfaction about some houses at Tangier.[19]

A.H. said that it would be best to keep Mansell still lodging at his house in order by that means to get some information from him to my advantage, which would be lost if this proceeding of theirs should be discovered and he removed.

After he had, and Harris, said these things, he promised to continue informing me from time to time of what he could recollect of old and gather of new that might concern me; and so we parted, he saying that he would come and wait on me again about the beginning of the next week.

After this I heard nothing from J.J. or A.H. till Tuesday the 10th of February, when by a note from A.H. to W.H. enclosing another to himself from J.J., both of that date, I understood that his sickness would prevent my seeing him till the next week.

But I did not hear from him till Ash Wednesday the 25th of February, when by a note from A.H. to W.H. now paying the Chest at Chatham[20] (which I opened) and at night by A.H. himself coming to me, I understood that J.J. is sick to despair of life. That upon a note of that import this day by his sister, he went to him this evening and, upon view, believes that he cannot live 40 hours. That J.J. declares himself to be in much quiet of mind at present in his condition upon the score of his being reconciled to me, and my having forgiven him. That he was desirous to speak to Mr Hewer in order to his communicating to him something that might be of great moment to me. That W.H. not being in town, A.H. proposed to J.J. successively (he desiring somebody might come to him whom I might trust) Atkins, Walbanke and Gibson,[21] but J.J. excepted against every one of them, adding that he would have somebody that understood something of the law in order to its being drawn up, it being something of very great moment. A.H. said that he seems to be in some disquiets for fear, notwithstanding A.H.'s present kindness and promise of more, lest when he were dead A.H. should not take care to have him buried, which A.H. put off by saying that Mr Hewer would take care of that, no doubt. After which A.H. came to me and, telling it me, proposed Mr Castleton as being one that J.J. would be satisified with, which I approved of; and sending for him presently by A.H. (though 10 at night) came to me and answered that he should not probably be in town all the next summer, and so we should be in danger of wanting his evidence if our case should require it the two next terms; next that an examination could be of no force in this matter unless taken by a Justice of Peace, and so proposed Justice Warcup saying that he was sure he would do it very readily and faithfully for me, as being to his knowledge entrusted by the court on like occasion, however he may be thought otherwise by the generality.[22] Upon which asking A.H. whether he did believe that J.J. would be willing to have it done by him, he said no, for some particular reasons which he knew. Upon which I proposed Mr Povey,[23] which both of them approved of, resolving to send to him and do the thing early tomorrow morning (I writing a letter thereupon to Mr Povey).[24] Then Mr Castleton taking his leave, A.H. stayed behind and, being alone, told me that his reason against Justice Warcup was that he did believe a great part of what J.J. would discover would be something of what he hath been privy to of the proceedings of the Great Club in reference to the King, of which club Col. Mansell who lodges at his house is one,[25] with whom nobody is greater than Justice Warcup, and so may not be so fit to be employed in taking this discovery.

Tuesday the 26th of February. A.H. comes betimes in the morning before seven and tells me he had been this morning with Mr Povey, who is making himself ready with all willingness to go about the business. After which he went to see how J.J. was this morning, and by and by between 8 and 9 returned, bringing me word that he was better, so as that J.J. hoped to be suddenly in a condition to write the whole matter himself, which he would do and leave it under his hand, but so as that he would have the keeping of it in his own possession till he was dead. That he did discover to A.H. much unwillingness to be seen by Mr Povey or anybody of quality in the condition he lies at his mother's, there being but one bed, as A.H. believes, for the mother, daughter and him to lie in. So I forbore to send anybody, A.H. promising to be watchful and bring me word from day to day how it fares with him, and to give me the original note sent him yesterday which he forgot to enclose to Mr Hewer, which A.H. says was but two or three lines under J.J.'s own hand, intimating J.J.'s being at the point of death and desire of speaking with him presently, which note J.J.'s sister has since owned to have been carried by her to A.H., but A.H. says he has lost it.

27th February. Friday. Nothing stirring. W.H. returned from Chatham late, so as I see him not tonight.

28th. Saturday. Nothing.

29th. Sunday. I acquainted W.H. with what had lately passed with J.J.

1st March. Monday. In the afternoon W.H. finding A.H. going with Atkins and one Strickland to visit J.J., goes with them, where J.J. desired all to withdraw but W.H., owning his having desire to speak with him; began and discharged his mind to him, desiring him with Mr Povey and Mr Hayes to come to him to that purpose tomorrow morning.

March the 2d. Tuesday. Mr Povey &c. took J.J's examination. J.J. gave W.H. two or three leaves he tore from his pocket-book about

Mr Southerne's[26] words and informers' names at Rochester, whither he was sent by Harbord, as also to Richmond to secure himself from S.P. for a time. Memorandum, I invited Mr Povey to this work today by a note or letter sent him this morning wrott by Lorrain[27] and sent by me. Also W.H. tells me that J.J. did desire that A.H. might not be acquainted with what he had declared concerning him.

March the 3d. Wednesday. S.P. swore his French witnesses.[28] Thence to Sir A.D. in bed about the jewel; thence to the watchmaker's, thence home to work with Joyne.[29] Frenchmen's last dinner here;[30] Mr Povey, Sir A.D. and Goldsbrough with them. After dinner complemented Gléreaux &c. This evening first charity to J.J. Late at work with Joyne. J.J. and his mother solicit us with a messenger, Jordan, to know whence the charity came, but are not answered.

March the 4th. Thursday. S.P. dines with Povey. First speaks with Dr L. Sends for A.H. against 3 in the afternoon, at home. Tells him of Dr Littleton's design for J.J., not naming him, but to propose it to J.J. to choose his own minister. Writes late at night to Dr L.[31] A.H. late with S.P. reporting J.J.'s illness and desire of the sacrament, and has appointed to do it tomorrow at 4 in the afternoon, choosing the minister hard by him, as A.H. thinks, of the New Chapel.[32] A.H. talking with me this night about Mansell, said that he did believe I did not know him, he having been but a little while in England,[33] that he knew not how his ill will to me should arise, but believed him to be an honest man, and had had it several times in his mind to offer me the bringing him to me, believing that he could prevail with him to do me right. To which I answered by declaring a total unwillingness (at least at present) to enter into any communication with one whom I did not know and had heard so much of.

March the 5th. Friday. Dr L. comes early to S.P.; is ready to do his desire, but with the knowledge of Dr Sprat[34] of the parish; is answered by S.P. upon A.H.'s being last night with me; Dr L. offers to be present, then parts. A.H. upon summons comes to S.P. at noon; carries a bottle of tent[35] of Mr Povey's to J.J. A.H. returns, saying the minister is not to be found, and Dr L. is accepted by J.J. Goes from S.P. to Dr L. to tell him this and bespeaks him, but mistakes; W.H. at the same time calls Dr L. to J.J., where J.J.

confesses &c., expresses his grief, desires the sacrament. Dr L. by A.H.'s mistake about the minister is not ready; suspends the duty till tomorrow morning. S.P. acquaints Mr Po. therewith at Sir John Holmes[36] his supper. A.H. his being unprepared occasions W.H.'s going to receive [*the sacrament*]. Sir John Holmes and Cotter dine with me today, and visited in the evening by Ladies M., S. [*Lady Mordaunt, Mrs Stewart*] and Higgins.[37]

March the 6th. Saturday. Dr L. with W.H. receive the sacrament, with J.J. again confessing &c., and declaring his late paper to be true; J.J.'s mother, a Dissenter, receiving with them, she and her son in tears. Dine at home. Pearse and Rolt with me.[38] See two acts of the new play *Orphan*.[39] Endeavoured in the afternoon to visit Dr L., but missed. J.J. distinguished to the Doctor which Harbord he meant, and of his own accord in addition to the paper added the story of the latter libel; the Doctor observing afterwards to W.H. the ill practices of our patriots. W.H. returning home about ten with this account, I having been writing a letter for A.D. to Lord B. [*Brouncker*], and having first carried it home to A.D., sent it away. About noon sought for Dr L., but missing him, went home. This day J.J. desired to have one Dr Curle sent to him, one noted by his bills [*advertisements*] for the consumption, and W.H. presently recommended it to A.H. to find him out that he might send him.

March the 7th. Sunday. To Dr L. before church, but miss him. Thence to Covent Garden.[40] Thence to Court, where in the Chapel Chamber spoke to Dr L., who told me yesterday's work, J.J.'s confession, its being enough to make him doubt the Plot; advised, and he promised, to write it. S.P. dined with Lady M. Thence to Covent Garden church, thence to Winchester Street,[41] and so home. Dr L. told me that J.J. had confirmed the paper he had signed, and added his confession of being concerned in the latter libel, which he had omitted in his said paper.

March the 8th. Monday. Late writing letters to France.[42] King supped in the City.[43] In the morning Wheeler kissed D.Y.'s [*Duke of York's*] hand.[44] S.P. dined at home, and after dinner Goldsbrough comes with papers. Before dinner to Winchester Street for tomorrow's play. This day (as I remember) A.H. owned to W.H. a conspiracy with J.J. to trepan [*lure/trap*] him into a coach and secure him somewhere unknown till they had brought him to his terms.

March the 9th. Tuesday. S.P. all the morning at Court with D.Y. to speak to the King about my Tangier treasurership, perfected after dinner at Lord Sunderland's, and Sir A.D.'s request granted there. Dined at home. Sir A.D. and Lady with us. After dinner to my Lord Treasurer's; moved and granted my assignment.[45] Thence to the play, and homewards with S.H. [*Sarah Houblon*][46] Thence late to the Court, taking leave of K. and D.Y. for Newmarket.[47] After dinner S.P. wrote a letter for A.D. to the Admiralty. W.H.'s visit this day to J.J. and second charity; owns imperfectly and with trouble the trepanned design upon W.H.

March the 10th. Wednesday. Dined with Lady M. on lobster pie, after being at Lord B.'s with Sir A.D. and Sir T.L. upon Lord B.'s letter to A.D. Thence to M.S.[48] Knightsbridge. Thence to Winchester Street late, Mr H. being ill. Find letter at home from Fairfax.[49] This afternoon Harbord was with A.H. at his house, very hot upon his having understood by his brother Russell[50] J.J.'s discovery and mine, and W.H.'s discourse of his bribing J.J. to swear falsely against me. Harbord would have him presently meet him at J.J.'s, but said he could not in a house, and that he would meet him in the Cloister,[51] where going he met Mansell, who was very reserved to him and said he needed not to go to J.J. However, after parting, A.H. did go where he found Hd., Dr Sprat, a Justice of Peace or two, and a clerk, where they writ something after Dr Sp. had said prayers; but the Doctor stopped them in having it signed or sworn to before I was there, as a party concerned, and so put it off to tomorrow morning, with notice to be given me by Hd., which he did by A.H.

At this time Hd. enquired of A.H. whether his accounts were yet passed or no, and being answered no, offered him his favour in it, saying that some of the Commissioners of the Admiralty would dine with him very soon, and he would speak to them in his favour.

March the 11th. Thursday. Meeting of Harbd. and the Justices &c. at J.J.'s. I having been first with Fairfax; and W.H. told me of A.H.'s being with him yesterday, and Harbd.'s speaking with him and visiting J.J. with Justices, and appointing this morning, meeting J.J.'s sister early with W.H. and he to J.J. where he found him asserting still the truth of his paper, but yields to Harbd.'s pressing him against bribery to speak falsely. S.P. and W.H. called at Dr L.'s, but he gone out. After the business at J.J.'s, S.P. follows Povey home; takes him to Lord B.'s. After dinner with ladies, to Exeter House;[52] thence to Winchester Street to see Mr H., thence to Salisbury Court, and there found Sir A.D. and W.H. Thence I home, and they from me into London. J.J. told W.H. this morning that he had moved a dozen or twenty times to A.H. to bring him to me to make this discovery before he could get him to do it. *Vide* the large following notes of this day.

Notes about James.

W.H. very early tells me of his being informed last night by A.H. of Harb.'s proceeding as before. J.'s sister had also been already with W.H. this morning to tell him what passed last night, and to desire W.H. to go presently to her brother. W.H. did, having sent first for Mr Hayes, while I went to the Savoy to Capt. Fairfax upon a letter of his last night saying he had something to say to me which concerned me, which I found to be to tell me from his friend Dr Sprat of what passed yesterday, and the meeting this morning. Thence to Mr Povey's, where I found W.H. and understood by him J.'s persevering to assert the truth of his paper of examination. Thence after digesting what to do this morning, Mr Povey, pursuant thereof, goes to Sir Wm Waller's[53] with purpose there frankly to open the whole matter to him of J.'s late examination. But whether he did or no, I know not. W.H. and I to Littleton's, whom not finding within, we went on to J.'s, overtaking in our way Mr Hayes; and finding nobody yet come, Mr Hayes and I asking J. how he did, who lay very weak in bed, and it being past ten a-clock by our watches and J.'s sister observing the Abbey bell, Hayes and I went out and walked around the new buildings in the neighbourhood; and at our coming back to J.'s found much company at the door, and Mr Harbord with W.H. and others in the chamber, where after salutation, Mr Harbd. and I, by consent, went down to Sir Wm Waller's, where Mr Povey was, and Col. Mansell, whom I never saw before. Harbd. said here that either A.H. or J. gave him this further reason of J.'s accusing Mr Harbord, that Mr Harbord did not prosecute Mr Pepys and Sir A.D. Here also Mansell said that J. had said to somebody that he was offered £200 to accuse him. Memorandum, that Capt. Fairfax told me this morning that he knew Mansell to be a very rogue in Ireland, and was cashiered there.

Memorandum, that A.H. answered me very scurvily when I appealed to him about Col. Mansell's tempting him to accuse me.

The persons brought by Mr Harbord were:

Sir Wm Waller	Dr Sprat
Justice Newman	Another divine
Another Justice	A clerk
Capt. Russell	and others

Persons brought by me were Mr Povey, Mr Hewer and Mr Hayes; there being also present J.J.'s mother and sister.

Dr Sprat took a paper out of his pocket, which he said was brought thither last night by Mr Harbord and a company that was then there, but he withstood the having it signed then upon account of Mr Pepys and Col. Mansell's names being concerned in it, who were then absent, and therefore bespoke this meeting today.

That he did then say his prayers with J.J.

Memorandum, the paper brought by Mr Povey, and read this morning, was taken as it fell from J.J.'s own mouth, whereas Harbord's was brought ready writ.

All that Harbord insisted upon this morning was that he might be cleared under J.J.'s hand of his giving him money to bribe him; he owning the giving of him money, and justifying it to the company by the King's own practice at this time to his witnesses, and his allowing dishes of meat to the Lords in the Tower.[54] And he still worded it that it was not for making him to swear anything falsely against me. Which there seems to be no reason for, neither myself nor J.J.'s paper charging him with giving J.J. the money to accuse me falsely. But upon his insisting on it, the fellow was prevailed withal to sign a paper in the presence of the company, wherein he acquits Mr Harbd. of his giving him money to swear or accuse me falsely, using some words importing its being given him upon charity.

And that being the thing to be signed to, the paper which was brought last night being now tendered again for his signing, it was observed that it was drawn up in the form of an examination before a Justice of Peace; which being judged fit to be altered, it was writ out again without that form. And that being done, it was observed by us that it was drawn without the word 'falsely'. Upon which we moved, and had it drawn over again with the word 'falsely' in, and so it stands.

Our paper of J.J.'s examination by Mr Povey being read publicly before the company, he did confirm every word of it but the word 'Chatham' which should be* Richmond, whither he retired.

And he declares, upon my demanding it, before them all that this declaration of his had been made by him at no solicitation of mine, but of his own choice only to ease his conscience.

And that this paper which Harbd. desired was only to explain the last clause in his paper before Mr Povey touching Mr Harbord, and does not seem to me to vitiate his said former declaration at all.

And the standers-by concluded and declared that in what J.J. now did he did both clear Mr Harbd. of the bribery and me of Popery, and what he had alleged concerning Morelli; which last concerning Popery and Morelli he upon demand did not only declare to be false that which he had testified to the Parliament, but did it afresh under his hand at the foot of the same paper wherein his former declaration was to Mr Povey, which was attested now by the standers-by as the other was on behalf of Harbord.

Harbord insisted upon the £3 mentioned by J.J., that he gave it him upon his petition which he said he had by him, wherein J.J. declares that it was to enable him to go into Ireland to get employment there. Whereas J.J. in his paper before Mr Povey calls it a letter showing his disappointments arising from his waiting so long upon Mr Harbord's promises. Q. the sight of the paper or its copy.

Harbord declared openly that he did not believe me to be a Papist or Popishly inclined,[55] and so did all the company.

Dr Sprat took notice to the company of his having talked yesterday or this morning with Dr Littleton, who has owned to him J.J.'s confessions and his having administered to him the sacrament.

Upon my taking this day the copy of the paper now signed by J.J. to Harbord, Harbord desired a copy of that to me, which I told him he should have from me upon his giving me copies of what papers he had against me.

Mr Povey began the business this day with reading my letters to him desiring him to visit J.J., and then went on to the giving the company an account minutely of every circumstance of proceedings at his visiting J.J., he having put the same down in writing which he now read, and was acknowledged by J.J. one particular after another to be every word true.

Sir Wm Waller, having some business, went away before the papers that were now signed were writ, the same being done now together at the latter end of all.

At our going away Mr Harbord proposed our giving J.J. each of us two guineas for his relief, he lying then sick in bed, out of which I believe he never rose afterwards alive, and accordingly we did so, Mr Povey lending each of us two guineas which were delivered for him to his mother.

Harbord then declared that he valued no other part of J.J.'s paper but that of the bribery to swear falsely, and did not deny any other part but owned all, even the giving of money to support just evidence.

After all was done Harbord came to me and privately said 'What rogues are these, for A.H. came yesterday to me of himself and told me what was passed'.

When Harbord found fault with his not being called to J.J.'s examination by Mr Povey, and Mr Povey answering that J.J. would have it done as it was and particularly insisted upon the paper being lodged in his own hand for privacy's sake till he was dead, J.J. did publicly declare the same to be true.

When the meeting was broken up and the company parted, Col. Mansell walked with me as far as Westminster Abbey, professing all the integrity that could, and declaring that he was able to do me a great deal of right in this matter, I never having had to do with him, nor he therefore any occasion of offence against me; and said he would meet me at any time to discourse with me, for that he had long observed this J.J. to be a rogue, and had advised Mr Harris and his wife to put him out of their house.

J.J. did to the last lay the whole roguery of his being put upon this work against me upon Col. Mansell (to his face) and A.H., they being both present, and Mansell appealing to him for the contrary and saying that J.J. came first of his own accord to him, often upon pretence of making discoveries of this against me, and he would not meddle with it.

J.J. being desired beforehand openly by me to make exception to any particular when he should have occasion for it in the paper he first signed to Mr Povey, and which he was now going to read, he made no exception thereto saving to the word 'Chatham' as before, and in the place where Harbord is said to have promised the merchants satisfaction out of A.D. and S.P.'s estates, he of his own accord cried out aloud when we were come to these words 'if the business did succeed', meaning Scott's information against us.

J.J. did also at the reading of one of the sums which Harbord gave him, did of his own accord interpose that it was given at the time when he sent a letter to Mr Harbord wherein he enclosed the libel to him of P. and H.[56]

I solemnly asked J.J. and he cleared me of his being led to this confession by any money, promises or rewards, but only a desire of easing his conscience.

Their subscribing what was now added at the foot of J.J.'s declaration of the 2d of March was proposed by me after they had agreed and drawn what J.J. was to sign to Harbord about the bribery, and this at my motion, we not opposing his paper, for J.J. does not in his former declaration nor do we pretend to say that J.J. accuses him of bribing him to accuse me falsely, and therefore Harbord's paper does not lessen mine, but confirms it rather, this last subscription at the foot of mine being writ and signed after his.

March 12th. Friday. Harbord early with Povey, speaking ill of the matter and insisting upon S.P.'s copy, met W.H. by and by at the Treasury; friendly to him; shows them both J.J.'s acquittance for the £3 upon charity. Thence set down W.H. at the Exchange. I dined with Sir T.A. [*Thomas Allin*] and Lidoct[57] upon ling. Thence to the Council with my memorial about Tangier treasury, which was granted. Thence to Winchester Street. Find W.H. well again. Thence to sup with Holmes, where Povey told me of Harbd.'s passages this day and his own surprise at W.H. Treasurer.[58] Hd. gave it to W.H. as an instance of his moderation towards me that he did not prosecute a motion of J.J. for seizing of my papers and searching of Morelli's closet for his hiding place and Popish trinkets.

March 13th. Saturday. W.H. being abroad at Whitehall and elsewhere is demanded by Sir R. Vyner, Sir D.G. [*Denis Gauden*], Mr Blayney[59] and many others about J.J.'s confession, the last saying that he first recommended J.J. to Sir H.G.'s [*Harbottle Grimston's*] service,[60] which was in the afternoon owned by J.J. to W.H., who visited him, J.J., repeating his desire about Dr Curle, whom W.H. went to at night against tomorrow morning; understood that Mr Harbd. had been there the day before with Dr Coladon his physician; at this or a former visit J.J.'s mother told W.H. of her meeting A.H.'s wife a good while since in the market, to whom she expressing some fear for her son's safety, A.H.'s wife answered that she needed not, for Mr Pepys would be soon hanged, or words to that effect.

March the 14th. Sunday. I was visited this morning very early by A.H., where he told me of his having been yesterday with J.J., and that Hd. had not been with him since he brought him his doctor the day before. That it was at Richmond where J.J. went the last summer to secure himself, as was pretended, and was there as he thinks about a month. That J.J. has been supplied by him with several sums of money, as a guinea and another time a crown, and several times a shilling or two shillings at a time, to spend, besides his diet and lodging for nothing for about half a year or three quarters, and at other times heretofore; when he had nowhere else to go, he was to come and lodge there. But that J.J. did never acquaint him all this while that he had any other ways (as now it appears, from Mr Harbd.) of being supplied with more. That in his absence waiting upon the Commissioners (at a launching, I think, or somewhere else out of town) J.J. sent to him to prevent his being arrested by Mrs Penny, my tailor, upon a bill of six pounds odd money, which he satisfied, but never could get any more than 40s repaid of it, supposed to be the 40s supplied him by Hd. upon occasion of an arrest. That J.J. owes still the remainder, and for his diet and lodging and other moneys lent and laid out for him, and [*in*] particular about 21 or 22s in satisfaction for a hat of a lodger of his which J.J. had worn past returning. That J.J.'s design of trepanning W.H. was, as he himself has told A.H., in combination with his brother J.H., and was upon inviting W.H. out of doors by a footman for whom he had provided a livery like Mr Houblon's, with a pretence of such a message as W.H. should not have scrupled to have come out upon, and with a coach ready to take him in, and a company provided to carry him by violence to a house that he had also secured on the right hand a little on this side Hyde Park gate, where they would have kept him their own time and till they had completed their own terms. That J.J. has several times shown him the place he had designed for this use, as they have been walking towards or from the park. That his brother J.H. being asked by him, has owned the thing to have been proposed to him, but that he, viz. J.H., did never intend to do anything in it without telling him first of it. That J.J. has expressed great dissatisfaction to him for his communicating this particular to W.H., W.H. having thereupon mentioned it to J.J., to whom J.J. did own it, but with no satisfaction (as W.H. tells me), A.H. also saying that J.J. continues his dissatisfaction to him for it to this hour. That Mansell is very great with my Lord Sha.,[61] and was with him last night, telling him so sitting by the fireside upon occasion of A.H.'s commending of a good fire, Mansell behaving himself very reservedly to him at this time.

This morning W.H. sends my coach betimes by appointment for Dr Curle, and goes with him to J.J. Myself to Covent Garden church, thence dining in Portugal Row, thence back to *ditto* church, thence to Hyde Park, the first time this year, taking two bottles of champagne in my way;[62] thence to Winchester Street, thence to Sir A.D.'s where, debating with him and W.H. the business of controlling the stores;[63] we home, W.H. by the way telling me of J.J.'s being well pleased with Dr Curle's coming, who had prescribed him something to drink and a fume to strengthen him, he finding him very weak.

At our coming home we find A.H. come thence, who surprises us with news of his being about three a-clock this evening to see J.J., and there found Mr Hd. and another man, whom he understood be one Needham of the College[64] and Capt. Russell, and by and by came in Mr Wormall, curate of St Margaret's Church.[65] But the paper which these gentlemen had got writ was writ and signed by J.J. before Wormall came. Wormall made difficulty to sign it till it was read again, which J.J. was unwilling to have done, and said that he might read it himself. So W. read it to himself and then signed it and took it up, saying that he would take a copy of it before he parted with it, and so seemed to carry it along away with him. Upon A.H.'s coming in and finding them busy, he was going to withdraw but Hd. said no, he might stay, and Capt. Russell came to him and pulled him to the place where the paper was, saying he must sign it. To which A.H. answering no, that he would not sign it, Capt. Russell said that he must and should sign it; and A.H. still refusing it, Capt. Russell was greatly in choler, and cried 'God damn him', A.H. was a great rascal. The paper, as well as A.H. can remember, was something towards the declaring that A.H. came to J.J. and gave him the several small sums of money which A.H. had from time to time supplied in order as they would have it to bring him to me. To which J.J. cried aloud 'No', telling them that it was he himself that came to A.H. to his chamber at Derby House, and desired him to supply him with moneys to answer his wants, and that he himself did first motion it to A.H. to bring him to me.

This morning at church after sermon, Sir John Baber[66] took notice to me of J.J.'s discovery, and asked me whether I meant or could think it reasonable with respect either to myself or our master the Duke, for whose sake, he said, I suffered, to be publishing anything relating to this matter. To which I answered him gently and sparingly that I did not design it, nor was at any time apt to put myself to the trouble of any unnecessary publication. At my coming home at night I understood by Mrs Hewer that one Mr [Mariott][67] had been here this afternoon to speak with me, leaving word that he had something of great importance to say to me; but who this [Mariott] is I could not guess, unless my Lord Duke of Norfolk's servant.

March the 15th. Monday. A.H. coming this morning early to see me, I began to recollect with him the steps by which he proceeded to bring this discovery of J.J.'s to my knowledge, and saying (as indeed it was) that his first motion therein was made by his brother J.H. to Sir A.D., he told me yes, but that nevertheless J.J. did several times move him, and they two did discourse together about discovering the truth to me before Sir A.D.'s being spoken with by his brother J.H. And as an instance of his own early designing to do it, he showed me a letter which he had wrott with a design of sending to me in June last to give me notice of J.J.'s proceedings against me, but for some reason or other forbore to send it; which draft of a letter, at my request, he gave me, and I keep it by me. He showed me also several small notes by way of memorandum which he keeps in his pocket-case, one of which I copied out and were in these express words writ with his own hand, viz. the eleventh of March last John James did tell me that Col. Scott's evidence nor Moon's would signify little without his help, for their whole dependence was upon him. Another note was to this effect, that J.J. had told him in December, and upon the 17th of January last precisely, that one Neve, a lawyer, had offered £200 not to come in against Mr Pepys, with a promise that care should be taken of him in the country; adding that one Sir John Fenwick[68] had spoken to him to the same purpose, but A.H. adds that J.J. has since told him that he did only make him believe so, it being his own contrivance.

A.H. being gone, Mr Mariott, my Lord of Norfolk's servant, comes up to me and in my study alone told me he had been here yesterday, and was now coming again from Mr Harbord as a friend to us both, to show me a paragraph in Muddiman his newsletter of Saturday last relating to J.J.'s confession,[69] and to desire to know whether the same was wrott by my order or designed to enter in a paper scuffle in print, which he did not desire but would provide for it if I did not. In answer whereto I temperately referred Mr Harbord to judge of my inclination in that matter by my not having yet upon all the provocations that have been given me troubled the world with one publication, as thinking it both beneath me and imprudent, not but that I shall without any difficulty, whenever I shall judge it necessary for my vindication; in the mean time declaring that I never directed nor knew anything of this letter of Muddiman's to the moment of his showing it me.

Then came Sir Nicholas Armorer to me,[70] giving me an account of Dr Sprat's fair discourse concerning me (he being his acquaintance) and that he understands it to be Harbord's purpose to do all he can for the keeping J.J. alive, and to sue him the next term if he recovers, for scandalizing of him.

Sir N.A. tells me also the whole story of Mansell's life, villainies and disgraces in Ireland, referring me for more to my Lord of Ossory.[71]

Memorandum also, that A.H. did this morning tell me that the paper signed to him by J.J. for ten pounds is not now extant, he having torn it, and that it was signed at a coffee-house.

Also that J.J. was two or three times retired at Richmond the last summer, and lay (as I take it) at the house of some apothecary here who has a dwelling there.

A.H. says likewise that his wife and J.J. have had several differences, he never liking him, but thinking him a rogue, his mother and she being at difference at this day about it.

He would have it thought that there was such a thing indeed as once coming to his house as from Sir Richard Mason to enquire after him according to his wife's affidavit.

He told me also something of one Richards, a kinswoman of Pett's, but what or who he is I have forgotten.[72]

He gave me also the history of Mansell with Damort,[73] and how he was cashiered.

He showed me also several notes he had taken in writing for his memory relating to J.J.'s proceedings, which he kept still by him, but gave me a letter which he says he wrote to me so long ago as in June last in order to his discovering the truth to me therein, but forbore to send it when writ.

Sir N.A. did also tell me more largely of Dr Sprat's owning to him J.J.'s clearing me of being a Papist and confirming his first paper to Povey, but that the money was given him by Hd. out of charity.

In the afternoon to Winchester Street, where understanding by Capt. Griffith the tavern-man at Chelsea that Dr Sprat and Mr

Harbord had been there with Dr Littleton, Mr Houblon and I went to Chelsea, where the Doctor read us his notes, which were very satisfactory, and promised me speedily a copy of them, declaring his readiness to make oath to the truth of them when desired.

March the 16th. Tuesday. All the morning at home with Sir A.D. about his present business of surrendering his office. And then Mr Blathwayt and I till night translating out of Dutch something out of the book of shipwrightry.[74] He being gone, came W.H. to me and tells me that he had been this afternoon with J.J., who grows weaker and weaker, and has been once or twice light-headed. Harbd. has been there since Sunday with Sir John Hotham,[75] who is J.J.'s godfather, but finding him ill said very little or nothing to him. Nor did W. Hewer now say much to him, his breath beating very short, though J.J. was going to give him an account of what Harbord did with him on Sunday, which was to get from him how J.J. and S.P. came first together. But J.J. has heretofore told W.H. that he did speak 12 or 20 times to A.H. to bring him to me before A.H. did. And this his sister (with whom W.H. had at this time some talk aside, her brother not being able to talk) did upon his asking what passed about the hard words the other night between Capt. Russell and A.H., say that Russell would have had A.H. sign the paper that they drew, and her brother did bid him not sign it and did say to Harbd. that he himself did first speak to A.H. to bring him to Mr Pepys before A.H. did do it, and said that Russell did call A.H. damned rogue or rascal, adding that for eighteen pence he would swear and unswear anything, or to that effect. Upon W. Hewer's motion she has promised to take care of her brother's pocket-book and papers, and giving him if he dies, they thinking that he cannot outlive tomorrow, and Harbd.'s doctor did say when he was there last that he could not outlive that day.

March the 17th. Wednesday. Being within all the morning, answering Mr Povey and conferring with Sir A.D. about instructions for stores, W.H. tells me of his being with J.J. W.H. brings towards noon *Mercurius Anglicus*, making the first mention of J.J.'s business, with a mistake about J.J.'s having made an affidavit.[76] Thereupon W.H. and I presently to him, and found him bettered by some sleep, his mother only present, he having talked idly in the night of W.H.'s telling that he should be lodged next door to the doctor's. We read the gazette to him; he was troubled at the word 'affidavit', saying he had never nor would ever have sworn it, though he had been pressed to it; hopes we would do him right in getting it rectified in the next, and the author found out; his mother and he complaining of the noise that Harbd. makes when he comes, and particularly his and Capt. Russell's rude behaviour on Sunday night late when they would have had A.H. sign the paper they then drew, which J.J. advised him not to do, and they said was but short, relating only to their enquiry how J.J. was first brought to give this information to me, which J.J. did upon my question declare again as he has several times heretofore done, that he had proposed it to A.H. to bring him to me before he could get him to do it, and this his mother, at my motion, took particular notice of, and said that she had formerly several times heard him say so. Thence into London, to Dr Kerne's, thence to Harford the bookseller's,[77] but found him not at home. Thence by invitation to Mr H.'s to dinner, where Dr L. met me, and after dinner writ and signed his memorial about J.J. from his own copy. Thence calling upon and finding Harford, set down the Doctor in Old Fish Street, and in my way homewards went with my cousin H.[78] and children to Chelsea; thence back home, where my brother St Michel entertains me with some discourse he met with today about Scott's life and practice at Surinam, his cheating of a Jew there and being a preacher, and his owing to one Penny, a slopseller[79] there, some money for which he would be glad to find him that he might arrest him. W.H. brings me word late of his having visited J.J. this evening, where he understands Dr Coladon had lately been, and spoke very civilly of me to J.J. and his mother. They have agreed of a meeting of him and Kerne tomorrow morning.

March the 18th. Thursday. To work early with Sir A.D. about the business of his stores. Lewis[80] comes with a discourse of some mighty discoveries should be made to me by a woman upon promise of concealing their names, and imparting it only to the King, of which he would say more to me anon.

Atkins reads over to me his case prepared by him very ingeniously for publication, but respited for the Captain's confession or trial.

Lewis owns to me now that he had heretofore been with Harbord, but would have me believe that it was as a spy. Dined with Lady Mordaunt. Thence homewards and met with Sir A.D. and W.H. in the middle Exchange, talking of Sir A.D.'s business. W.H. gave me an account of the conference between the doctors today, himself present, their agreement in all things, and Coladon's civility to me and his opinion of the irrecoverableness of J.J. Thence home, where Balty brings me one Ward, of whom he spoke last night, who knew Scott at Surinam, heard by an Independent aunt of his that Scott was a preacher there, and saw a Jew whom he would have cheated, kicked him. Mr Cranfeild can tell me more.[81] By and by comes Mr Hall, telling me of Harbd.'s discourse of an original bond he has* got and gives me a character of Hd. and Marratt [? *recte* 'Mariott']. Last of all comes Lewis, who told me who the woman was, and that she would come to me in a day or two. But neither liking Lewis nor Blood &c.,[82] with whom she was embarked, nor the matter being levelled especially against Lord Shaftesbury and Mansell, I put it off my hand, advising for its being communicated to the King immediately, or one of his ministers.

March the 19th. Friday. In the morning to Mr Povey's, communicating to him Dr Littleton's memorial, and recollecting with him the passages of the 11th instant at a general meeting of Harbd. and the Justices at J.J.'s, Mr Povey having committed the same to writing in a memorial, as he did that of his first visit to J.J. Thence to Mr Ashburnham's stable with W.H. to see a coach of his to be sold.[83] Thence home to work with Richard the joiner upon shifting my bedchamber and study. At noon Mr Bertie and Capt. Shales dined with us, the former giving an account of his late difference with Sir Robert Howard at the Treasury.[84] Then came in Sir John Banks,[85] glad of the story he hears of J.J.'s confession. All the afternoon and evening busy in removing as before. In the evening W.H. to J.J., and had a paper signed by him signifying his desire of having his late mistake in the *Mer. Angl.* about his having made an affidavit against me rectified, he and his mother having put W.H. in mind of it when he was with them this morning, and now pressed him again. This paper was deliberately read over, not only to him, and fully agreed to, but twice to his mother, that she might the better remember it, he being grown visibly worse beyond hopes of living many hours. The paper is signed by W.H. and his clerk Thomas, who attended him, and by his sister, his mother not being able to write. W.H. with the paper to Harford the printer, but found him too late, as he fears to get it printed against tomorrow.

March the 20th. Saturday. Up very early, and all the morning with the joiner upon yesterday's work. The *Mer. Angl.* this day does not take in what was designed about J.J. Dine with Lady Mordaunt. Thence by water to Vauxhall, and so home, where came to me J.J.'s mother and [*her*] daughter, her son dying this morning; the mother bringing me J.J.'s pocket-almanack containing several notes, and particularly the days of his receiving moneys from Mansell and Harbord, she telling me that he has left no other papers behind him. She also very largely told me how sensibly and frequently during his sickness he would speak concerning his wronging and betraying of me, saying it was Judas-like, he having eaten my bread, as* also expressing great satisfaction in his having made his peace with me before his death. The daughter gave an account of her carrying a note from her brother upon Ash Wednesday to A.H. to call him to him. They both took notice of the rudeness and noise of Harbd.'s coming into J.J.'s chamber the first time and afterwards, and particularly Capt. Russell's cursing and swearing at A.H. the last day for not signing the paper, saying 'God damn him', he was a rascal, and that for eighteen pence he would swear or unswear anything, and that J.J. himself did at the same time advise him not to sign it. But the mother seems to say (and I presume she has been prevailed with to declare some such thing to Harbord) that J.J. had declared to Mr Povey, though not down in his paper, that Harbord had not given him the money to tempt him to swear falsely; both mother and sister promising to be ready at all times to testify the truth in these matters whenever they shall be called thereunto.

March 21th. Sunday. Marratt the porter of Derby House comes to me in the morning, telling me of Capt. Priestman's speaking ill of me and calling me rascal before Capt. Saunders, Walbanke, &c., the latter reprehending him for it.[86] He puts me also in mind of Lieut. Byron's doing the like before Capt. Tyrrell.[87] Mr King of Harwich[88] also comes to tell me what Capt. Thornhill told him yesterday of Sir John Hotham's discourse to him of what he would do against me in Parliament when it should meet for my foul play with him and Harbord in the business of James. Thence to church to St Giles's. Thence home to enquire after W.H., who is ill of a cold. Thence to Lady Mordaunt to dinner with my Lord Berkeley and his family.[89] Thence to Covent Garden church. Thence to Sir Francis Boteler's,[90] so to the park, thence to my Lady Banks's, where I supped,[91] and so home.

March the 22th. Monday. Most of the morning with Richard the joiner settling things in my chamber. At noon drew a fresh paper to be put into the *Merc. Angl.* of J.J.'s being now dead, in the room of that which missed of being printed the last Saturday, drawn while he was alive. Then with W.H. by coach to Blackwall, leaving this paper in our way with Harford, who promised to print it in the next *Mer. Ang.* At Blackwall we dined at the launching of the *Exeter*.[92] Thence homewards, carrying Sir John Matthews[93] to St James's, where the D. is just now come from Newmarket to meet the Duchess of Modena from Flanders, who is hourly expected.[94] So at night home after having walked an hour late in St James's Park with Mr Povey, who I find more concerned at Harbd.'s discourses to the lessening the credit of J.J.'s confession and censuring his, the said Povey's, part therein than I think either reasonable or convenient, adding his having spoken to Sir Jon. Baber to propose to me the accommodating the business between Mr Harbd. and me, which I declared to him an absolute refusal of, and so home.[95]

March the 23th. Tuesday. All the morning Lewis with me writing and signing his information. At noon to St James's to attend the D. at dinner, who asked me whether my man James was alive, and told me he had heard at Newmarket the story of his confession. In the afternoon upon the water and to the Neat-House.[96] In the evening home, where A.H. came and I took from him in discourse the heads in shorthand of his information, and read it to him, which he agreed to, and began to write it fair.[97]

March the 24th. Wednesday. All the morning finishing A.H.'s information, and read it to him, he declining his asking of pardon, so I rectified that. Dined at home. After dinner to Mr J. Houblon, and with him to Hyde Park; thence set him down in the Strand, and I home, where A.H. and his brother came, and after his approving my corrected draft of his said information, he signed it; and I drawing up from J.H.'s mouth the story of W.H.'s trepan, he signed it, and the brothers mutually attested them.

March the 25th. Thursday. Morning Dr Gale visiting me.[98] Thence to meet W.H. at a coachmaker's. Thence into London to set him down. Thence to my stationer's in Cornhill. So to Little Brittany. So dine at Lady Mordaunt's. Mrs Stewart ill. So to the play.[99] So with Mr Wynne to Little Brittany,[100] and so home, where J.H. came for and had a copy of his brother's general information. So to settle my papers, and so to bed.

March the 26th. Friday. Busy in the morning till ten, thence to Whitehall Chapel; thence with my Lady M., Stewart. and Higgins to Vauxhall, and dine. Thence by barge to Putney, thence to Wimbledon, and from thence home by water. Busy at night drawing a paper for Balty to the Admiralty, and so to bed. This afternoon J.J.'s mother met W.H. and there herself took notice of the reason of the paper's being not printed in her son's vindication, and pressed that it might be done tomorrow, and was promised it by Harford's chief man, himself being from home.

March the 27th. Saturday. Early to my Lord Br. about Balty. Thence home and found J.J.'s vindication from perjury inserted in the *Mer. Ang.*, joined with another advertisement put in in favour of Mr Harbord.[101] So to work in my study till noon, then to dinner, when Mrs James and her daughter dined with us, invited by Mr Hewer, where they told me many things; and in particular the mother told me that the day that her son was buried Mr Harbd. sent for her, where she found Sir John Hotham with him, and learned by their discourse that they do chiefly rely upon two things, the one to make it believed that the charity of Harbd. to J.J. was only in pursuance of his godfather Sir John Hotham's desire to him, when Sir John Hoth. went out of town, that he would from time to time relieve J.J. to keep him from starving, saying that he, as being J.J.'s godfather, would reimburse Mr Harbd. what he should supply J.J.

with, recommending it also to Mr Hd. to endeavour to get J.J. some employment; whereas his mother tells me that Sir John Hotham is indeed his godfather, but never gave him anything, either at his christening or at any other times of his life, nor ever took any care of him in all his life to this very day before, but on the contrary, Sir John Hotham did very lately (if not the very same day) say to her that he always found her son very neat and spruce, and did not take him to want anything, but that he did say to Harbord 'Thou art a bustling fellow about the town, and mightest get this young fellow an employment'. Besides, she took notice that there could be no pretence for them to say that it was to keep him from starving, he being so able in his trade as a butler and then in good health, besides that he was always welcome to the D. of Buck.'s to eat and drink, and her and his sister to resort to in case of need, who would not have let him starve, nor did not, when he did come last to them from Harris's upon a falling-out between him and Mansell, whom he used to complain of to her to be a dangerous rogue. She concluded this point with saying that Sir John Hotham pretends now to be very kind to her, and that Harbd. did make his excuse for his not coming to see her, saying that it was for fear of its being taken for bribery. 'For you see' (says he) 'what ill construction they make of what I have done'. As to the other point, of their pretending that Harris was the occasion of all this confession, she says in the first place that her son did often say in his sickness that he begun it to Harris, and to the last hour of his life did speak of it as a matter of great joy to him that he had eased his conscience and made his peace with his master, both mother and daughter affirming this, and that it was the greatest joy to him to see Mr Hewer come in, and afraid and troubled to see Harbd. complaining to A.H. that he should send him to him, Mr Harbd. having said that A.H. directed him thither, and that Mr Hd. always came in like a lion, constantly insisting upon having their hands to something or other, and the same thing over and over again to the provoking the young woman to observe it once to him somewhat rudely. The mother says that she had not seen her son so cheerful for some months together before as he was at his coming home after he had been with me and declared himself to me, and had my pardon. The mother moreover has forgotten the date of Harris's note for the £10 which her son gave him up, but does believe with me that it is true what A.H. says, that A.H. gave it her son after he had made his peace with me, and the daughter seems to remember that it bore date upon the 27th or latter end of February, the mother two or three times observing to me that the worst thing she liked in A.H. was his denying to Harbd. in their presence his ever having given her son any such note, which I wonder at in him, he having owned it to me under his hand. But above all she told me alone, and confirmed it afterwards before W.H. and her daughter, that he had several times expressed to her (before A.H.'s and his joining in it with one another) [his]* trouble for what he had done to me, and how glad he once was when he understood that when I was once in court at Westminster Hall it was declared that his testimony against Mr Pepys was only about his being a Papist, which they both say he did declare he never would swear although he was pressed to it. But beyond all that, the mother does expressly declare, and will be ready to make it good when called, that several months ago, and as she remembers about October or November, and before ever her son proposed this business to A.H., he did once in a particular manner express to her the trouble of his mind about me and his desire of being at peace with me. Whereto (she now confessing to me that she was not then very forward that he should do it) she replied 'How can that be done?' He answered 'By going to him'. To which she returning the like question, he answered yes, he could go to Mr Pepys, but then added there would be then no staying for him here (either in London or England, I do not know which), whereto she asking why, he answered, because of Harbord and A.H. This being over, they told me how Capt. Russell's man, without using his master's name, came and gave them notice of the first mention of this business in *Mer. Ang.*, saying 'You see what a paper they have put out against your son', and this very morning meeting with Mr Harbord by chance at Justice Newman's, he said something like it to her.

March the 28th. Sunday. Nothing; only in the morning young Mrs James came to me, showing me two original letters, one of

Harbord's to the E. of E. [*Earl of Essex*], and the other of the D. of B.'s [*Duke of Buckingham's*] to Sir T. Lee and Mr Vaughan on behalf of J.J., the former of which she left with me, the latter I took a copy of and left the original with her.[102]

March the 29th. Monday. I set forth towards Brampton.[103]

April the 3rd. Saturday. I returned to town.

April the 5th. Monday. A.H. coming to visit me at night, discoursing generally of this business, and I observing to him that old Mrs James had forgot but her daughter did remember that the note he gave her brother bore date in February last. He answered yes, that he had recollected that it bore date about the 14th of February.

April the 7th. Wednesday. Old Mrs James came to tell me that she was likely to come into some trouble about a debt of her son for lodging which she had taken for him the year before the last, for which his landlady comes upon her, amounting to twenty-five shillings, praying me to help her in it, and saying that if her daughter could have received about three pounds which is due to her from somebody for wages, she would not have troubled me. Upon which I told her it was a thing that I ought to do very tenderly, but that I would think of it and give her an answer two or three days hence.

April the 10th. Saturday. She came to me again, repeating her request; and it being a holy time, and the eve of Easter Day, I supplied her with the sum by the hands of Thomas, W.H.'s clerk, taking her receipt for it, as so much lent her by Mr Hewer to enable her to discharge this debt.

1. The Admiralty building, between Whitehall and Westminster, which had been Pepys's office and home from 1674 to 1679. John Harris's employment as porter was terminated at Lady Day 1678. His brother Alexander was still head messenger there; he was dismissed (while Pepys was out of office) in 1682: Sainty, p. 129.

2. Nicholas Belbin: Collinge, p. 85.

3. Richard Marratt was to succeed A. Harris as head messenger in 1682; no porter is recorded in immediate succession to J. Harris, but evidently Marratt was filling the post: Sainty, pp. 69, 72, 138. Beckwith is not found on the Admiralty establishment.

4. A committee of the Privy Council investigating the plot.

5. The trial of Pepys's clerk Samuel Atkins as an accessory to the murder of Sir Edmund Berry Godfrey; see principally J.H. Wilson, *The Ordeal of Mr. Pepys's Clerk* ([Columbus], Ohio, 1972).

6. Wynne was the son of Pepys's close friend James Houblon and his wife Sarah (née Wynne); all were called 'cousin' as courtesy by Pepys. Bryant (*YP*, p. 314) understood this entry as an elliptical reference to Wynne's wife, but Tomalin (*Pepys*, p. 323) accepts the simpler reading. *Diary*, X, p. 193 states that Wynne married another Sarah. In Houblon, *Houblon Family*, I, pp. 201 n. 3, and table at rear, the only Sarah is Wynne's mother, and Wynne himself is shown as dying unmarried.

7. By Sir George Etherege; Pepys had seen an early performance in 1668 (*Diary*, IX, pp. 53–4), and retained a copy of the text published that year: PL 1604(9). This is the only reference to its 1680 performance, which is assumed to have been by the King's Company at Drury Lane: *The London Stage 1600–1800*, I, *1660–1700*, ed. W. Van Lennep (Carbondale, IL, 1965), p. 283 (all references in this work wrongly locate the Mornamont MS in Cambridge University Library). Text in *The Plays of Sir George Etherege*, ed. M. Cordner (Cambridge, 1982), pp. 105–208. Cf. D. Underwood, *Etherege and the Seventeenth-Century Comedy of Manners* (New Haven and Oxford, 1957), pp. 59–71.

8. Grey, *Debates*, VII, p. 307.

9. Fox was a Treasury Commissioner; Mason was Clerk Comptroller of the Greencloth (a post formerly held by Fox, who retained a clerkship). Both men were also currently Commissioners of the Stables: *Hist. Parl.*, II, pp. 356–9; III, p. 28. The implication is that James was sent to the Prince of Orange with some official message. Pepys told the Commons that he employed James on Mason's recommendation: Grey, *Debates*, VII, p. 307.

10. I.e. since the gold was not touched, it was unlikely that smaller moneys had been stolen.

11. Lee and Winch were Admiralty Commissioners; Thomas Hayter, one of Pepys's original Navy Office clerks, succeeded him as Admiralty Secretary, May 1679 to February 1680; John Walbanke had served Pepys at the Admiralty, and would become Chief Clerk to Hayter's successor: Sainty, pp. 21, 130, 155. *Hist. Parl.*, II, pp. 718–23 (Lee); III, 742–4 (Winch).

12. The allegation that the *Hunter*, fitted out by Deane with Pepys's connivance, had piratically taken the English merchantman *Catherine of London*: *CJ*, IX, p. 628.

13. A cottage at Parsons Green which Pepys and the Houblons rented for summer weekends: Bryant, *YP*, pp. 183, 360.

14. William Garraway alias Garway, MP; at the debate on 20 May 1679 he accused Pepys of being at the centre of a 'Sea-Plot': Grey, *Debates*, VII, p. 305. *Hist. Parl.*, II, pp. 373–80.

15. The commemoration of the execution of Charles I.

16. Sir Hugh Bethell, a moderate Whig, and Capt. Peter Rich, more usually a Court supporter: *Hist. Parl.*, I, pp. 647–8; III, pp. 326–8. The Mitre, on the corner of Lime St, was well known to Pepys as Rawlinson's in the 1660s: *Diary*, X, p. 424. The merchants were those claiming against Pepys and Deane for goods seized from the *Catherine*.

17. Col. Roderick Mansell, an agent for the Whig leaders. In *Pepys and the Navy* (p. 133) I wrongly made him an MP.

18. By Fleet Bridge. The goldsmith was James Heriot, whose later partner was *Harboard* Heriot: A. Heal, *The London Goldsmiths 1200–1800* (Cambridge, 1935), p. 173.

19. Edward Neville alias Scarisbrick, SJ: *ODNB*.

20. The fund for naval charities.

21. Richard Gibson had served Pepys at the Navy Office and remained one of his most trusted agents; he was currently Clerk of the Cheque at Deptford: Collinge, p. 103. *Diary*, X, pp. 155–6.

22. Warcup took many depositions relating to the Plot. He also kept a relevant journal, but it has no entries for 1680, and none concerning Pepys: 'The journal of Edmund Warcup, 1676–84', ed. K.G. Feiling and F.R.D. Needham, *EHR*, XL (1925), pp. 235–60.

23. Thomas Povey, Pepys's predecessor as Treasurer for Tangier, and (apart from a rumbling disagreement about Povey's pension) a long-standing friend: *Diary*, X, pp. 344–5.

24. Printed in Howarth, pp. 91–2.

25. The Green Ribbon Club, most prominent haunt of the Court's opponents. Pepys later copied its journal (from the original which had come to the King's hands): PL 2875, pp. 465–91; it mentions (p. 484) Mansell being deputed to collect the Romish vestments needed for 'the solemnity of Pope-burning' on 17 November 1680, Elizabeth I's accession anniversary. Cf. J.R. Jones, 'The Green Ribbon Club', *Durham University Journal*, new ser. XVIII, no. 1 (December 1956), pp. 17–20.

26. James Southerne, Pepys's Admiralty clerk and later (1690–4) himself Admiralty Secretary: Sainty, p. 151.

27. Paul Lorrain, Pepys's private clerk, better known as a literary translator; though a Huguenot, he was himself accused of popery because of his association with Pepys: *ODNB*. Bryant, *YP*, p. 352.

28. Depositions dated 3 March sworn by the *sieur* des Gléreaux (Paul Thévenin, M. Pellissary's nephew) and Claude Moreau, Pellissary's late porter: PL 2881, pp. 463–82.

29. John Joyne, a watchmaker living in Paris (where he was cheated by Scott), one of Pepys's key witnesses; he made several depositions on 3 and 4 March, including a journal of his proceedings with Scott, 24 November 1679–21 February 1680: PL 2881, pp. 209–325 (with matter from Joyne at other

times). *John Joyne: A Journal (1769)* [*sic*], ed. R.E. Hughes (Augustan Reprint Society no. 75, Los Angeles, 1959).

30. Joyne and other witnesses brought from France at various times over the past few months; they were all expected to be at Dover awaiting return passage the next day: Heath, pp. 152–4 (Pepys to St Michel, 4 March).

31. Adam Littleton, Canon of Westminster. Pepys wrote at 7 p.m., having had no reply to a message sent an hour or two earlier, but still hoping Littleton would bring James the sacrament: Howarth, p. 92. Pepys knew Littleton as a scholar, and may already have bought his *Linguæ Latinæ Liber Dictionarius Quadripartitus* (1678; PL 1895–6). *ODNB*.

32. Later known as Broadway Chapel; built in the 1630s as a chapel of ease for St Margaret's, and replaced in 1843 by Christ Church, itself now a ruin: cf. *Diary*, VI, p. 162 n. 2; fuller note in H.B. Wheatley's edn (1893–9), V, p. 19 n. 1.

33. From Ireland: cf. p. 95.

34. Thomas Sprat, Canon of Westminster and lecturer at St Margaret's Church; later Dean of Westminster and Bishop of Rochester. Pepys had bought his *History of the Royal-Society* (1667; PL 1529) on publication, and later acquired several of his other works: *Diary*, VIII, p. 387. PL 492, 1137, 1432(6, 7, 9–10).

35. Dark red wine, generally from Spain.

36. Younger brother of Adm. Sir Robert Holmes: *Hist. Parl.*, II, pp. 568–9.

37. Elizabeth, widow of Sir Charles Mordaunt, Bt, and then of Francis Godolphin; by convention known by the superior style derived from her first marriage. She and her sister Mrs Stewart (also widowed) were distant cousins of Pepys, and had been his regular associates since the death of his wife. Mrs Higgins appears to have made up a four from time to time: *Diary*, VII, p. 403 & n. 3; X, pp. 249–50.

38. Two of Pepys's oldest friends, one first met in the other's company: James Pearse, naval surgeon, and Capt. Edwart Rolt, courtier to and ambassador for his kinsman Oliver Cromwell: *Diary*, II, p. 108; X, pp. 310, 356.

39. *The Orphan: or, The Unhappy Marriage*, by Thomas Otway, played by the Duke's Company at Dorset Garden, with William Betterton as Castalio. The prologue (ll. 25–36) celebrates the Duke's return from Scotland (24 February), but this performance seen by Pepys may have been the premiere: Van Lennep, *London Stage*, pp. 285, 286. *The Works of Thomas Otway*, ed. J.C. Ghosh (Oxford, 1932), I, pp. 47–8; II, pp. 1–87 (text).

40. St Paul's Church.

41. Great Winchester Street, where James Houblon had a grand house.

42. Sent via St Michel at Dover, where the returning French witnesses were being detained by contrary winds: Heath, pp. 154–5.

43. A prolonged civic banquet welcoming the Duke of York back from Scotland, producing many hangovers blamed on the City's bad wine; but the Duke

politely said it was excellent: *London Gazette*, no. 1493 (8–11 March 1680). *CSPD 1679–80*, p. 414.

44. Probably Francis Wheler, appointed ensign in the Holland regiment on 29 March: *ibid.*, p. 425.

45. Pepys surrendered the treasurership of Tangier in return for settlement of income due, which was never honoured. By 'Lord Treasurer' he means the First Lord of the Treasury (Lawrence Hyde).

46. Play not identified: Van Lennep, *London Stage*, p. 286.

47. The King and Duke of York left between 4 and 5 next morning: *London Gazette*, no. 1493.

48. This has been thought to be a reference (the only one in any diary) to Pepys's mistress, Mary Skinner: Bryant, *YP*, p. 328 (tentative); Tomalin, *Pepys*, p. 323 (confident). I think it more likely indicates again Lady Mordaunt and Mrs Stewart. They did not live in Knightsbridge, but no other connection there is known for Skinner.

49. The Hon. Thomas Fairfax, a Captain in the Yorkshire militia: *Hist. Parl.*, II, pp. 293–4.

50. Capt. Edward Russell, later Admiral of the Fleet, Earl of Orford (1697). Harbord's brother-in-law: *Hist. Parl.*, III, pp. 359–60.

51. Of Westminster Abbey.

52. In the Strand; built by Lord Burghley and his son the 1st Earl of Exeter.

53. MP and Westminster JP, living at Strutton Ground; son of the parliamentary general, and himself famous for the vigour with which he pursued papists: *Hist. Parl.*, III, pp. 658–60.

54. The Earl of Powis, Viscount Stafford, and Lords Arundell of Wardour, Belasyse, and Petre, who had been imprisoned for alleged complicity in the Plot.

55. In May 1674 Harbord regretfully assured the Commons that he had 'collateral proof . . . that he [*Pepys*] is not of our religion': Grey, *Debates*, VII, p. 304.

56. *Plain Truth: or, a Private Discourse betwixt P. & H.* [Pepys & Hewer], containing a scurrilous dialogue which James admitted concocting at Mansell's instigation, and then sold to the printer Benjamin Harris for 20s. This first hit the streets on 13 October 1679: PL 2882, p. 1248. Bryant, *YP*, pp. 279–82, 302–6. Subsequently reissued as the second part of *A Hue & Cry after P. and H. and Plain Truth* (n.d.; Wing H3282). Pepys retained only a MS copy of the second part, variant from the printed version in title ('closet' for 'a private') and other small details: Bodl. MS Rawlinson A. 173, ff. 180–183v.

57. Possibly John Lidoct, occ. December 1678: *CSPD 1678*, p. 621.

58. I.e. Hewer's appointment as Treasurer of Tangier in succession to Pepys. Povey had an interest because of the pension from his own previous tenure, for which he would now hold Hewer liable.

59. Vyner was a goldsmith-banker, a former Lord Mayor and one of the great men in the City; Gauden was another City magnate, but best known to Pepys as Navy Victualler, from which post he had retired in 1677: *ODNB*. *Diary*, X, pp. 154–5, 464. Robert Blayney was a minor figure, but with important connections from his time as secretary to Lord Ashley (later Shaftesbury); he worked as a court stenographer, and supplied Pepys with a report of Atkins's trial: PL 2250(1). *Diary*, X, p. 33.

60. A moderate Whig: *Hist. Parl.*, II, pp. 445–8.

61. Mansell certainly associated with the Whig leader, but he merits only three passing references in K.H.D. Haley's substantial *Shaftesbury*, pp. 521, 555, 575.

62. Not necessarily sparkling, but still a luxury. The name is not found in English before the 1660s, and Pepys (despite a considerable alcoholic repertoire) never used it then.

63. Deane was to be moved from Comptroller of Victualling Accounts to Comptroller of Storekeepers' Accounts w.e.f. 30 April: Collinge, p. 96.

64. John Nedham, official of Westminster Abbey; he had a reversion to the post of Receiver-General, to which he succeeded in 1681: *The . . . Registers of the Collegiate Church or Abbey of St. Peter, Westminster*, ed. J.L. Chester (Harleian Soc., X, 1876), p. 257 n. 2.

65. Bartholomew Wormall: WAM 12030. I am grateful to Dr R. Mortimer, Keeper of the Muniments of Westminster Abbey, for supplying Wormall's forename from this document of 1677; Wormall does not appear in published lists of the St Margaret's clergy.

66. Physician in Ordinary to the King and Gentleman of the Privy Chamber; he lived in King Street, Covent Garden, close to St Paul's Church: *ODNB*. *Diary*, X, p. 16.

67. MS here and next 'Marratt' by mistaken association with the Marratt already mentioned, whose identity Pepys would not have queried.

68. Sir John Fenwick, Bt, Gentleman of the Privy Chamber: *Hist. Parl.*, II, pp. 307–9. Pepys kept the literature relating to his trial and execution in 1697 for conspiring to assassinate William III: PL 1435(8), 2180(1, 3).

69. *The True News: or Mercurius Anglicus* [ed. Henry Muddiman], no. 34 (13–20 March 1680).

70. A shipbuilder in Ireland: Tanner, *Naval MSS*, IV, pp. 331–2 and *passim*.

71. Heir to the Duke of Ormond, Lord Lieutenant, and himself a major figure in Ireland.

72. Perhaps the wife of Solomon Richards of Westminster, gentleman, who had deposed his hearing James much maligned by an unnamed visitor at Harris's house (8 July 1679): PL 2881, p. 31.

73. Not traced.

74. Nicolaas Witsen, *Aeloude en hedendaegsche scheeps-bouw* (Amsterdam, 1671; PL 2220), recommended to Pepys by Brouncker: *Naval Minutes*,

p. 127. Passages of English interest worth translating from 'the Dutch book the shipwright's art' (demonstrably Witsen's work) had been drawn to Pepys's attention a few months earlier: Bodl. MS Rawlinson A. 173, ff. 12–13v (James Houblon to Pepys, 18 Oct. 1679). Cf. Houblon, *Houblon Family*, I, pp. 207–8. Blathwayt was currently an Extraordinary Clerk of the Privy Council; his competence as Secretary for War (1683x1704) mirrored that of Pepys at the Admiralty: *Hist Parl.*, I, pp. 667–8.

75. Yorkshire baronet and MP for Beverley; as a member of Harbord's committee, he joined in the accusations against Pepys: Grey, *Debates*, VII, p. 305. *Hist. Parl.*, II, pp. 584–7.

76. Above, n. 69; the article claimed that James had made affidavit that Pepys 'kept a Romish priest in his house' (meaning the musician Morelli).

77. Robert Harford of Cornhill, who printed *Mercurius Anglicus*.

78. Sarah Houblon.

79. A supplier of cheap clothes for seamen.

80. Pepys's clerk Phelix Donluis alias Lewis: as above, p. 48.

81. Edward Cranfeild was Principal Commissioner for Surinam: Tanner, *Naval MSS*, IV, p. 66 & n. 2.

82. Thomas Blood, a double agent best remembered for an audacious robbery. See D.C. Hanrahan, *Colonel Blood: The Man who stole the Crown Jewels* (Stroud, 2003).

83. William Ashburnham, Cofferer of the Household, had died on 9 December, and this must indicate a sale of his effects. He had lived in the fine house, now part of Westminster School, in Little Dean's Yard: *Hist. Parl.*, I, p. 554. Cf. *Diary*, VIII, pp. 198–9 & n. 1; L.E. Tanner, *Westminster School: Its Buildings and their Associations* (1923), pp. 14–25.

84. The Hon. Charles Bertie had succeeded Howard as Treasury Secretary; John Shales was a Treasury clerk with special responsibility for naval accounts: *Hist. Parl.*, I, pp. 639–43 (Bertie); II, pp. 595–604 (Howard). Sainty, *Treasury*, pp. 30, 113. Baxter, *Treasury*, pp. 73, 181–3. Tanner, *Naval MSS*, IV, p. 45. For Shales see also below, p. 180.

85. A leading financier; as an MP he had supported Pepys when his election was contested in 1674: *Hist. Parl.*, I, pp. 590–1. *Diary*, X, p. 18.

86. Capt. Henry Priestman (to whom Pepys recently transmitted a reprimand) and Capt. Francis Saunders alias Sanders: *CSO*, pp. 367, 393. Tanner, *Naval MSS*, III, pp. 289–90 (no. 3311); IV, p. 362.

87. Lt Richard Byron and Capt. John Tyrrell: *CSO*, pp. 68, 448. P. Le Fevre, 'John Tyrrell (1646–1692): a Restoration Navy Captain', *MM*, LXX (1984), pp. 149–60.

88. Thomas King, MP for Harwich 1661–79: *Hist. Parl.*, II, pp. 684–6.

89. George Berkeley, recently advanced from baron to earl, and his countess, Elizabeth; one of their daughters (presumed to be the eldest, Elizabeth) had turned the heads of Pepys and Louis XIV: *Diary*, VIII, p. 338 & n. 1; X, p. 27.

90. Hertfordshire JP. Mary Skinner was his wife's niece, and had been brought up at the Boteler's seat at Hatfield Woodhall. Lady Boteler rented a house in Crane Court off Fleet Street, though the family may have had another London house: *Hist. Parl.*, I, pp. 691–2. Tomalin, *Pepys*, p. 307.

91. Elizabeth, wife of Sir John. They lived at Arch Row in Lincoln's Inn Fields: *Hist. Parl.*, I, p. 590.

92. A 3rd-rate, built at Blackwall by Sir Henry Johnson, who had been knighted when the King visited the yard on 6 March: *London Gazette*, no. 1492 (4–8 March 1680). Tanner, *Naval MSS.*, I, p. 268.

93. A London merchant and Worcestershire grandee: *Hist. Parl.*, III, p. 33.

94. Duchess Laura, the Duke of York's mother-in-law, arrived at St James's from Ostend on the afternoon of 23 March; the Duke returned to Newmarket the following morning: *London Gazette*, nos 1496–7 (18–22, 22–25 March 1680).

95. Baber was a courtier but also close with the Presbyterians, so was looked to as an honest broker: Haley, *Shaftesbury*, p. 385.

96. Place of recreation at Chelsea (one of several so known).

97. Copy (though not Pepys's autograph) in PL 2882, pp. 1257–68.

98. Pepys's cousin, High Master of St Paul's (Pepys's old school), and later Dean of York. He and Pepys corresponded extensively on scholarly subjects in the 1690s, and Pepys stood godfather to Gale's youngest son (Samuel). Cf. *Priv. Corr.*, I, p. xii and *passim*.

99. Not identified: Van Lennep, *London Stage*, p. 286.

100. MS 'Mr Gwin' (Wynne Houblon). The place is Little Britaine Street, Smithfield.

101. *Mercurius Anglicus*, no. 37 (24–28 March 1680), p. 102 (a sheet occurring in some prints only).

102. Copy of Buckingham's letter (though not Pepys's autograph) in PL 2882, p. 1273.

103. The Huntingdonshire property which Pepys had inherited, and where his father now lived. On 27 March Pepys wrote to his father and to Morelli reporting the conclusion of the James affair, and saying he would be riding north on Monday, principally to attend the King at Newmarket: Howarth, pp. 92–4.

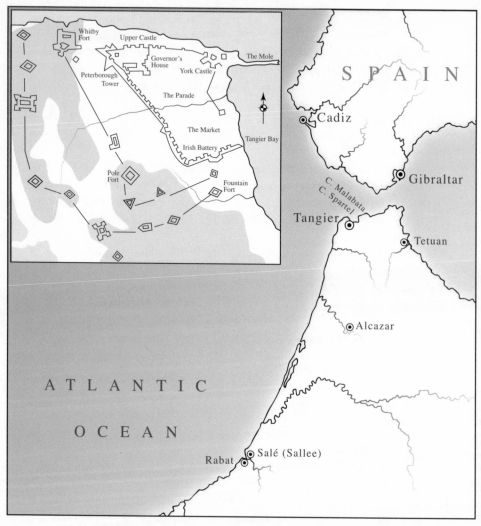

Tangier, showing (inset) the fortified lines of the English occupation *c.* 1680, and the principal places mentioned in Pepys's text. Drawn by Bow Watkinson from *TP*, facing p. 17, and Routh, Tangier, facing p. 194.

F O U R

The Tangier Journal
30 July–1 December 1683

Tangier, in the modern kingdom of Morocco, was a possession of the British Crown from 1661 to 1684, having been ceded by Portugal as part of the dowry of Charles II's bride Catherine of Bragança. British ships, naval and merchantmen, were increasingly present in the Mediterranean, and acquisition of a base for refits and provisioning had previously been considered. Tangier itself had been recommended by Admiral Blake in the 1650s. The 1661 marriage treaty brought this desired object without a fight. Such an outpost would, it was supposed, also assist operations against the Barbary corsairs who preyed on European shipping in the Mediterranean, and occasionally beyond. Once the seaways were secure, Tangier could be developed as a thriving entrepôt, a place of profit in itself, and establishing Britain as a significant fixture in the Mediterranean economy. For all these reasons, and simply because it enhanced British prestige, the new colony was well received. Few, perhaps, stopped to wonder why the previous owners were contentedly parting with it. The Portuguese had been there since 1471, which in itself is a reminder of how far ahead of the British they were in imperial experience.[1]

There was an immediately complicating factor because Spain, to which Portugal had been annexed between 1580 and 1640, refused to acknowledge Portugal's new independence, and by extension her competence to cede dependent territory. So Britain's new colony faced a large unfriendly presence to the north. To the east, south and west were the people of Morocco, who naturally resented this European enclave in their country, and made repeated attempts to recover it. These could sometimes be thwarted by exploiting local rivalries. More generally, the British approached their new neighbours with a policy of kicks and ha'pence. The Moors made their most determined effort in 1680, but the garrison withstood their siege. Two years later a Moroccan ambassador was welcomed in England; and in the last months of the occupation there was an uneasy peace. Tangier lies surrounded by mountains to landward, so command of the heights was essential to its defence. The British drove out a system of earthworks and small forts which created an outer bastion. The Moors beyond still overlooked them; and although they lacked the artillery and general organisation to take the town by storm, they were well placed to conduct guerilla operations.

A more serious problem came exclusively from the west. The prevailing winds off the Atlantic meant that Tangier was an inadequate anchorage for the large ships which the Navy needed to station there. This was recognised from the outset, and the solution was the construction of a stone breakwater, the 'Mole'. It was a colossal undertaking, quite beyond anything the British had ever attempted so far from home, and much of the history of the colony revolves round it. The site was chosen by Sandwich when he took possession of the town in 1662, and the Swedish engineer Martin Beckmann designed a 400-yard pier terminating in a return arm. The project suffered many setbacks, and underwent a radical structural change when caissons (chests filled with masonry) were introduced. The outward part had to be longer than was first planned, and the return limb, though shown in many illustrations, was never built. The structure was nevertheless extremely sound, as was to be demonstrated by the great effort required to demolish it.

All this consumed a prodigious amount of money, for very little return. Tangier never developed as a commercial centre. There was no productive hinterland, and trading was in any case impeded by political and security considerations. The garrison and the civilian community therefore had largely to be supplied by sea, which turned the whole purpose of the place on its head. Instead of having a base to support a naval presence in the Straits, it became the main purpose of the Straits squadron to maintain the base. That itself did not prove really necessary, as the Navy continued to make use of Leghorn, Port Mahon, Malta and other friendly foreign ports for repairs and victualling.

After twenty years there was very good reason for closing down the experiment, and several of the King's advisors made this point. Charles's early enthusiasm had lapsed, and so he needed little persuasion. Since Tangier had come to him personally, he was expected to pay for it from his existing revenue. Only after the 1680 siege did Parliament offer supply, and this was made conditional on the King's acceptance of the bill to exclude the Duke of York from the throne. Charles refused this gambit, and his own device of assigning Tangier to the Irish budget did not work. By the end of 1682 the decision was made to withdraw. Tangier was offered back to Portugal, and to Spain, who both declined. So in 1683 Charles ordered a scorched-earth evacuation.[2]

At this point Pepys re-enters the Tangier story, with which he had been associated from the start. He received dispatches from Sandwich himself and others describing the first British landing in 1662. When, later that year, a committee of the Privy Council was formed to administer the colony, Pepys was appointed to it by Sandwich's means. Three years after that Pepys became the committee's Treasurer, and he retained this post alongside the Clerkship of the Acts until his fall in 1679. The Tangier work brought him new and useful contacts, and a great deal of money. On his resignation he arranged for the post to go to Hewer, whose own fortunes were similarly improved. Since Pepys then went to live with Hewer, it may be said that Tangier continued in some measure to support the roof over his head.

All this time neither of them had actually been to Tangier. That opportunity came only when they were ordered to assist in the withdrawal. A fleet commanded by Lord Dartmouth was to evacuate the garrison and the civilians, and to destroy the fortifications. Hewer, as the incumbent Treasurer, had a clear function. Pepys was appointed to Dartmouth's staff, with special responsibility for assigning compensation to those whose private property would be abandoned. This was Pepys's first public employment since 1679, and marked his rehabilitation after the Popish Plot allegations. It was rather a menial job for someone who had run the Admiralty for six years, but Pepys accepted it and performed it with characteristic professionalism.

The mission was kept a secret until the fleet was at sea. When he embarked at Portsmouth on 1 August 1683 Pepys thought they were going to reinforce the garrison. Having once loved Tangier as 'one of the best flowers in my garden', he must have been hoping it was about to blossom again.[3] He had no idea what his own function was to be, and his more immediate interest was the prospect of a lengthy voyage in congenial company. His fellow passengers would include people he already knew: the divine Thomas Ken, the Admiralty lawyer William Trumbull, and the military engineer Henry Sheres.[4] This would be easily the longest journey he had ever made, and that alone may have prompted him to begin keeping daily records again. Dartmouth did not show Pepys the King's commission and his own instructions until 14 August. It was not until 2 September that Pepys explained matters to Hewer, and then only obliquely. Trumbull, who was to be Pepys's particular colleague, was not told until some days after that. Pepys meanwhile had overcome his initial shock and disappointment, and had set to work. He made a summary of Dartmouth's instructions (25 August), and drafted a justification for the withdrawal, which would form the basis of Dartmouth's public announcement to the Tangerines (3 September). In this instance he was working to Dartmouth's specific order, although he was not his secretary. Later there are indications that he overestimated the extent to which he was required to serve.

The first part of the journal is principally an account of the outward voyage. Pepys had the satisfaction of sailing aboard one of the ships from his own great building programme of 1677. He is revealed as a poor sailor, but remains a reliable witness: the accuracy of his record is confirmed by comparison with the Captain's log of the *Grafton* (appended to the Navy Record Society's edition of Pepys's Tangier MSS). Pepys makes a few observations of a nautical kind, and enjoyed some of the customs of seaboard life. Mostly he entertained himself with the familiar pleasures of music and reading, wine and conversation.

When Pepys at last sees Tangier for himself (14 September) his first reaction is astonishment that such a place could ever have been thought defensible. This was astute enough, yet also curious from someone who for twenty years had collected every map and picture of the place he could find, and had spoken to countless people who had been there. It would later impress him that the hills really did look blue in the evening sun, just as painters had shown him. So it is hard to explain why the fundamental topography came as a shock. On the other hand, once ashore (17 September) he seems immediately on familiar territory. Pepys arrived with detailed knowledge of the civic buildings and fortifications, and he does not describe them. He is in any case not writing directly for an audience. If he did have some travelogue distantly in mind, he could have pasted in the local colour from other sources. Nor is the journal much concerned with his main work in assessing compensation for property. This is the subject of a separate official register, preserved among Dartmouth's papers now in the National Maritime Museum. Personal details aside, the second part of the journal is chiefly about the Moors and the Mole.

Pepys took his first look at the Moors by telescope before disembarking from the safety of the *Grafton* (15 September). He would later become more venturesome, and his game of chicken with the sentries in no-man's-land adds a comic touch; he felt almost insulted that they did not think him worth shooting or capturing. There was serious danger, all the same. An army under the command of the Alcaïd of Alcazar had recently arrived in the mountains, and new hostilities were thought to be imminent. Dartmouth's position was extremely difficult. He did not want to fight a major defensive action over a place he was about to abandon; nor could he retreat unobserved. He therefore needed to maintain amicable relations with the Moors, the most overt expression of which was a grand parley on 28 September. For a while Dartmouth had toyed with the idea of taking the Moors into his confidence; they would, after all, soon be able to recover their territory without effort. But his instructions were that they must not be left the use of the fortifications; in particular the Mole, albeit incomplete, could not be presented to the corsairs. Pepys claims (21 September) that he and Sheres dissuaded Dartmouth from divulging his instructions. As a result further contacts with the Moors were kept to a minimum. This reduced Pepys's opportunities to observe and comment; what he does say of Arab custom and demeanour reflects his usual curiosity and openness. He found much to admire in graceful manners and martial skills (22 September, 28 September). We should, however, not invest him with modern notions of inter-racial understanding, or be surprised that he does not sound like a high-Victorian imperialist.

A good part of Pepys's working life had been spent organising the construction of the Mole, and in paying the thousands of men who had been engaged on it. He had no direct responsibility for its demolition, but took a lively interest all the same. Dartmouth had supposed that the whole work of destruction could be completed in a couple of weeks. This, as Pepys knew as well as the engineers, was simply not feasible, and the operation went on throughout the winter. Pepys reports several stages in the dismantling of the Mole, and he also inspected the other buildings being mined. On one occasion (18 October) he was led on his knees beneath the principal fortress, Peterborough Tower, where the powder and fuses had already been laid. Towards the end of the journal everyone has to take cover as debris from the explosions rains down on the rooftops (31 October).

Pepys did not stay through the whole process. Once his official work was done he was anxious to begin a holiday in Spain which he and Hewer had long planned. They left on 6 December, a few days after the last entry in the journal. Pepys made some entertaining notes on the Spanish trip, but they were never developed into a diary.[5] A more substantial memorial was a chestful of Spanish books: plays, ballads and ephemera, including two carols heard in Cadiz Cathedral on Christmas Day.[6] Pepys and Hewer did not witness the final moments of the first British rule in North Africa. At midnight on 6 February, in bizarre parody of later imperial farewells, Dartmouth ordered the detonation of the last mine, and took to his boat.[7] Pepys has preserved for us copies of the awesome drawings by Ensign Thomas Phillips, reproduced here, which show the scenes before and after the final explosions.[8] The latter view would have greeted Pepys and Hewer on their return to the fleet, still anchored in the bay, a few days later; and it would have been their final image on the morning of 26 February as Dartmouth's ships weighed anchor and turned for home.[9]

The text derives from Bodleian Library Rawlinson MS C. 859, a collection of notes and papers predominantly deriving from Pepys's visit to Tangier and Spain. All the material is in his customary shorthand, the 'tachygraphy' of Thomas Shelton, embellished with some characters of his own, save that names and unusual words are written in longhand. It is partly in pencil, but mostly in ink, on slips of paper, some $3 \times 7\frac{9}{10}$ ins, the rest $8\frac{3}{10} \times 11\frac{1}{2}$ ins. The sequenced journal itself is about one fifth of this material (ff. 207–234v), much of the rest consisting of supporting documents and undated observations. There are also several fragments which supply lacunae in the journal or duplicate the main text (some also in Rawlinson A. 190). The C. 859 MS has been split and bound in sections: C. 859a (Parliament Notes), C. 859b (miscellaneous Tangier and Spanish material), C.859c (Tangier Journal and related fragments). The Diary of 1660–9 began from just such a mixture, but because Pepys never worked up the Tangier Journal in the same way, there is no definitive text.

The first publication was by John Smith, who had made the original transcription of the great Diary.[10] Smith went far beyond the acceptable conventions of editorship by retrieving what he could from the dated fragments, and mixing them in with the core journal to form a fuller sequence of his own devising. He cut and shaped Pepys's text without notice, and made a large number of straightforward errors in transcription. Smith's text was reprinted by R.G. Howarth in 1932. Howarth removed the correspondence with which Smith had also intercut the journal text, and supposed he had thus restored its 'proper continuity'. He made no new examination of the MS.[11]

A new transcription of all the Tangier and Spanish material was made by Edwin Chappell, and was published by the Navy Records Society in 1935.[12] Chappell was scathing about Smith's work, and in his new version of the journal he removed all that did not to his satisfaction belong to the main sequence. In only one instance (22 September) does he consciously break his own rule by incorporating a detached segment.

While Chappell was at work the American scholar William Matthews was making his own new transcription. As soon as he became aware of the duplicated effort, Matthews generously abandoned his own work, and allowed Chappell the use of his draft text. (Matthews would in due course make a complete new transcription of the great Diary, and co-edited with Robert Latham the new edition published 1970–83.) Chappell collated Matthews's text with his own, as acknowledged on the title-page of his *Tangier Papers*. Matthews deposited a copy of his typescript at the Pepys Library.[13] Chappell's typescript, meticulously checked against Matthews's version, is also now preserved there.[14]

The present edition is a slightly reduced version of Chappell's text. I have cut out some repeated matter and a few frequently occurring phrases. Some awkward passages, which might have taken more trouble to interpret than their content seemed to merit, have also been omitted. All such cuts are again shown by the | symbol. The reduction is also made as a courtesy to the NRS, so that the Society's text should not be supposed redundant. I have been unable to attempt reinterpretation of the shorthand, but I have re-examined the Matthews and Chappell typescripts. In most cases of dispute Chappell preferred his own original choice. The same shorthand symbols can represent different words, so some editorial decision is necessary. In a few cases I have felt it of interest to note the Matthews variant; but it must be remembered that Matthews never revised his own draft against Chappell's, and might not necessarily have adhered to his original readings. Very occasionally I have preferred Matthews's word on grounds of sense. All these points are flagged by * and explained in the diplomatic notes on pp. 204–5. I have also used Matthews's transcript to reintroduce Pepys's abbreviations of personal names, extended in Chappell's edition, and the forms of dates within the text. The MS date-headings are too heavily abbreviated to serve here, and so I have followed Chappell's editorial versions. The annotation derives some detail from that of previous editions, but is here substantially advanced.

1. The essential account of the occupation remains E.M.G. Routh, *Tangier: England's Lost Atlantic Outpost* (1912), thoroughly documented but necessarily reliant on the only version of Pepys's journal then published, Smith's unsatisfactory transcript of 1841. The subject is well summarised by C. Lloyd in *Diary*, X, pp. 407–16. The military history is more fully narrated

by J. Childs, *The Army of Charles II* (1976), pp. 115–51. Tangier's maritime role is re-evaluated in Hornstein, *Navy*, esp. pp. 155–208, and P. Le Fevre, 'Tangier, the Navy, and its connection with the Glorious Revolution of 1688', *MM*, LXXIII (1987), pp. 197–90. Cf. Davies, *Gentlemen and Tarpaulins*, pp. 192–6 and *passim*; R. Luckett, 'A sea-change: Samuel Pepys and the evacuation of Tangier', *MCMR*, no. 43 (1998–9), pp. 40–9. There has been no separate study of Pepys's overall work in the administration of Tangier.

2. J. Miller, *Charles II* (1991), pp. 339–40. R. Hutton, *Charles the Second* (Oxford, 1989), pp. 393, 415, 426–7.

3. *Diary*, V, p. 280.

4. Howarth, pp. 151–4 (Pepys to Evelyn, 7 August, and reply, 10 August).

5. *TP*, pp. 251–63. W. Matthews, 'Samuel Pepys and Spain', *Neophilologus*, XX (1935), pp. 120–9.

6. Principally PL 1545–6, 1553, treated in E.M. Wilson, 'Samuel Pepys's Spanish chap-books', *Transactions of the Cambridge Bibliographical Society*, II, ii (1955), pp. 127–54; II, iii (1956), pp. 229–68; II, iv (1957), pp. 305–22, and Wilson and D.W. Cruickshank, *Samuel Pepys's Spanish Plays* (1980).

7. *TP*, pp. 285–6.

8. Colour plates II–V.

9. *TP*, p. 289.

10. *The Life, Journals and Correspondence of Samuel Pepys, Esq., including a Narrative of his Voyage to Tangier* (1841), I, pp. 325–456.

11. Howarth, pp. xvii (editorial policy), 379–449 (text of 'journal').

12. *TP*, pp. xii–xix (editorial policy), 1–57 (text of journal). A memoir of Chappell is given by his great-nephew R.A.M. Dale in *Halcyon Days: Recollections of Post-War Vintage Motoring* (Haddenham, Cambs, 1999), pp. 5–6; I am grateful to Mr Dale for kindly giving me a copy of his book.

13. PL reference collection, bound volume marked 'Tangier Papers'.

14. PL reference collection, Chappell Papers, parcel 12. Deposited by Mr Dale.

A Journal towards Tangier begun Monday July 30. 1683.

July 30. Monday. Set forth at Lambeth. Lay at Godalming.

31 Tuesday. Dined at Petersfield and lay at Winchester.

August 1 Wednesday. Dined at the college there and lay at Portsmouth, where we came before my Lord Dartmouth, who came not till Friday following, and was sent for to Windsor upon Monday and returned to Portsmouth upon Wednesday following, where he entertained my Lord Gainsborough and his lady that day at dinner on board (I and my company dining at our lodgings, Dr Grundy's) and so we all went on board, for good and all, the next day, being—

9 Thursday. Went and lay the first night on board the *Grafton*[1] at the Spithead, my Lord lying on shore. Capt. Gunman[2] came into the port this evening and saluted us, but never came or saw my Lord.

10 Friday. My Lord came on board for good and all this morning, and we sailed with all the ships in our company to St Helens.[3]

11 Saturday. A council of war on board this afternoon the while I and some of our company went on shore at St Helens.

12 Sunday. Prayers and sermon in the morning by Dr Ken,[4] and prayers in the afternoon. In the evening came the *Cleveland* yacht with the money for Tangier. Sir J. Berry sailed and came to anchor again.[5] |

13 Monday. The wind hitherto all at West and overblowing so we could not stir. In the afternoon my Lord in his cabin first broke to me in discourse the truth of our voyage for the destroying and deserting of Tangier. The first moment he ever spoke or I ever knew or [? supposed]* that to be the intent of our going, having writ the contrary in my opinion to Mr Houblon.[6] He will shortly show me the King's commission to him and instructions,[7] telling me that the King has appointed me to be his sole counsellor in the matter and Col. Kirke[8] when we come to Tangier.

After going upon the quarter-deck fell out the accident of the [? pilot's]* falling down from the ropes in his coming from the maintop.

14 Tuesday. Up by times to send off letters to Portsmouth for the post. Then into my Lord's cabin, where he took me into his closet within his bedchamber and gave me his commission under the great seal and his instructions referred to therein, both the one and the other writ under Mr Secretary Jenkins's[9] own hand, to look over. At noon to dinner and then into his cabin, where I slept; and after sleep he asked me whether I had read those papers. So, answering that I had not, I took a time by and by to leave him and went upon the poop quite abaft, and there alone not overlooked by anybody, I read them over and over both the one and the other, the contents whereof are very particularly and well digested for the work. And so down upon the quarter-deck, where I walked with my Lord. The weather very troublesome. And in the evening we observed at a distance guns to be fired from the *Oxford*, Capt. Wylde,[10] who by want of looking out was tailed aground upon the edge of the Deane sands, and great trouble it gave us; and several boats were sent on board her so as late at night word was brought us that she was got off safe.

15 Wednesday. This morning Capt. Wylde, the Captain of the *Oxford*, came on board, and my Lord was dissatisfied with the account he gave of their last night's misfortune, as seeing plainly that it arose from ignorance or neglect. All this day nothing extraordinary.

16 Thursday. All the morning and forenoon writing my last letters to all my friends,[11] thinking that we should by the weather have sailed today, but we did not. Only in the afternoon my Lord weighed and removed from his berth, and came to another a little more to the seaward over against Dunnose. In the evening came on board Col. Wyndham with his yacht[12] and some friends, and lay on board this night.

17 Friday. This morning the Turk, for an attempt of buggery before we came on board, was whipped severely at the capstan and his beard* burned with a candle. After dinner my Lord and several of us went on shore into the bay of St Helens and went up upon the

Downs and walked back again, a long dirty walk. And so on board Col. [Wyndham's]* yacht | and in supper with a syllabub of the milk we brought this evening on board. I to bed. This day Berry sailed out again and got quite out to sea.

18 Saturday. This morning the Mayor and several aldermen of Portsmouth came to visit my Lord with a compliment of a promise to choose Will. Legge, my Lord's brother, into the next Parliament.[13] At noon Mr Sheres,[14] W.H. [*William Hewer*], Dr L. [*Lawrence*][15] and myself to dinner to the *Mary Rose*, Capt. Ashby,[16] to a pole of a ling. After dinner many songs among the gentlemen and commanders that dined here, then home on board.

19 Sunday. Fair weather but the wind very bare. We weighed and stood out to sea with the fleet,[17] it blowing fresh all day, so that I was at night sick so as to vomit | but was well presently when in bed. No sermon today, but prayers twice, as we have had every day since the second that we came on board, by Dr Ken. By reason of a flyboat wherein were all our miners not being able to come up with us, we lay by for her all the night; and in the morning the [*miners*]* were taken on board us and then distributed to other ships.[18]

20 Monday. The weather very fair, and the wind better for us so as we had a pleasant day of it, all day under sail. Walking, talking, reading and music, and a fine moonshine evening. So about 10 to bed, the ship continuing under sail very little for the sake of the other ships astern of us.

21 Tuesday. The wind came to the E. of S. very fair, so as we were come by the morning over against Portland, and by the evening off the Start, making as much way as wind would permit, which was but little in the night.

22 Wednesday. In the morning fair, with the land off the Start, and after dinner, in the afternoon came to anchor in Plymouth Sound. Where my Lord staying on board, Dr Trumbull,[19] Dr K., Mr Hewer &c. in a boat on shore. And after seeing the citadel and giving order about washing of some of our linen, leaving W.H. to visit his relations here, Dr Tr. and I slipped aside and went alone by our barge to Mount Edgcumbe, where Sir R. [*Richard Edgcumbe*] being gone to see my Lord on board, I visited my Lady and her child,[20] and she received me extremely kindly. Viewed her house and garden and park, a most beautiful place as ever was seen. And in the evening took leave, and we to visit St Nicholas Island and my Lord Lambert.[21] Thence to Plymouth to take in what of our company we could find, and at night home on board. My Lord having played the good fellow with some visitants, and was gone to bed.

23 Thursday. All the morning on board, Sir R. Edgcumbe coming on board again, and several strangers, and dined on board. And after dinner, in the afternoon, all our boats and their linen* being come on board, we weighed anchor and sailed, our company taking leave.[22] At night early to bed, I having rose early this morning to write and send away my last letters, particularly that to Sir A.D. [*Anthony Deane*] |.

24 Friday. Up and stayed long for my doublet, having my sleeves altered according to the sea fashion. After dinner and some discourse together in the great cabin, [I] to mine, and there alone copied out in shorthand my Lord Do.'s instructions to keep by me. At night, after supper in my Lord's cabin, to bed.

25 Saturday. This morning there came by us Capt. Aylmer[23] in the [*Anne*][24] yacht from Tangier going for England. He was confounded to meet this fleet and persons bound for Tangier, as knowing nothing for it. My Lord thought fit to keep him with us, and so gave him order to go back with us. In the afternoon, copied out alone in my cabin my Lord's patent, and did abstract his instructions so much as relates to the commission he will give me and Dr Tr. about the propriety [*property*] of the houses &c. in T. [*Tangier*]. So at night to bed a little sickish, the weather being bad, and very bad indeed it was all night, we being then about the Land's End. And one of our merchant vessels, the *Welcome*, was in distress, and the *St David* was like to have fallen foul of us in [the] night.

26 Sunday. Very much out of order with last night's weather and the noise at my head from the steersman.[25] I kept my bed till the afternoon. Then up, and in my cabin did some business upon notes for my Lord Do. Then he to visit me and discoursed his business* about his commission. Then to prayers. To walk on the quarter-deck. Down to sit in my Lord's cabin and supper, and then at night sat late, a fine moonshiny evening, till 11 a'clock, and talking with the French Lieutenant,[26] he telling me several things of the methods of the French Navy. So to bed. My Lord sending Aylmer with his yacht to Plymouth to refit, she being ready to sink with her leaks, and so to follow us to Tangier.

27 Monday. The wind still fresh, but against us so as we made very little way. I up and to my Lord by agreement for him to take my notes* from me in his own hand, but the motion of the ship was such that I could do nothing there. So up upon the quarter-deck, and there walking all the morning, the sea running very high. My stomach so ill I could not go down to dinner, but in my cabin talking with Dr Tr. all the afternoon. In the evening till midnight upon the quarter-deck seeing the seamen dance to the harp and song, and late talking with my Lord, and then to bed.

28 Tuesday. All the morning upon the deck. And after dinner, I being pretty well and the sea a little smoother, my Lord and I locked up together in his cabin, and there he did finish what we only begun yesterday of his taking from me the heads of the commission he is to give to me and others about examining the proprieties of the houses &c. at Tangier. In the evening after supper long upon the deck, and then to bed.

29 Wednesday. My Lord did this morning with my advice put into Dr Tr.'s hand the heads he took from me yesterday of the commission he is to give us, and this the Doctor is to do* into form, we doing this now principally to entertain him, he being troubled that he is not yet privy to the design and, as we suppose, taking it ill that he found us locked up together yesterday. But this, my Lord tells me, do please him. And then indeed I had rather he should have the drawing of the commission than myself. This morning my Lord put into my hands Beckmann's project of a method of proceeding in the destroying of T., which I read by myself in the afternoon.[27] I being pretty well all this day, but the wind quite* against us. This day I read over the two first books of *Hudibras*.[28] | Dr Tr. being out of humour, we have had no merry chat these two nights.

30 Thursday. Up, taking it for Sunday. I visited my Lord abed, the wind being all last night and this morning very high and still against us, so as my Lord had a meeting of the Captain[29] and Master to advise how to proceed – I perceiving by their drafts that we are running towards the coast of Ireland over the mouth of St George's Channel. After dinner the weather continued bad and rainy and thick all the day, and so I forced to sit in little Mr Sellers's[30] side cabin upon the deck all the afternoon to keep me dry and not sick. At night to bed, being not able to go in with the company to sit with my Lord. And Mr Hewer also was all this day and last night very seasick.

31 Friday. The wind came fair in the night and continued so, and the weather very fine all day, so as I was pretty well, but Mr H. still much out of order. After dinner in the cabin a good deal of music and good humour. All the afternoon upon the deck, walking with my Lord and company. And in the evening Dr Tr. and I alone in our cabin reading of Dr Zouch's his book of the Admiralty, with great pleasure in our mutual discoursing thereon.[31] |

September 1 Saturday. Up by times, and in my cabin copied out Major Beckmann's project. | Then to breakfast, the wind being come again in a great measure against us, and continued so most part of the day till night. Then the wind and the weather fair, and my Lord and I walking upon the quarter-deck till midnight.

2 Sunday. Up by times, and the weather* fair, and upon the quarter-deck. Mr Hewer and I (by appointment last night) met, and I the first time communicated to him by implication, and not in clear words, | our business to T. and the destroying of it. At which, he expressing some doubt of its weal for His Majesty in the construction that would be made of it, I told him there was several necessary accounts to be given of the reason of doing it, but told him not then the particulars. Towards noon at prayers we had the King's declaration publicly read to the company about the late plot.[32] Then to dinner. The wind* fair all this evening and greatest part of the night, but high, so that I was a little sick. Tonight at supper with my Lord we entered into discourse | with Dr Ken about spirits, he asserting that there were such, and I with the rest denying it, but was referred to another night's discourse.[33]

3 Monday. Up and with Dr Tr., he in his bed, reading further in Dr Zouch's book of the Admiralty, with very good talk between us

upon that business. All the morning upon the deck till prayers; then
to dinner, the wind being bad all this morning. After dinner, music
and talk in the great cabin. Every ship of the fleet coming by
command under our stern to receive orders, and Capt. Priestman[34]
came on board and stayed all the afternoon. This evening my Lord
and I alone in his cabin, and he took from me in writing with his
own hand my notes towards reasons for justifying the present
demolishing of T.,[35] after which he gave me them back with a paper
of others that he had brought with him that were agreed upon at the
King's Cabinet; desiring me to put them together in order. This
evening also much mirth among the seamen at dancing. And so at
night to supper and to bed, I not well, the sea running high.

4 Tuesday. Lay long. The wind for us part of the night, but all day
against us. This day in the morning Dr Tr. [*and I had*] great pleasure
in reading on in Zouch, and discourse thereon. After dinner and
sitting with my Lord, he and I to it again. This day my Lord gave me
de Paz his paper about preventing and having an account of false
intelligence abroad in Holland.[36] At night supper and good
discourse in the great cabin, and so to bed, myself pretty well having
vomited this afternoon, but my Lord a little troubled with a cold
and headache.

5 Wednesday. Up by times, the wind fair, to copy out the paper
my Lord gave me of Mr de Paz touching an office of intelligence to
be instituted for Holland, and then to visit my Lord, who is well
again today. Then into Sir W. Booth's cabin to breakfast, and alone
with Mr Sheres and W.H. did hear many good things of the roguery
of Herbert.[37] At noon to dinner, and in the afternoon in my cabin
with Dr Tr. reading Godolphin upon the business of the Admiralty,[38]
so sillily writ that we left him off, and so to walk on the quarter-
deck till night, then to supper and to bed. The wind most favourable
to us all this day, and all night due South.

6 Thursday. Up and upon the quarter-deck all the morning, the
weather very fine and good wind, so as we have sailed 126 miles
between yesterday noon and this. So to dinner and then the great
cabin.[39] This morning my Lord tells me he has at a distance broke
the business of our voyage for the destroying of T. [*to Dr Trumbull*],

with the reasons whereof he seems to be well satisfied, but seems unsatisfied with the putting of the Recorder of T.[40] into the commission with us about settling the propriety – my Lord and I think, upon the score of his being a common lawyer, and the competition between that and the civil, but I do think it will not be fit to leave him out to be of counsel against the King, wherein my Lord agrees with me. And so upon the quarter-deck after dinner, we having had a mighty shoal* of young porpoises of several thousand swimming by our shipside today. At night late upon the deck, it being little wind, and so to bed.

7 Friday. This morning and last night I begun the first time to feel the alteration of the heat of the climate, we being now come to the latitude of the North Cape.[41] And very warm it was all last night, and this morning we first begun to put up our awning, it being calm all day. At noon, the sea being very smooth and pleasant, Sir W.B., Mr Sh., W.H. and myself to dinner to Sir J. Berry on the *Henrietta*; and after dinner he and a reformado[42] on board played on the violin, and a good deal of good talk about the bad discipline of the fleet at this date. In the evening on board our ship again, and late looking upon the stars to learn them, it being very calm to our great trouble.

8 Saturday. Up, it being very hot and a calm all night. I to set down my notes in my memoranda, and then upon the deck, where we dined under the awning first. And after dinner the whole ship fell to exercise their small and great guns, and particularly the latter quite through* the ship, as if they were really in fight, drawing in and out of the great guns and showing the manner of loading them &c., which was very pretty but very confused. In the evening my Lord too told me first that he had now acquainted Dr Tr. with my being privy as from this day to our business, and accordingly would have me discourse of it to him that he may not know that I am a greater confidant than he, for fear of discouraging him. Dancing with music upon the quarter-deck at night, and then to supper and late talk, and so to bed. This evening we had our experiments in the sea with a [? bottle]* let down to 120 fathoms.

9 Sunday. Up and to read some chapters in the Bible by myself, and by and by to prayers, this being the day of thanksgiving for the

King's late deliverance, and Dr K. gave us a very good sermon of the duty of subjects to their prince. And then to dinner. In the afternoon I to read, and then on the quarter-deck with the Comptroller[43] [*who*] was carried up to the maintop [. . .] much awed,* and there left alone to fright him, and so there he lay while we were at prayers upon the quarter-deck. After prayers he was brought down. So to walk till night, when Sir W.B. treated my Lord and me and the rest of our knot with wine &c.,* to drink the King's health till late, and the ship's company had a great vessel of punch, but one man [? drunk]* and that was Mr Session,[44] who quarrelling [with] the Lieutenant, was set in the bilboes all night. So my Lord and I a great deal of talk of our business upon the [quarter-]deck, having had a very fair wind all this day.

10 Monday. A fair and fresh wind all night and this morning when I rose. And so I to my Lord's cabin, where he showed me the first draft of Dr Tr.'s providing (from the notes which I had given my Lord unknown to the Doctor) of the commission about the houses and lands at T. Then upon the quarter-deck, where we this morning first made land, which was the Burlings,[45] and had great information in what I observed upon the comparison I occasioned the making of the several accounts kept of the ship's way, of which I have take[n] large account in my extra minutes,[46] to the discover[ing] the mighty imperfections of this art to this day. After dinner up to the quarter-deck, where passing by the Portugal shore all day, and about the evening we came by the rock of Lisbon. Then my Lord Do. took Dr Tr. and me down to his cabin, and first mentioned together to us the business, reading and discoursing the whole business of his commission, instructions, and the commission we are to have; and taking into our hands several things to be digesting of, he the commission and I the abstract of my Lord's commission and instructions, and so to supper, talk, and to bed. We having had a very fresh and fair wind all this day and still such.

11 Tuesday. Up and to do something upon my Lord's business, and so upon the quarter-deck, where finding my Lord going to send a ship away before us to call in at Cadiz (we being now every hour expecting to make the South Cape[47]), I went down and wrote a letter to Mr Gough[48] and with Mr Houblon's letter of credit for me to him, and also other of my friends in England. Dined in my cabin, being busy about my letters, which when done I gave to Capt. Ashby.[49] And so upon the deck all evening. After supper in my Lord's cabin Dr Ken and I were very hot in the dispute about spirits. Then upon the quarter-deck, and so into Sir W. B.'s cabin with my Lord Do. to drink a glass of wine and water, and mighty pretty music upon the flutes in the night, and so to bed. |

12 Wednesday. Most of this day in my cabin with Dr Tr. to digest a commission for him and I about the proprieties, and I to digest the arguments in order for the King's destroying of Tangier, the former of which my Lord and we did read and agree upon together in his cabin in the evening. Then to supper, and after that to talk, Dr K. producing his argument for the existence of spirits, which was from the ancient acting of the oracles, which I took upon me against the next time to answer. So to walk upon the deck all toward midnight, and so to bed. We supposing ourselves to be now the length of the Barbary shore, the wind having been very fair for us; the night very hot, so I rested very ill.

13 Thursday. Capt. Villiers[50] waked us early with news of his making the land of Cape Spartel, so up to see it.[51] Then to my cabin to finish my collection of arguments for the destroying of T.[52] By and by my Lord Do. came to Dr Tr. and me and run over several things of our business, I propounding his present communicating it to Mr Sh., | which he did by and by, by taking him alone into his cabin. I upon the quarter-deck, where we were come now fair in sight of the entrance into the Straits between the two shores, and therefore the customary money was collected of everybody that had not been before in the Straits.[53] In the afternoon towards these,* my Lord did communicate the matter to Sheres, and afterward did tell it me that he is greatly satisfied with his having done it, Sh. taking it with great discretion the news of it. Then my Lord and I alone in his cabin for him to write down in longhand from my notes in shorthand, which I read to him, my arguments for the destroying of T., which he is very greatly pleased with. Then upon the deck, and my Lord, because of a levant coming up just as in the evening we came off Cape Spratt [*Spartel*], caused the fleet to come to anchor under it [and] there lay all night. My Lord and I finished his writing out my notes late at night, and so to bed.

14 Friday. Up by break of day, | seeing the shores on both sides at our entering the mouth of the Straits, which I did to my great pleasure. The levant keeping still very strong. About 10 a-clock we got well within the Bay of T., where Kirke the Governor having had some days' notice of our coming by a ship we left behind us that came hither before us, he did salute us with all the guns of the town.[54] We found here the Alcaïd[55] with his army encamped near the town. But Lord! How could ever anybody think this place fit to be kept at this charge, that by its being overlooked by so many hills can never be secured against an enemy? By and by K. came on board, to whom before dinner my Lord broke the business by themselves, and afterwards told me that he do most seemingly collectedly bear it, and very cheerfully. Then to dinner, where abundance of officers of the place. And all say that my and Mr Hewer's coming makes more talk than my Lord's, for they have had for a good while discourses of the place's being to be deserted,* and Kirke told us how the talk arose. After dinner my Lord took K. and Dr Tr. and myself into his bedroom, and there opened the matter to us all together; and I find K. very forward in all appearance in the matter, and offered several reasonable things towards the expediting of it, on which we agreed and resolved for the putting them in practice. Then upon the quarter-deck full of officers walking and talking, and among others my brother St Michel[56] came, who is mightily altered in his looks – with hard usage, as he tells me. At night upon the deck my Lord told me it was well we were come, for the Governor and the Alcaïd would have broke out into a rupture within these 10 days, K. did carry himself so hot in all his business. To bed, and the scuttle being open, it blew very hard into my cabin upon my bed all night; but being at anchor, we lay much more still than hitherto, and so I slept well.

15 Saturday. In the morning up by times to look with a glass upon the Moors' camp. Then my Lord and I in his cabin to dictate to him an abstract of his instructions, which he took in longhand from me for his better memory and execution of them. Then we had our first council of four in his cabin, that is to say my Lord, Dr Tr., Mr Sh. and myself, to debate of matters, of the actions* of which I did and shall take particular memoranda.[57] Much company at dinner. In the afternoon my Lord called a council of officers to consider the disposition and orderly keeping of the fleet when he shall be on shore, which he thinks to be on Monday next.[58] Mr Hewer went first ashore this afternoon, I not intending to go till my Lord goes. The evening as usual in the cabin and on deck, a most pleasant night for weather, and the Pole Star do evidently appear lowered. So to bed.

16 Sunday. Up and breakfast with Sir W.B. This morning came in from cruising Sir J. Wyborne,[59] and full of company from shore all day.

17 Monday. Writing letters all the morning for England by a vessel.[60] About 10 on shore with my Lord for the first time, all the ships firing guns, and the town. And met and conducted in great state up to the castle, where we dined; and after dinner see the Lady[61] mightily changed. The place [an]* ordinary place but overseen by the Moors, so as to be amazed to think how that the King has laid out all this money upon it. Infinitely bit with clinches tonight. Good grapes and pomegranates from Spain.

18 Tuesday. Mightily out of order from my being bit last night in my face &c. | After dinner rode out with my Lord and K. to see the town without, and did it with no pleasure, but great danger, I thought, and so did W.H., and wondered all the way at the folly of the King's being at all this charge upon this town. No water in our command about this town. Tonight I used several ways to preserve myself against the clinches, as the lime, candles, removing my bed, but still bit. At our coming back into the town tonight we saw the Moors' exercise hour upon our shore.

19 Wednesday. In the morning the Mayor &c. presented their petition to my Lord. I having been at the bath, and found at my return that Moors from the Alcaïd come to visit my Lord. | The commissions signed by my Lord this afternoon, and a proclamation of my drawing for a meeting tomorrow. And in the evening rode out | with Mr Sh. to the Mole and on the shore. And in the evening music of the harp and guitar and dance with Mr Sh. in his garden with mighty pleasure. Lay tonight upon chairs and my hands and face covered, but yet my neck and other places bit, and my eyes. This evening I began to have milk at 8*d* a quart. Some Tuniseens this day came to us and were well used by my Lord.

20 Thursday. I this day put on my first [? stuff]* suit and left off [. . .]* after many years. With Dr Tr. and B. [*Frederick Bacher*]⁶² to the Town House and there the Mayor present, I opened the business entered in our journal.⁶³ And there for a little while seeing the confusion of the business we are going about. And so to see the Popish church and library, and so home and dined at a dinner by ourselves from my Lord. This afternoon all the afternoon in my chamber, Mr Sh. going this day to the Alcaïd and come home at night with great reports of his civility and a wild boar hunted and sent in by the Moors. This afternoon I first opened my long glass. Lay tonight in my bed again with my hands and face covered, and bit but a little. Most admirable grapes and pomegranates brought among other things by Mr Sheres from the Alcaïd, and sweetmeats [and] fowl roasted by them.

21 Friday. In the morning to the court, where the Portuguese brought their titles in Spanish, which we ordered to be translated;⁶⁴ so having nothing ready to go on with, we home and there I found a letter coming to me to enclose a letter of my Lord's to Secretary J. [*Jenkins*] to show to Dr Tr. and have advice thereon, which we gave him | and advised him to be more pressing about victuals, in both which he agreed with us, and I took a copy of it. After dinner by ourselves, again to the court and there the afternoon to little satisfaction; and so in the evening Doctor [*Trumbull*] and I with Dr K. to walk to see the Parade, and so home. And in my chamber Sh. came and opened to me great things of the works to be done and the time it would take, and my Lord came to us and discoursed on the same, and particularly surprised | us with a motion of presently communicating our business to the Alcaïd, which we opposed and he yielded. Then | after I doing some public* business, to his side and merry at supper with wine in saltpetre. Spanish onions mighty good. Sh. tells me and shows me the mines cannot be done in less than three months. | Our drills better than those brought from

England. A popish friar this afternoon went with us. A Moor ran away from their army into this city and desired to become a Christian, but upon examination do find his coming away to be by reason of his having killed a man.

22 Saturday. Up, little bit tonight. Keep to my milk evening and morning. To my Lord with Dr Tr. for some directions for clerks about our business, and so to our court, where little done. My Lord come to us and Mr Mayor and some order taken for summons and papers against Monday. And so all the morning late doing something against Monday by papers. Here Dr Tr. and I spoke of the silliness of our having a table by ourselves and the little pleasure or any use of it, and resolved to put an end to that foolery. Here we got and six clerks at work all day till night. [At] noon to dinner at our particular tables again, and sent victuals to the clerks at the court. I there all the afternoon till after candlelight. After going home from our office at night, at supper with my Lord we had the Moorish young man that is run away from them to us and my Lord entertains him, he having recommended himself as he thought to us by saying that he had killed a Moor and so run away, it being an act of merit in them to kill a Christian. He was servant to the Alcaïd to wait on him a-horseback, but his secretary and other Moors being here this afternoon, they told my Lord that there was no such thing as the boy's killing a Moor or any other hurt concerning him that, upon enquiry since his running away, they can find. The law between us giving each of us liberty of receiving runaways from either party, as they do our men. So at supper at my desire my Lord called for the boy and there we examined him by an interpreter concerning the killing of a Moor, which my Lord did take as an objection against his entertaining him or making of him a Christian, which the boy seems to desire and to make the only reason for his coming to us. But upon examination the boy did at last come to confess that it was wholly untrue what he had upon the other account pretended of his having killed anybody, or done any evil, saying that if any such thing could be proved of him, my Lord should hang or do anything with him. He seems a very sober, good, well-looked youth, and says to my asking him that it was God only that put it into his heart to be a Christian, and he has laboured several days to get to us, and could not till last night. I bid him show [us] the manner of his saying his prayers, and he did it with so much reverence in his manner, speech, the motion of his hands and eyes, | his voice, and most of all in his prostrations, that I never was more taken with any appearance of devotion in my life in any person of any sort or religion. We saw the manner of his putting on his *alhaque*, which is strange to see how dexterously he do it, being so large a piece of cloth, and we also saw his manner of sitting on the ground and eating his victuals without a knife or serving his mouth with his left hand at all. Upon the whole my Lord is reconciled mightily to the youth and will take him into his own service, and his servant Gargrave will have him in my Lord's livery tomorrow. So to bed.

Mighty talk of spirits in York Castle, mighty noises being heard by the minister and most intelligent men and particularly Dr Lawrence, who told me that he was now begun to be convinced of spirits, this having continued for some time past and appearing every three or four nights, but nothing since we come to this | Saturday, a good argument against Dr Ken's argument from the silence of the oracles.[65]

23 Sunday. Up and the first time shaved myself since | coming from England. When ready I sat down to read with great pleasure in my Micrography.[66] Thence with my Lord, attended by all the officers of the garrison and Mayor and aldermen of the town, to church, where Dr Ken made an excellent sermon that is full of the skill of a preacher, but nothing of a natural philosopher, it being [all] forced meat. I saw very few women of any quality or beauty in the place. The Mayoress and two sisters of his and hers being the only women that appeared gentlewomen. At home to dinner and dined with my Lord, whereas we had for some days dined, Dr Tr. and myself, at a [? table] by ourselves, but to so little content that he and I are resolved to break it off from this day. After dinner to read again in my chamber, then to church, where the parson of the parish[67] preached. Here I first observed crawling upon the side of the church windows some lizards, and sticking in the windows to bask themselves in the sun. And at noon we had a great locust [leapt]* of a sudden on the table; and this morning in my chamber the most extraordinary spider that ever I saw, at least ten times as big as an ordinary spider. Such things this country do mightily abound with. But above all that was remarkable here, I met the Governor's lady in the pew (a lady I have long admired* for her beauty, but she is mightily altered. And they do tell stories of her on her part, while her husband minds pleasure of the same kind on his), and after sermon I led her down to her chair, and asking her how Tangier agreed with her Ladyship, she told me well enough for the little time she had to stay in it, by which I see she knows the mystery. From the church to walk in the garden of the parson of the parish, and so down with Dr [*Trumbull*] and others on the brigantine within the Mole to see the nature of a galley. And so by boat with Sir J. Berry we rowed to Whitby,[68] in some danger as Dr Ken, who was with us, seemed by his fear to think, to see the place. And so home to my chamber to read and then to [supper] where I of late have so far eat with the rest as related to grapes and pomegranates; here we had wine cooled in saltpetre which made it very cool and refreshing, and this done in a vessel used, they say, in Italy on purpose for it, being a square vessel of cork. At night to bed. Dr Tr. and I being a little* under some disdain to hear my Lord speak to us a little too pressingly touching the business of dispatch in the matters of our commission, when we take so much pains as we do, and the delay is only people's not bringing in their pretences [*claims*].

24 Monday. Up by times in my chamber, as we have every morning since our commission done with Mr Hunter to prepare business for our meeting, and so to the court, where all the morning. My Lord coming at our desire and according to order on Saturday to declare* a day within which everybody should bring in their papers. And we had got above six score copies of our papers of enquiry to disperse to everybody that pretended to propriety, and Thursday next is appoint[ed] for the day, and that published by proclamation. All the morning with little to do but preparing books with columns, then home to dinner, once more to our table, we having taken no care to unbespeak it, though Dr Tr. and I did last night tell my Lord of the unusefulness of having any such table kept to the increasing his change; so tomorrow we will begin and eat again with my Lord, we

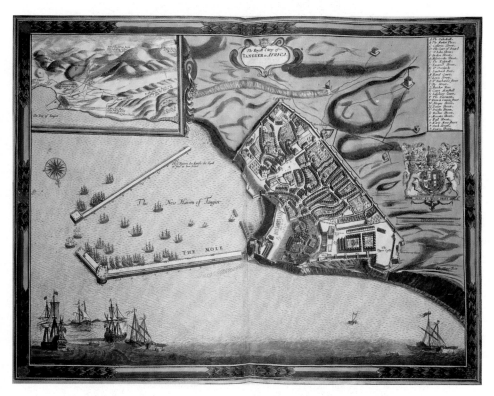

I. *Map of Tangier*
From John Seller, *The English Pilot* (1677) [PL 2928(2)]. *(Pepys Library)*

Overleaf:

II–V. *Four views of Tangier, before and after the destruction 1684.* Engravings by Nicholas
Yeates and John Collins from originals by Ensign Thomas Phillips, who accompanied Pepys
on the 1683–4 expedition. They were advertised in the *London Gazette*, no. 1997 (5–8 Jan.
1685) as sold by four dealers in London and Westminster. Each is engraved on two
interlocking plates. Pepys's copies are hand-coloured (probably as purchased), and trimmed
for binding within one of his largest albums [PL 2895, pt ii, pp. 294 × 307; (a) 475 ×
1120mm, (b) 417 × 1195mm, (c) 389 × 1190mm, (d) 380/390 × 1190mm]. They are
believed to be the only such copies to survive. *(Pepys Library)*

II

III

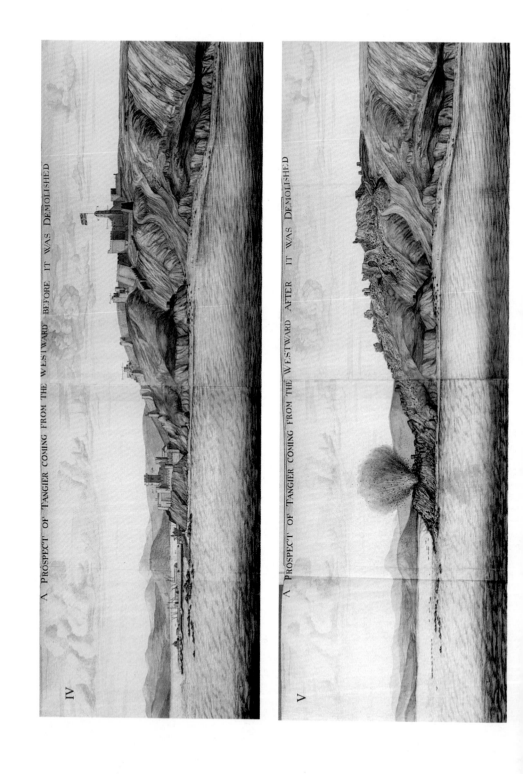

IV   A PROSPECT OF TANGIER COMING FROM THE WESTWARD BEFORE IT WAS DEMOLISHED

V   A PROSPECT OF TANGIER COMING FROM THE WESTWARD AFTER IT WAS DEMOLISHED

having this day had foolish company come to us and stinking meat. After dinner immediately to the office again, where we sat till 7 or 8 at night without stirring, though little work yet brought to us, but we preparing of books.[69] At night my Lord sent for us home to supper, and after supper I to my chamber, having got a mosquito net of my Lord. Before I was abed my Lord come to visit and sit with me, and very melancholy I made him with my discourse and observing to him himself (while talking of the despondence of Dr Tr. and Mr Sh.) my observing him himself to be sometime melancholy; he answered to me how could he be without thoughts to find himself sent with such promises of every sort of supplies, and particularly of victuals, by my Lord Rochester[70] (as he has heretofore told me) and be in this condition, which I magnified by my telling him Sir W. Booth's discourse of that matter to me today after dinner in my way to the office, he telling me his dreadful prospect of the condition of the fleet in a few days when the seamen shall know what provisions they have and no more, and what they are to do before they go where they may have more. He told me too that he had now stated the victuals of the fleet to my Lord clearly, which is three months from this at six to four men's allowance, and nothing as he hears in the garrison, or very little, to spare for the fleet, nor anything for the inhabitants and their families, wherein he tells me there is full 400 children, and therefore advises that three ships should by all means | presently be sent to Plymouth as the surest and speediest way. But for sure I am sure there is no sureness in it, and for speed my Lord told me it could not be depended on in less than ten weeks. I told my Lord also of Sh.'s saying that the blowing up of the Mole could not be done in less than three months, to which he excepts as saying that Sh. do not know the ways of doing these works in great, though he do in little. But my Lord do express, however, great trouble to be upon him, and apprehensions of the success of what he comes about, and is sometimes speaking of his present opening all to the Alcaïd, against which I offered, and he yielded, that it ought to be well thought on, and that he would not do it but upon good and joint advice of those he should think fit to consult about it, I putting him in mind of the express clause in his instructions to tell the Moors of it as late as may be;[71] I offering it to him to consider the distress he would be in if he should have the Moors to oppose without the walls at the same time while he has this work to do within it, and at the same time be under the further distress of danger of starving. All which put together made him very melancholy, though I laboured in the end to submit himself to God Almighty while he did all that a faithful and diligent officer can in his station, according to his best prudence and the best advice he can get. So he left me and I to bed, where I was worse troubled than any night since my coming but the first with biting, notwithstanding the net.

25 Tuesday. Up by times, being uneasy with the clinches or mosquitoes in the bed, and walked forth with Dr Lawrence and saw | some little foolish work our men are doing by direction of Major Beckmann (then present) in the sea near the Devil's Tower to secure the wooden work in the sea. There he told me how ill we were provided with everything here for the great work that we came about. We neither having materials of all kinds necessary, nor tools nor hands, and saying therefore how weary he was of his employment, and of himself took notice of this to be one of the great occasions of the greatness of the King of France, that for all his works there, both by land and sea, his magazines are double or treble what is necessary, so that they never want any success or dispatch from the want of materials; whereas in England we think as much of having a dozen of links beforehand as he do of 100,000. So walked to the office and there dispatch all the business that came, we having divided the work thereof into three parts and begun thereon this morning, Dr Trumbull and my[self] for the leases and Mr Bacher for the freeholds; but our business comes in very slowly, so as at this rate it will never be done. At noon home to dinner, we this day returning to dine at my Lord's table, it being much more pleasant to us and in every respect better. And from dinner presently to the office, where we sat close till 8 at night and then sent for home by my Lord to supper. So home, and after supper with my head troubled to see so much trouble to do so little business at the office, through the slowness of people to come and ignorance of those that do come. So to bed.

26 Wednesday / 27 Thursday. From Wednesday morning to Thursday morning continually busy till 8 or 9 at night without an interval but only to dinner, and then presently again to receive the claims of people to propriety. But in one word so silly and supine from all of them, even the people of most understanding among them, that it is plain there was a habit of disorder and forgetfulness of all method and discipline in [all] they did, even in their own private concernments, taking such evidence for their security as would not be worth sixpence in Westminster Hall, nor would be here if any of the right heirs [of] the parties they have their titles from would give them any trouble. So that I think it is impossible for us to give any tolerable report of them to do either the King right or them, in which Dr Tr. and I do greatly agree and discourse of it. Dr Tr., who has of late been mighty open to me of things that he takes hardly of my Lord (and especially of his bringing him upon this errand thus far from home, contrary to all his professions touching the place and business he was to go upon), did on Wednesday morning complain mightily of his going in to my Lord in hopes to have his letters, which are brought this day from Cadiz with my Lord's, and my Lord's refusing to give him them presently, with some kind of rebuke for his impatience; which was indeed a little hard, though I know (by Sam Atkins, who brought them from on board the vessel that fetched them) that my Lord do it to avoid the world's knowing that there are any come, because my Lord would delay their having any news from England of our errand. But by and by he had his letters sent him, and I a packet from Mr Gough at Cadiz, enclosing divers letters to the several places to give me credit in every place where I am likely to come if I go thither, which I take mighty kindly of him. This Thursday we did by proclamation expect that all claims should be brought in to us, or at least this night, according to a special proclamation made yesterday, and therefore we did sit very late to finish all, and I did and the rest (as we think) receive very near the whole, not but that there are many defects in them to be made good to us by the several proprietors. And so home to supper and to bed, the whole talk tonight being about our going to an interview of my Lord and the Alcaïd tomorrow morning, the same being adjusted between them.

28 Friday. Did not go | to the office at all, but walked forth a little in the morning for to stretch my legs at the Parade, there to see our seamen come on shore and putting on their new clothes in order to their mustering today in the field as soldiers. And so they and their officers did make for so many, which was about 1,000, as good an appearance and gave as good, or better, a volley with their small* shot than the soldiers themselves.[72] About 11 a-clock my Lord went out and us of his family on horseback all with him, without the town, where upon the hills we had a mighty fine sight of our army finely disposed among the hills and wholly down to the sea just without the town walls. We also had several small ships and boats armed lie close along the coast of the bay, where by and by the Alcaïd made his appearance, and we down to the strand to meet him; and my Lord and he shook hands, and by interpreters did talk together for about half* an hour, the Alcaïd and his company appearing like very grave and sober men, and his discourse and manner of speech very good, and with more presence of mind than I thought our master did, though he did also extremely well. Their appearance and habits I liked very well. His son a pretty youth, who in particular exercised by and by very neatly, and sometimes attacked his very father himself, and now and then the father (who is no old man, not fifty, though his habit makes him appear otherwise) would hit him with his lance. His son bareheaded, not so much as a cap which they all wear. My Lord moved the Alcaïd and he readily and very civilly shook hands with Kirke. Their style extremely fine and so for compliment. They agreed upon a treaty to begin between them by persons to be chosen on both sides tomorrow. His army was drawn up not so thick as ours, being but two deep and that in but few places very artificially to make a greater show than us, though we believe they had not [above]* 2,500 in the field and we full 4,000, but they a great many horse and we few. Their hallo is an odd sort of noise, nothing so mellow nor cheerful nor strong and full as ours. Great shooting with the small shot on both sides, and upon our parting both the fleet and the city saluted them with all their great guns in mighty triumph. After their discourse ended with great civility, they went and exercised for half an hour, which showed great dexterity of horsemanship and handling of their lances, but very confused in the order of it, and yet they fight just so. And so we parted, and we home to dinner, breaking the carriage of one of our field pieces by the way. And in my way home Kirke and I did go aside to see some hand granadoes* shot off and flung about* 300 yards off with an instrument lately invented for that use.

After dinner, in the afternoon my Lord sent for me and Dr Tr., and with the Governor did discourse of the treaty he is entering into, and declaring that he intended the Doctor and I for two of the persons [*? parties*]. I said nothing, but did submit to his determination, only I wished that he might have the designed effect of this treaty, which is the getting of time enough for the work he is to do, whereon I was doubtful because of the different judgements I meet with in our people that are to execute the business of blowing up, which I said they did some of them declare could not be done in four, others six months. My Lord presently replied to me very short that they understood not the business, for he had a way of his own in reserve that should do it within a fortnight without fail, to which Kirke immediately added 'God damn him, he would do it all in a fortnight or he would be contented* to be hanged', saying that he had nothing to fear but want of water and the coming of the rains, with which my mouth was stopped, and so said no more. Whereof I after took notice to Dr Tr., and he did also tell me that he did take notice of my Lord and K.'s speaking so peremptorily of the time wherein they would do this work. So to my chamber, and in the evening to walk a little out of the house for air; and so to supper with my Lord, though I never eat anything but continue to my milk, and so to bed.

29 Saturday. Up by times and to the office,[73] where busy receiving what were brought us of answers to any of our difficulties by people concerned therein, but never surely was ever any town governed in all matters both public and private as this place has been, as appears by the strange imperfections in their titles to all they have. At noon home to dinner, where I find that the Alcaïd's son is received on board my Lord's ship today[74] and will be here in the afternoon to visit my Lord and a banquet was prepared for him; but upon second thought his wiser officers that his father sent on shipboard with him would not permit him to come on shore. This afternoon my Lord sent for me and Dr Tr. and there showed us the foul draft of a letter ready drawn without any knowledge or advice of ours to the Alcaïd (it seems upon a message he sent this day that my Lord would proceed with him by first sending him his proposals he had to make for this treaty in writing) giving (after compliments for his favour yesterday in coming at my Lord's entreaty to a peace with K.) three points whereon he has to insist on behalf of our King, viz. the ratifying the present treaty on foot, the giving us ground to fortify, and the treaty marine. I did tell my Lord that I had never to this day read or seen any of the transactions between our King and this, and so could give no advice in it, but if his Lordship did know and had considered all | I could make no objection to what [was] wrote, only I proposed my Lord's making use of [the] Alcaïd's voluntary promise yesterday to negotiate for the ratifying of the treaty, and that all other things should be granted that my Lord should propose for the satisfaction of our King, which my Lord and the whole company mightily liked of, and would have me to order it for de Paz to sign the draft accordingly, which I did, and offered to transpose my Lord's first compliment about K. from the beginning to the conclusion, as indeed thinking it a very little thing for him to speak so greatly of; but my Lord did tell me that he had reason to put more weight upon it and place it as the introduction of all he had to do with the Alcaïd, and so it rested in the place it was, and the letter left with de Paz to translate the whole into Spanish; and so I suppose it was, and sent away, for I never saw nor heard more of it. [So]* going presently to my office to work in taking more answers from the people about their proprieties, and there continued upon this business till nine at night. And so home to supper and slept mighty well, and the better that the business of my being employed in a foolish treaty is over.

30 Sunday. Up and to work at the office till church time, drawing up a report from us to my Lord about having a commission for the surveying of the houses and preparing the form of the commission. So to church and heard a very fine and season[able] sermon from Dr Ken in reproof particularly of the vices of this town, so as I was in pain for the Governor and the officers about us in the church, but I perceived they regarded it not. From church to the office again till dinner,[75] and immediately from dinner thither again till church time and so to church, where we had a foolish sermon of Hughes, but had the pleasure of seeing fine Mrs K. again better dressed than before, but yet short of what I have known her. From church back to the office, and there finishing my matter, I walked out in the evening with Capt. Giles[76] to the high garden that overlooks the town, of the Governor's, where he largely told me the whole unfortunate history of this town from the neglect and self-interestedness of the several governors, showing me what this place would without deceit have really been by this time for trade, if it had not been for their taking away its being a free port by their duties set on goods, so as the place is much worse than ever it was.[77] When it grew dark I walked home and there supped with my Lord, who tonight has declared that (the Alcaïd having this day returned answer to yesterday's letter from us that he would have us propose some persons to be sent to the Emperor[78] upon the business demanded by us, which my Lord will not agree to, for that were but to put people into his hands to be their slaves when we should be found doing what we design to do) from this day he will no longer hinder the public knowledge of his design, and that he will openly go to work to prepare his mines and doing all things towards the great work. My Lord troubled with the headache (as he said, with going into one of the mines that is begun) left the company at table and went to bed. And I and W.H. to my chamber, where we sat and talked over matters an hour, and so he gone and I to bed.

October 1 Monday. All this morning (the Town House being taken up by the town for civil causes) within doors bringing up the journal of our public commission to this day with Mr Hunter our clerk,[79] and doing several other things at the call of my Lord, and particularly preparing and getting signed by my Lord the commission we his other Commissioners do advise him to about surveying in general all the houses pretended to in propriety in the whole town. At noon to dinner, where my Lord did not dine, he having been ill ever since last night and so keeps his chamber. There dined some of the Moors with us, and now they begin to grow troublesome to us by their coming every day, and cannot come but to spy what they can and learn of our proceedings; but now they bring a letter from the Alcaïd wherein they principally* desire his appointing some persons to accompany him to the Emperor to settle things of the peace, but my Lord will not trust him* therein, nor send anybody, but give[s] him a put-off as to that. And to that purpose some things were discoursed on by my Lord to K. and the Doctor and I, but I told my Lord that, we having never read the treaty, we could not judge anything of it, nor [indeed] do I desire to be informed, but only we agreed to his refusing to send anybody to the Emperor; but his letter that he gave us in answer we did not then debate nor afterwards saw, but let it be as he pleased. Towards evening Dr Tr. and I to prayers in the town church, and also did see a burial in the Romish church. And then he and I walked down to the Mole and there saw the pontoon launched, but most bunglingly; and so to the head of the Mole and saw the beginnings of mines digging in one chest [*caisson*] by my Lord by Capt. Leake[80] and the next by Mr Sheres, but it is very hard and slow work. Then home | to supper with my Lord and talk, and then to read and to bed.

2 Tuesday. Doing much business of different kinds | for my Lord, and towards noon to the office and there dispatched some little business of our commission, and drew orders also about demanding from the storekeepers an account of what materials they have laid out in the repairing or new building of any private houses in the town. At noon home to dinner, where my Lord told me he had been writing something that he must show me, which was what he was to say in the public Town House when he speaks to them about the business of destroying the town. After dinner there came in some Moors and went up, where my Lord alone with them in his chamber; and looking in by chance, my Lord called me in, and I was a witness of their high talk to my Lord and his as high to them, and yet they always ended with expressions of desiring peace, and yet now and then mixing that they should have another army come to them. My Lord answering that he cared not for what all Barbary could do to him. Their great difference was about my Lord's not telling them what his errand was here with this force and fleet. | But my Lord would tell them no more than that the Alcaïd had an army near us which could have no business but against us, whereas we had a fleet that could have nothing to do with them, they having nothing to do at sea, but a little war with us as to Sallee, which needed no such fleet, but that the King had other affairs with other neighbour princes that did require this fleet, and whenever the Spanish fleet shall return home this way, they should then know what business he had. However they persisted to know, and my Lord to deny. They to say they knew it from Spain though they would not tell it, and my Lord to tell them that the Spaniards knew as little what he came for as they did. After long bandying in no order about this matter and other general matters, they broke up, both professing purposes of peace, and my Lord appealing to them whether he had or did do anything contrary to the peace.

So Dr Tr. and I by and by walked out down to the Mole and there saw the little advance made in either of the mines since last night. But the weather promises* very foul, and we were no sooner walked home but it begun to rain very hard. | By and by my Lord sent for me to supper, where K. and several others, and | it was discoursed by my Lord and them that from the nature of our discourse with the Moors this day and their parting with us, they bringing a letter from the Alcaïd charging my Lord with not performing his word (in not opening of commerce because that his Moors that he sends are conducted directly to my Lord and not suffered to walk up and down the town) that certainly they would break with us, and that they would do it this very night or very soon. But my Lord and K. made nothing of it if they did, not seeming to think they or the whole army of Barbary could do us any hurt. Besides we have the satisfaction of my Lord's having assurances, as he tells, from Duncombe[81] out of England that three vessels with victuals are upon the way to us from Ireland. And then Capt. Gifford is newly come from Santa Cruz upon an errand he was sent to Mulaï Hamet[82] and tells us for certain that the Emperor is thereabouts still and makes it demonstrable to my Lord (as my Lord and K. says) that if the Emperor would come hither with his army he cannot be here these two months, and therefore do believe that the Alcaïd is in trouble of mind concerning us and puts on a face [only] of bravery, whereas they have reason to think that by our refusing to send anybody to their Emperor, and our being able to [send]* him (as we did yesterday upon the coming of Gifford) fresher news of the condition of his Emperor and where he was than he himself knew (upon which he sent to us to have an account of what account we had from his master) he will be driven at last to secure himself by fleeing to us for his security.

After this the company broke up and went away, and my Lord took me and Dr Tr. into his closet and there did show and read to us his draft of his speech that he intends to make to the town in a day or two upon his opening to them the truth of his design about destroying the place, which I observed to be wholly taken out [of] my notes that I gave him, but with many good improvements that were really very good and wise, and shows him | a man of very good understanding and consideration. After reading he put it into our hands to consider and give him our observations | tomorrow morning; but before we parted I asked him (upon occasion of something Dr Tr. told me the last night, that he had really understood that it was discoursed in England that the King did disown the thing by saying that he was urged to it against his own inclination) whether indeed the King was himself satisfied in this business, for accordingly we should be able to give our advice to him in reference to what he might expect from it whether the success of it was good or bad. He answered me in plain words, the Doctor being by, that the King was the first mover of it at the time that it now begun to be last taken up, which was about ten months ago, but that it was first proposed by my Lord Sunderland about three years since (by the same token Dr Tr. answered that he like[d] it the worse for its being of his proposing) and that it was taken up again upon my Lord Sunderland's coming in again.[83] That the King was the fondest man in the world of it, and had declared to him (I mean my Lord Do.) at his coming away that it was the greatest service

146

that any subject he had in the world could do him; and upon my Lord's adding that he understood that some persons at Court did nevertheless labour to render this thing ill to the King, thereby to do him hurt, though he in all his life had never deserved it of them or anybody, I took occasion to say something of my being sorry for it, but that he was not the first that had been so used in obeying the King's commands and labouring to serve him. He answered that it did not much trouble him (though at the same time I saw by his looks and manner of speech sufficiently that it did) for he was sure they had not durst to use him thus before the King, for the King would do him right in it, and did at this time discourse publicly of the folly of keeping Tangier any longer.[84] Adding that he must and would do the thing though it cost him his life and the laying of his bones here, so that the work might be well done. I thereupon said that the well doing of the thing did not lie in flinging away himself, but preserving himself to see it done, for I did not know what would become of it if he should fail. Upon which he answered that he did not intend to fling away himself, for he too well remembered the case of my Lord of Sandwich and Sir Wm Berkeley[85] and others, and what they got by it when they were dead and out of the way to do it, but would labour to do the work so as that his life should not be spared if that were necessary for the accomplishing of it. This said, we took leave, and the Doctor and I after a turn or two in my chamber discoursing of what had now passed between us, to bed.

3 Wednesday. All the morning in my chamber doing several things upon the score of the public business, and particularly of getting signed and sent away our orders to the storekeepers about an account of the King's materials spent upon private houses,[86] as also Dr Tr. and I reading and making reflections upon my Lord's draft of his speech read to us last night, | which we went with to my Lord, and upon reading it over again with him in his closet, he approved of every one of them and saw them all altered in Dr Tr.'s hand. Dr Tr. also and I did prepare for the commissioners of the survey a letter to give to the Portuguese priests upon the difficulty they make to value the lands and houses of their church, it being not their own private propriety but their King's. We also had committed to us a letter he [*Dartmouth*] designed to send away this day in answer to another of the Alcaïd's yesterday giving reasons for his not thinking it necessary for him presently (as the Alcaïd desires) to send persons with [him] to the Emperor before he has an answer from the King our master to letters he had wrote to him since our arrival here, as also [to] justify our not permitting his Moors to go up and down in the town, but to be brought directly with his messages to my Lord. This my Lord upon our advice did think to make some alterations in the draft drawn of it by de Paz (to de P.'s great trouble) and accordingly I did with the concurrence of the Doctor and Kirke (who did come in just in the season) propose some alterations in it. | And so it went away to be put into Spanish and send to the Alcaïd.

My Lord being not yet very well was let blood this morning, and yet did go on board Sir John Berry to dinner and give orders about Killigrew's[87] commanding in the other's absence who was going to Cadiz to stop some leaks. But I was sorry for it, the weather being very bad for my Lord to go out in, it having rained very much the last night (the first time that it has since we came, and being the time of year that the rains should be here) but he having public business to settle did go; and so we of the family did dine without him, and the same company with us. Mr Sheres also did this morning come and tell me that he had delivered my Lord his paper, whereof he did show me his foul draft of the ordinary objections made against the Mole, improved the most he could to justify the King's destroying of it; though he do tell me privately that he is able to answer them all, and therefore by my advice has not given them in in his own hand, lest it should one day rise up against him in judgement after his having published to the world his discourse upon my instance in defence of Tangier and the Mole. And he added this of his being ready to show that what he wrote on that subject was at my request, that I also might, when time of trouble shall come, be able to prove my fondness for the thing, and therefore frequent[*ly*] desires to have [me]* publish something in defence of the usefulness of the place and the King's cost bestowed and to be bestowed on it.[88]

After dinner up to my chamber to carry on this my private journal to this time and place ever since Sunday last, and so to read it. Still very foul weather ever since last night, | and it is [*to*] be feared will continue to the great interruption of our works upon the Mole, though we cannot but hope that it will be as [*bad*] for the enemy in the field.

4 Thursday. All the morning at the office hard at work. | In the afternoon my Lord coming and opening the great secret in the Town House, with general joy and content to all. He gone, we continued at work. At night home and there took care by Jos.[89] to copy my Lord's speech by stealth out.

5 Friday. All the morning busy at the office.[90] Home to dinner and most of the afternoon writing letters to go by the post from Cadiz. To Mr Houblon a very grave letter, owning the secret and saying some things thereon.[91]

6 Saturday. Up to Pole Fort, which is now beginning to be pulled down. Then to work till noon and so to dinner, and thither to work again till 9 at night.

7 Sunday. In the morning with my Lord by horse riding round the town to see the mines upon the Mole and about the walls, and out of the walls Kirke led me to see some old Roman little aqueducts, of which there are many ruins, and some pans worked out of the rock like tanners' vats.* Thence to church where Dr K. made a weak sermon upon the great business of our being called home. Thence home with my Lord, and from him carried by Mr Sh. to his lodging, Mr Cuthbert's,[92] and gave me a Spanish dinner very good and neat, and the finest Spanish woman, Mr Cuthbert's wife, that ever I saw. Thence to church and heard a silly sermon, and so to the Town House a meeting there till night,[93] and so home to sit with my Lord Do. and Mr H. in my chamber talking about our businesses here, and so to bed. My Lord told me this day that he doubted not to have all done within three weeks, though I cannot imagine it yet. He speaks how much he is troubled with Dr Tr.'s being so sheepish and weak a man, and reproached him with his saying that the first day of the term he should have got 10 guineas.

8 Monday. Extremely busy at the office all the morning, when news brought of my Lord's fall and his being put to bed and let blood. At noon to dinner some few by ourselves, my Lord being ill abed, though there was great preparation for a dinner for the Mayor and town to deliver their address. To the office in the afternoon and about 4 a-clock to my Lord to see the delivery of the address, but it was not read, but a foolish speech of the Recorder, with a great cold, about our values set upon their proprieties, to which I answered.[94] Then into the garden to a collation, and I and Dr Tr. with them, in good humour. | At night to my Lord and sat with him, who was in great pain. And there Nich.[95] told us many stories of the Moors by my Lord's bedside, and we read the town's address, wherein a great deal of repetition of imprisonment and captivity, which I do not like. So sleepy to bed.

9 Tuesday. All the morning very busy in my chamber with Mr Hunter fetching up our journal. Then towards noon to the office where several things done, and then home to dinner. | After dinner to the office again and there very busy till night. Thence home and supped all by my Lord's bedside, he being much better able to move his fingers and rest. At night to bed and slept ill by reason of the clinches again. [*Margin*] Pleased after dinner with the discourse of Mr W.H. and the Comptroller.

10 Wednesday. Up and to walk the first time into the fields over Fountain Fort, seeing the Moors' sentries and people treating at the stockades, and the folly of this place in being overlooked everywhere, I seeing the very soldiers going in and out of the Castle gate, the strange diligence and patience of the Moors. So to my office where busy all the morning, but now in a fair view to have done. | After dinner to see my Lord, who grows every hour better and better and sits up. From him to the office close till the evening, when we all three waited on my Lord with our reasons for our rates proposed for the proprieties, which my Lord was pleased with.[96] Thence to my chamber, and by and by to supper by my Lord's bed and sat late talking with him. And at last, being alone, he took notice of Dr Tr.'s ridiculous degree of melancholy continuing, and I proposed by the by his going home; which my Lord was fond of, and said he should if he would by the *Swallow* – I telling him, and my Lord observing it to me himself, that he saw that I did all the work and he signified little. Thence to bed.

Memorandum, that having lately heard Mr Phillips[97] | say that he feared we should lack powder, and he answering to my question what powder my Lord sends to Mulaï Hamet to Santa Cruz which is not gone yet,[98] he told me 50 barrels, I did this day ask my Lord whether he was sure he would have powder enough. He told me yes, or if he wanted he could borrow of the fleet, to which end he had given order for their forbearing any more salutes.

11 Thursday. Up by times and again to walk, and particularly upon the sands at the stockade, and I ventured a little way within it to see a boat a-mending by the Moors and some of our carpenters lent them, but would not venture too near them for I had been good prize, and I saw their sentries mighty close and intent upon me. So to the office busy till noon, when I hear the Moor that was Secretary to the Ambassador that was in England[99] is just come to my Lord, but I do not see him, he staying all the time that I was within alone with de Paz. So I after a little nap after dinner (where the Portuguese fathers dined with us) in my chamber Mr Budgeon[100] come to see me and told me several pretty passages of his Captain, young Aylmer.[101] So to my office till evening and so home to my Lord to supper and bed, I having a mighty cold that made me dumb. This day we had a foolish answer from the Mayor in the name of all the proprietors about the valuation of their houses.[102]

12 Friday. Up, my cold being greater than it was, so as I was not able to speak and therefore did not go out of my chamber all the day till towards the evening, when I walked out into the fields up the hills and there ventured very near the Moors' sentries almost round our bounds, and in the evening too, when they might have come and snapped me and nobody have seen that they took me within our bounds, having only my man with me. In the evening supped with my Lord and sat talking with him after all were gone. This day Dr Tr. owns to me that my Lord has offered him to go home with his expresses for England in the *Swallow* and is mighty brisk upon it, which I told my Lord of and he laughs with me at it, this being upon my advice to my Lord. So to bed and first lay in my drawers, and what with that and pinning my sleeves close, I was not troubled tonight at all with clinches.

13 Saturday. To the office this morning and there busy the greatest part of the day providing against the public meeting that we have proposed to my Lord to have with the proprietors to justify our proposals against their objects thereto.[103] At night to supper and discourse with my Lord and his company, and so to bed.

14 Sunday. Up by times and walk to the stockade, where there was landed from Smyrna some Turks or Armenians with their wares, and laid on the sand to be by them [carried]* into Fez for sale. Here I talked with them in a kind of Frank,[104] and I liked their habit and countenances very well. Then home to dress myself and to church, where Mr Hughes preached his farewell sermon to the town, a very good and pious one, wherein among other things he found it necessary to purge himself against some ill reports it seems he had lain [under]* declaring in the presence of God that he in his time with them had [never]* done injury to man or known unlawfully any woman, but he did it very handsomely and gravely. From church on board the *Grafton* and dined by invitation with Sir W.B., and after dinner Dr Ken gave us a sermon there. Here Sir W. Booth gave me an account of the [? *trouble*]* he has had with some of Herbert's young fellows to get the paper signed my Lord desires about the Mole and harbour of Tangier.[105] In the evening on shore, where I stayed walking on the Mole with Mr Sheres till it was late by moonshine, talking of several matters, and here I had the pleasure to see in the night the volleys of great and small shot round the town towards the sea, it being the Duke of York's birthday, and it was very pretty.[106] This day also all the military officers presented an address to my Lord for the King upon the subject of the King's deliverance from the Plot, and what is now doing here and his calling them home,[107] they dining also today with my Lord. Thence being wet with the dew that every evening falls, I went by appointment to the Comptroller Erlisman's with others to discourse the business once more of our proposals of rating the proprieties, to fit myself against the public meeting thereon tomorrow. So home, there being several bonfires tonight, and to my Lord to supper and talk and bed. Dr Tr. being very ill of the flux, but more in his mind, and so my Lord resolves with me to send him presently home, as being but a trouble to him, and a man of the meanest mind as to courage that ever was born.

15 Monday. All the morning busy in my chamber upon the public business till dinner, and after dinner to walk in the garden with my Lord, talking of the silliness of Dr Tr. with reference to his poorness of spirit, and that he will send a ship away with him on purpose, for Dr K. tells me today that he is not to be supported but by sending him home. In the afternoon to the Town House by appointment with my Lord, and there the matter of the proprieties and their valuations were debates by me against them before my Lord, and ended in standing by my rates, with room left for more if, when they come into England, the King shall be prevailed with to give them more. Thence home, where my Lord called for the draft of a letter he is writing to the Alcaïd, wherein my Lord is for provoking of him to break. But the Governor and Dr Tr. (who is come out of his chamber upon the news of his going home) did join with me in altering it, showing the inconvenience that may attend it, and none that can the keeping our peace longer with him; and my Lord was content to delay it a week longer and then, he declared, he would not care for all the strength of Barbary. Thence I to walk in the evening till within night by moonshine in the fields under the wall, thinking of all our affairs here. And here I found a glow-worm shining, but a very small one compared with what we have in England. I stayed till the gates were ready to be locked, and first observed the manner of placing the turnpikes without the gates for fear of any horse surprising them in the night. And so home to supper with my Lord, and so to bed.

16 Tuesday. The business of the rates of the proprieties being settled last night, we applied ourselves this morning and all this day to the adjusting with the Portuguese, and did it very fully; and presented it at night to my Lord, with which he was well pleased, their money coming to near £600.[108] | At night to supper and discourse with my Lord. Dr Tr. being now quite well again upon his being to go home. |

17 Wednesday. Up and to walk a little up to the Castle to look upon the progress of the mines, which appears not great, but there I was taken with rain, and so to the office where very busy till noon, providing for the present casting up the value of all the proprieties in the town by way of abstract. And it was done by night, and amounts to about £11,000. | In the afternoon I walked down to the Mole, which advances I think very slow. At night to supper where were all the engineers discoursing merrily every man of his work, and my Lord discoursing as if a week or ten days more would put all things a good forwardness about the walls of the town, so as they will be subject to no interruption from the Moors if they should come, and then they will spare all their miners to the Mole, the want of which Capt. Leake and Mr Sh. do much complain of. This evening Mr Sh. brought to my Lord the report of the commission appointed to survey the fortifications, and they make the works necessary by land to make the place secure to come to a great deal above two millions of money. After supper to read and to bed.

18 Thursday. Up and in my chamber at work all the morning. This morning the *Dover* is come in with a Turk's colours under his own, but not the prize, she having only made her run on shore, where they rifled her after she was deserted by her company and was broken a-pieces. This is Capt. Deering.[109] | After dinner with Dr Trumbull to show my Lord the state of our commission now upon his going, which is finished in everything but what is to be done by the officers of the King's Revenue, and so it has been these twelve days, and for the setting of the rates which was concluded on on Monday. But now to see how weakly and yet impudently would this Doctor pretend to interpose in discourse with my Lord upon it when he knows and owns to me, and so do my Lord too, that he has done nothing in the world in the thing but I let him do it. After dinner to read till the evening, and speaking with people that come to me of the commanders to desire my favour much against my will, I not seeing one that has virtue enough to deserve it. And then walked out round the fields again, as I had done this day once before, before dinner, to Peterborough Tower. And there by Capt. Silver[110] was led upon my knees into a mine which is finished, the powder being laid in and the trunk and fuses in it, and the trunk now bringing out to the outside of the wall, he explaining to me the whole method of it. Thence home and to read and discourse with Mr Hewer; and so to supper, where full of discourse of Dr Tr.'s going away, poor man, tomorrow, with so impudent a degree of professed fear as never man did of his quality and in public commission. My Lord did this evening read to us his long letter of two large sheets of paper to Sir L. Jenkins, giving a general and very good state of matters here by Dr Tr., with all the advices and other public states of surveys that can inform him in everything. But that which did trouble me tonight at supper, and when I waked in the morning, was some words my Lord let fall that he should not be able to spare Mr H. to go to Spain with me. I had much good discourse this evening with Mr Sh. about the evil arising to the Navy from Good Voyages.[111]

19 Friday. Up by times, and after entering some notes, I walked a little abroad, and then home and fell to my letters to England by Dr Tr., who is impatient with my Lord to be gone today.[112] Thus to dinner and then to the same again. About 5 a-clock I went to the Mole to see the first trial by Capt. Leake of two bombs under the arches in the Mole blown up, but by the looseness of the earth above they did little or no execution, which makes us fear more mistakes in the greater works, since the Master Gunner of England can be so mistaken. So home again to my letters and then to my Lord to supper, where everybody laughing at Dr Tr.'s foolish impatience to be gone, but my Lord's letters are not done. So to bed.

20 Saturday. Up, and all the morning making an end of my letters to England. Dr Tr. still playing the fool and making himself ridiculous in his impatience to be gone, but it was the afternoon before my Lord had done his, or I mine, and therefore after dinner both he and I up to end our letters, and then my Lord and all of us with all seeming respect took our leaves of him, my Lord giving himself the trouble to treat him with all the respect in the world because of his going, that he might be useful in England, and therefore came with him to my chamber and there drank a parting bottle to his good voyage, the Governor K. being also with us, and so we all, my Lord and all, walked down and saw him in the boat and gave him several guns from the town.[113] And so the fool went away, every creature of the house laughing at him. Then my Lord and we upon the Mole and saw a small mine blow up of Mr Sh.'s, which did good execution and had liked to have hurt my Lord and me had we not stood within a little house hard by, but it did hurt Col. Boynton's eye.[114] And so home and to read, and supper, and to bed.

21 Sunday. Walked out with my Lord down to the Mole before church, and there saw the little advance (I thought) thereon. Thence back and to church. | Dr K. reading the prayers, Mr Hughes preached an ordinary sermon instead of what was expected of a farewell sermon to the garrison. So home to walk alone with my Lord in the garden till dinner. And then | to my chamber to read and sleep a little, it being most excellent weather. In the evening my Lord berode the first time a-horseback since his hurt in his arm, and I and de Paz a-horseback to ride out into the fields; and meeting with an officer riding out, he carried us round the very brinks of our bounds close by the Moors' sentries, to whom we talked, and several times out of our bounds, as we were told when we came home, and might have been shot or taken prisoners. But this I am glad I have once done, to know the most of the place, some of the history of it against the Moors, | seeing the present condition of Pole Fort, which is stripped of everything within, only in appearance to the Moors it is as it was, and here a mine ready to blow up when we desert it. So home, meeting my Lord at the town gate, sitting with the Governor on a bank. | At supper my Lord did come to a resolution that pleased everybody, which was to have all the hands off the works about the town (which are almost all finished) and take them this very fair weather and moonshine nights to the Mole; and this the engineers now all at supper did themselves offer, and it was taken by my Lord, he saying that he had several times wished it, but durst [not] propose it to Phillips and Beckmann for fear of offending them. So to bed.

22 Monday. Up and to the office to work all the morning at ruling a finishing book to be the ground of our report to my Lord. But first I walked down to my Lord to the Mole where I saw a second experiment of his with a gun in blowing up, but it did nothing. Then I saw to the office till noon, and then down again to the Mole, where Mr Sh. showed me the whole process of a mine made and blowed up with a drill, and the manner of plugging up the hole, which was done so as to do mighty execution. Then he and I | by appointment off to the *Mountagu* to dinner with Killigrew, where we dined most delicately, his being the finest ship one or other and the neatest kept, and his manner of living the neatest and most like a gentleman that I ever yet saw of any man, and his civility to me extraordinary. After dinner and a glass or two, Mr Sh. and Dr Lawrence and I away, he giving us guns contrary to a late order against salutes. And I having set them on shore at the Mole, I went alone in the boat round the bay and saw the ruins very plain of old Tangier and the river of Tangier, and several Moors all along upon the shore gathering of driftwood, and the manner of their huts, seeing some near the waterside. And so coming to Malabata Point, turned about to go to my Lord, who dined on board the *Grafton*, but he going off before we got to him, I to the Mole and there saw several more mines blowed up of Sh.'s with very good execution even to wonder with so little quantity of powder. Coming back upon the water I first saw how blue the remote hills will look in evening about the sun's going down, as I have sometimes seen them painted but never believed it natural. | My Lord at night to my chamber, troubled to lose so extraordinary a moonshine night and have no work done in it upon the Mole, but at supper he settled it for tomorrow and so onward to have all hands night and day there.|

23 Tuesday. Up by times and to set down my journal for two days. Then to the office, where hastening my clerks in the things to be prepared towards my report. And then down to the Mole to see all the hands taken from the walls now to the Mole, and great riddance they in appearance make, but it is but upon the slight part of the Mole and not upon Mr Sheres's chests, which go on but slowly yet. So meeting my Lord there, I home with him and to dinner, and after that to my chamber to read, and then a little to the office, and so to the Mole and saw great execution done with two drills. I also went down into a mine, the first made, to try the business of the iron cylinders. | At supper with my Lord, well pleased with the appearance of dispatch upon the Mole, and particularly with his cook Atkins[115] taking all his and our servants this afternoon and pulling down a house and wall upon the Mole. After supper, it being a very fine moonshine, I proposed walking down to the Mole, which my Lord did, and I saw the manner of giving the word to my Lord as General by all the officers of the guards. And my Lord told me of the strange mistake in the discipline of this place in their giving to every guard both within and without the town both words, that is to say the In and Out words, which he showed me the extreme ignorance of. So back and to bed.

24 Wednesday. Up with a great cold in my throat [that] I could hardly speak or swallow. To walk, however, a little [in] the fields, and then to the office awhile, and so home to read and set down several things that I had heard of Kirke that vex me to see so great a villain in his place.[116] At noon to dinner, and notice brought us of Mr Sh.'s mine going to be blown up, so we up to [the] top of the house to see it, but I down to the watergate and saw it blow up, and it was a wonderful distance [the] stones did fly to the endangering all the small vessels in the harbour. Going down to the Mole I saw the effects of the blow, which was very great, some parcels of the iron cylinder making their way quite through the side of the Mole and making a crack in one place quite across the Mole from side to side, and yet there was not full a barrel and a half of powder. Thence I took my man Anthony[117] with my long glass and entertained myself the first time therewith in the fields, it being a fine evening, and saw the whole camp of the Moors and their huts, and manner of walking up and down in their *alhaques* that they look almost like ghosts all in white. Thence as it grew dark I went home and there met with letters by the [? yacht]* just come from Cadiz. My letters are of the 24th of September, being just a month, and blessed be God, all our friends well and writing mighty kindly, moving me mightily with joy and trouble to be so far and long from them. So after supper to bed.

25 Thursday. Up, my cold still upon me, and first took a walk upon the walls about [the] Irish Battery, being led thither to see the mortar pieces drawn up thither and placed to annoy the Moors if they should come, which my Lord do now and then think they will, and the more for that none of them have lately been with us as they used daily to be; but I see nothing like extraordinary in the fields near us that they are doing. Here I walked a good while, pleased with it. Thence to the office till noon, and back again after dinner, never stirring till 11 at night, making up a report for my Lord upon every one of several petitions he has referred to us, and I was [? glad]* to rid my hands of them. But this sitting up so late did increase my cold mightily, that I had an ill night of it, my throat being so sore.

26 Friday. Up and to my Lord, showing him my last night's work about reports, which he was mightily pleased with, saying it was surely the first time ever such a general report was ever done upon petitions, and I believe so too. Thence to the office, where he said he would come presently after me to give people their answers according to my report, but he met with business upon the Mole. And at noon dined upon the *Mountagu*, and therefore being a little ill and troubled at so much loose company at table, my Lord not being there, I dined in my chamber, and Dr Ken for the same reason came and dined with me there. And a great deal of good discourse we had upon the viciousness of this place and its being time for God Almighty to destroy it. Besides, my Lord gives me an extraordinary case today to examine upon a petition of one Mings complaining of his being laid in prison and his wife ravished.[118] | So to the office after dinner, where towards night my Lord came and run through all the petitions and gave answers to them accordingly by our report. So at night home and after supper, being full of my cold, I to my bed.

27 Saturday. Up very ill in my throat with my cold, but yet I was obliged to go to my office, and there all the morning preparing another general report upon petitions to clear the coast, the Mayor being to go away on board today. | We have news brought us of hurt done this morning at the Mole by ground falling in, so that two or three men are killed quite outright and several spoilt in their limbs and carried to the hospital. | To work again in the afternoon to finish this report against the evening, when my Lord came and there we run it through and answered everybody. And that done, I by my Lord's desire to write a letter to Mr Secretary Jenkins for him to sign in behalf of the Mayor. | I away to bed by 9 a-clock because of my cold, and about 10 I heard the Mayor take his leave of my Lord and the company, and so with the *St David* he and the best families of the citizens sailed away at break a-day for England.[119] This day, after a week's silence and absence of the Moors we used to have daily come to us, my Lord had a letter from the Alcaïd of mighty compliment and offering the civility of the country for us to ride out or hunt, which was very surprising, though none of our blades, I see, dare trust him with themselves.

28 Sunday. My cold continuing upon me, I did not go to church, but stayed in my chamber very busy setting some papers to rights with my clerk Lawson. And noon very high discourse between Dr Ken and me on one side and the Governor on the other about the excessive liberty of swearing and blaspheming we observe here, and it seems the Doctor had preached upon it today. | After dinner to read and then to walk out a little in the graft [*ditch*] under the walls to avoid the wind because of my cold, and there read an hour (the first time I was ever yet there); and so home to my chamber and to fetch up my journal thus far. So to supper and to bed.

29 Monday. Still very ill of my cold, so I was not able to do anything, but only in my chamber, to state the business of several petitions.[120] And entertain myself in Hakluyt,[121] which I do nowadays to mighty pleasure. At night to supper with my Lord, and much talk among the engineers about their dispatch of their mines. Mr Sh., I fear, beginning now to be the most in arrear, by reason of the good weather lasting beyond all imagination. So to bed.

30 Tuesday. Still as ill as ever or worse of my cold, and so keep my chamber and work there as yesterday all day upon petitions.

31 Wednesday. The like at my chamber all the morning. I at noon with my Lord to dinner at Mr Sh.'s lodging upon a Spanish dinner, Mrs Cuthbert being however gone away for Spain, but a good dinner, and so home, and then down with my Lord to look upon the great chest at the head of the Mole that is to be blown up tonight. And it was worth seeing the care that is taken to bind the mouth of it close with timbers. In the evening with my Lord to Capt. St John's,[122] to a good supper and a harp well played on. After supper home and stayed up till 11 at night, when my Lord and I standing looking out at our dining-room window, we observe the going off of the great chest, which though four chambers yet made but one blow, and that no great one, but the stones flew up and down upon the top of our house very plain, but no hurt done. But by the people that came to us afterward, we find it has had all the success imaginable, at which we were all glad. And so I very ill with my cold to bed.

November 1 Thursday. All the morning till noon at home, when a great cry of Capt. St John's house being afire, which gave me much care for W.H.'s papers and books and himself, but they were presently brought to my chamber with several chests of money, and I went out thither to look [for] him, but he was within disposing of Mr St J.'s goods and papers, so as I could not come to him, which because they talked of blowing up the house, did give me great pain for Mr H. So home to dinner, and by and by W. Hewer came in very well and has saved all his own and Capt. St John's books and papers; and the house (which we supped so well in but last night) is now a few days before its time burned down. And not without some fear, I saw by W.H., that is by some ill design of Col. K.'s, for his not knowing (but by my Lord himself, who sent for him thither) of his entertainment last night. After dinner down with my Lord to the Mole, and there surprised to see the mighty effect of the last night's blowing up of the great chest, it tearing it up from the very bottom. So my Lord and I, Mr Sh. taking him from the Mole, rowed to old Tangier and round the bay, very pleasant. And so back and home, and I to look after my cold which yet troubles me. |

2 Friday. All the morning in my chamber for my cold. At noon with my Lord to Capt. Priestman on board the *Bonaventure* | where we dined very handsomely, and ship very neat, though not quite so well as Killigrew's. Thence home in the afternoon and I to my chamber to keep myself warm. And so after supper with my Lord, to bed.

3 Saturday. All the morning busy in my chamber about office business, and particularly till noon with Hunter fetching up the journal thereof to this day.[123] | In the afternoon down to the Mole to walk with my Lord, but I found it so cold that I came back and kept my chamber, and went to visit Dr Ken, who keeps his chamber, being very ill of an headache. So after supper, being very much out of humour with my cold, I to bed.

4 Sunday. Kept my chamber reading all the morning, a little better of my cold than I was, since I made use of my old powder to keep the phlegm from falling down into my stomach and come out of my nose. Down at noon to dinner | with my Lord, | declaring himself, upon both messages by Cuthbert and by letter from the Alcaïd, that we shall meet with no disturbance from the Moors, which do give me a great deal more quietness of mind, though I speak not of it. In the afternoon Mr Hewer, S. Atkins, Capt. St John and I on horseback ride out round about our bounds, where with great pleasure I received an account from St John of every considerable action that has happened in any place about the town since the beginning. So back and | read till late, not being willing to go to supper to my Lord's for fear of taking cold.

5 Monday. Very much better of my cold, but did not stir out of my chamber all the morning, but read Hakluyt to my mighty pleasure. At noon down to dinner, | my Lord having first shown me his letters and papers going this day by the *Dartmouth* for England, giving a particular account of the state of our works at this day, and his assurance of meeting with no disturbance from the Moors. After dinner I all the afternoon writing to my friends in England; and that done and given my letters to Lt Usher,[124] I out into the fields to my usual walk before the Marine Battery, and so home to my chamber to fetch up my journal to this day |, Mr H. sitting with me a good while this evening.

[*19 Monday*]. I have been so much out of humour with my cold and therewith kept my chamber for the most part, that there has happened very little worth setting down in my journal. Only now and then I have dined aboard some ships with my Lord and gone by water with him in the bay and a-fishing with him afterward, and particularly on Wednesday, Nov. 14th, dining on board Capt. Wheler[125] in the *English Tiger*, my Lord and Governor K. and I went in his barge at my single instance as far as Alcazar Bay, without our bounds, and in our return it was a thousand to one we had not been shot by the Moors, as we must if they had not begun with us too soon, and thereby prevented our going further into the bay as we intended to have heard our trumpets, of which my Lord writ a complaint the next day to the Alcaïd, and had an answer. In all this time the work of the Mole, by the fairness of the weather, is much advanced, but yet much to be done to it. These two days much rain but no wind, and this day fair. I now preparing for my journey to Spain, having finished and delivered my Lord our great report upon our commission the 12th instant.[126] This is the first day that, by putting on something extraordinary to keep my feet warm, I feel my cold a little and immediately abated. And this day the guard house at the end of the Mole is expected will be blown up. |

19 Monday to the 22 Thursday. Nothing, but stayed within doors, my cold remaining upon me, and it being very wet weather without doors. Myself preparing matters for my journey to Spain against the vessel comes in with letters by the last post from England. Yesterday in the afternoon, being the 22nd, the guard house at the end of the Mole was blowed up in my sight at my window with very good success, yet no great noise. | And now the Mole do begin to look indeed as in a way of destruction, this being a great mark of its standing all this while, but is now gone. My Lord has been ill also these two or three days and keeps his chamber of a great cold, only was with me this afternoon to see the house blown up.

24 Saturday. Nothing, but as before keeping in my chamber, the weather being very rainy in mighty showers and drops, with a great deal of thunder and lightning. The work of the Mole going but ill during this weather, and yet no storms to break it down; the moon at nights very bright so as to give me opportunity to observe that I could read very plain, even this thick hazy rainy weather, by moonlight. The vessel with our letters from Spain | not come in yet, being thought to be driven into the Straits with the W. wind, so that Mr H. and I are stopped in our journey to Spain, being unwilling to go without hearing first from England. A mine blown up this morning as by mischance in the fields, to the frighting of the Moorish sentries, of which we sent an excuse to the Alcaïd as of a mere accident, for which the Alcaïd sent my Lord thanks for his advice; but thereby we show them what they are [to] expect if they come near our ground. Mr Sh. in great trouble at the friendly plainness* of my Lord with him about the backwardness of his work, in which I think my Lord has reason, and that he is a little too obstinate in not complying more with my Lord. My cold much better upon the coming down of the rain.

25 Sunday. Mighty wet and thunder in mighty sudden claps, and hail and lightning this morning. Fair all day, and I within doors, | my Lord not well and coming and sitting a little while with me talking. Mr Hewer ill all day of his headache, and I twice at his ill lodging to see him, and mightily troubled I was to see him lie in a room great and wide and cold, rain coming in all over the house, and no glass windows, but shuts [*shutters*]; but he better at night. Our letters came today from Gibraltar by the ship's boat that could not herself come in,[127] but no letters [to]* Mr H. nor me, nor indeed to anybody but one to my Lord of an old date of the 15th October,[128] whereas we looked for letters of the 22nd. | So if Mr H. be well enough tomorrow, he and I mean to be gone for Spain. Up late putting things in order for our going. |

This day my Lord told me with great pleasure the good condition of his affairs, that the Alcaïd now could not hurt him, nor designed it, he having yesterday sent him a present of fowl, and that indeed he had once orders from his King to set upon us, but upon an answer from him to the King, the King countermanded it. And that rains must now have raised the rivers in the country so that the King himself if he [would]* cannot come with his army against us. All which made this the proper time for me to be gone and to stay no longer, lest the opportunity be lost. My Lord is very earnest for my coming back soon as I can, and seems to expect it in fourteen days; but he having once said three weeks, I say I will come as much within the three weeks as I can. But Mr de Paz tells me today that the Alcaïd do insist upon hostages for our performance of treaty as to the powder when we go, but my Lord would put it off (as himself today told me). But the thing seems most reasonable, and if my Lord gives me opportunity, I will advise it.

26 Monday. Mightily frightened this morning with my cold swimming in my head at my rising and most of the morning, which makes me melancholy, and a fear also of my right foot being lame; but I hope in God it will both of them go over, and that it is only the weather.

30 Friday. From the last, still ill weather till today pretty fair, but the night before last several of our ships drove out of the harbour, and hurt done by one of them[129] the *Mountagu*, so that she must go to be fitted at Cadiz. And so because of the floods apprehended to be in Spain upon these rains, I do resolve to begin our tour by Cadiz and to go thither in her, and this my Lord and I agreed to do with Capt. Killigrew. But such weather for wind, thunder, lightning, rain and hail all together for eight or ten days I never saw in my life. This day I wrote many letters to clear my head of matters to my friends in England, and among others a merry, roguish, but yet mysterious one to S.H.[130]

My Lord did tell me this day that he do find that the Moors are designing us mischief, the Alcaïd being all last night, as bad as it was, in the fields about our bounds, and yet but a few days ago he told me that all was well with them, and would be so, for that the Alcaïd has let fall his pretension to hostages, and had called back the Jews again from Tetuan to his camp, which is a sure sign of their designing nothing against us. | But yet I doubt we shall be found in the wrong and that my Lord do break the treaty in not giving hostages, and that the Alcaïd do not let the thing fall so much as put the consequence of it upon us, and will break with us for his own safety rather than suffer us to go away without paying the powder and giving hostages for the doing of it. By a calculation also made by Mr Sh. two days since in my chamber, he do show me that the Mole cannot be brought down even to high-water mark in less than three months, according to the rate that we have wrought hitherto all in fair weather, and this without taking in the tarras work[131] that has been done in this time also, which is sad consideration. Within these last four days have come in some victuallers from England, which have given us much relief, we being likely otherwise to have been under great difficulties. A turkey being come to be sold for six dollars, and some soldiers actually mutinying at their having pilchards given them for flesh. And our men dropping down sick with the rains and great labour and short provisions, and not of good kinds. And the seamen all at short allowance.

Four or five nights we have fallen to play at cards, by which my Lord will want me the less. This night I washed my feet and thighs with brandy, being I bless God in very good health again, and so to bed.

December 1 Saturday. Up and to get my things together to be gone this morning on board the *Mountagu* towards Cadiz, but by and by it become so stormy.

The journal ends here. Pepys and Hewer did not sail for Spain until 6 December.[132]

1. See plate 11. The Captain's log of the *Grafton* (24 May 1683–19 April 1684) is printed from PRO, ADM 51/407 in *TP*, pp. 267–98.
2. Capt. Christopher Gunman of the *Mary* yacht: *CSO*, p. 192. *TP*, p. 111.
3. They sailed at 9 a.m. and anchored at St Helens about 11: *TP*, [Appendix I, *Grafton's* log], p. 268.
4. Thomas Ken, DD, Canon of Winchester and Chaplain of the *Grafton* for this voyage. At Dartmouth's suggestion he became senior Chaplain on the Tangier station, the first such appointment within the Navy. Bishop of Bath and Wells 1685–90: *ODNB*. G.C. Taylor, *The Sea Chaplains: A History of the Chaplains of the Royal Navy* (Headington, 1978), pp. 105–7.
5. Berry, in the *Henrietta*, had to shelter from the westerlies before proceeding to Plymouth for provisions: *TP*, pp. 268, 269.
6. Cf. Houblon's reply, 11 August: Howarth, pp. 154–5.
7. Commission (2 July 1683) and instructions (2 and 27 July) printed in *TP*, pp. 58–67. Abstract in HMC, *Dartmouth*, I, pp. 83–4, 86.
8. Col. Percy Kirke, Acting Governor of Tangier.
9. Sir Leoline Jenkins, one of the two Secretaries of State.
10. Capt. Charles Wylde: *CSO*, p. 482. Cf. *TP*, pp. 268–9.
11. Including one to James Houblon, printed in Howarth, pp. 156–7.
12. Francis Wyndham, Royal Horse Guards, an equerry to the Duke of York, was an enthusiastic private yachtsman: *TP*, p. 110. *Hist. Parl. 1690–1715*, V, pp. 938–9. PL 2877, pp. 281–4 (refusal of Wyndham's request to wear the King's jack on his yacht, 1685).
13. Legge, Royal Horse Guards and supernumerary Groom of the Bedchamber, was duly elected for Portsmouth, his brother's former constituency, in 1685: *Hist. Parl.*, II, p. 727.

14. Henry Sheres, military engineer, Kt 1685: *ODNB*.
15. Thomas Lawrence, MD (Padua), Dartmouth's physician: Foster, *Alumni Oxon.*, III, p. 889.
16. John Ashby, Kt 1689, Admiral of the Fleet 1690: *CSO*, p. 11. *ODNB*.
17. At 7 a.m.: *TP*, p. 269.
18. Ten miners from the *Delight* flyboat boarded the *Grafton* on 20 August and were discharged the following day. The flyboat was then returned to Plymouth for more ballast: PRO, ADM 33/108, f. 32v. *TP*, p. 269.
19. William Trumbull, DCL, Clerk of the Signet, with some practice in the Admiralty Court. Designated Judge-Advocate for this expedition; Kt 1684, PC, and Secretary of State 1695: *ODNB*. *Hist. Parl.*, III, pp. 608–9. PRO, ADM 33/108, f. 27v.
20. Or 'children' (Howarth). Lady Anne Edgcumbe, daughter of Pepys's cousin and first patron Lord Sandwich, and thus Pepys's own kinswoman. Her child is perhaps the future 1st Baron Edgcumbe (b. 1680): *ODNB*.
21. 'Sir Nicholas [Acland ?]' (*TP*) and 'Sir Nicholas Holland' (Howarth) are both imaginary; the reality (first noted in Ollard, *Pepys*, p. 352 n. 18) is much more interesting: Maj.-Gen. John Lambert ('Lord' only by Cromwell's elevation), imprisoned since 1660, was moved to St Nicholas Island in Plymouth Sound in 1667. Pepys must have been among his last visitors, as he died in the following winter: R.J. King, 'Lambert, the "Arch–rebbel"', *Notes & Queries*, [1st ser.], iv, no. 105 (1 November 1851), pp. 339–40.
22. There were 9 warships (*Grafton, Henrietta, Mountagu, Oxford, Woolwich, Mary Rose, St David, Bonaventure, Greyhound*) and 12 merchantmen: *TP*, pp. 269–70.
23. Capt. George Aylmer: *CSO*, p. 14. Cf. *TP*, p. 270. George was the brother of Capt. Matthew Aylmer (text, p. 151).
24. MS blank. Cf. *TP*, p. 270.
25. High winds between 2 and 6 a.m. made it difficult to steer the *Grafton*; then the *Anne* noisily announced that she was taking water: *TP*, p. 270.
26. Probably Abel de Verdun, entered in the *Grafton* as a midshipman extraordinary, having served as a volunteer under the Duke of Grafton: *TP*, p. 106 & n. 1.
27. Maj. Martin Beckmann, a Swedish artillery officer and engineer, serving Charles II since 1660, chiefly in the fortification of Tangier. His scheme of demolition, dated aboard the *Grafton* 28 August, is printed in *TP*, pp. 67–71.
28. Pepys bought the first part of Samuel Butler's comedy in 1662, and further copies of this and of the second part the following year, but repeatedly pronounced it humourless: *Diary*, III, p. 294; IV, pp. 35, 400, 411. Clearly he was enjoying it by 1683, and bought another copy (3 parts, 1689) retained in his library: PL 889.

29. Captain: Sir William Booth: *CSO*, p. 41. *ODNB*. Master: Benjamin Hoskins: PRO, ADM 33/108, f. 13v.

30. John Sellers, entered in the *Grafton* as volunteer extraordinary: PRO, ADM 33/108, f. 27v. Thought unlikely that this was the cartographer John Seller (colour plate I) since Pepys records no relevant discussions with him: *TP*, p. 9 n. 3; cf. pp. 107, 108, 248.

31. Richard Zouch, *The Jurisdiction of the Admiralty of England asserted, against Sr. Edward Coke's Articuli Admiralitatis* (1663; PL 785).

32. *His Majesty's Declaration to all his loving subjects concerning the treasonable conspiracy . . . lately discovered* (1683; Wing C2998), also issued in the *London Gazette*, no. 1848 (2–6 August), and ordered to be read in churches. The Rye House Plot, by which the King and the Duke of York were to be pistolled on the Newmarket road.

33. The Diary of the 1660s shows Pepys already sceptical of *other people's* ghost stories, though he could be frightened by a cat in the night: *Diary*, II, p. 68; IV, pp. 185–6, 227 VIII, p. 553.

34. Capt. Henry Priestman: *CSO*, p. 367.

35. Revised 12 September (text, p. 130); printed in *TP*, pp. 75–83.

36. Samuel de Paz was Dartmouth's Spanish secretary; his scheme for collecting intelligence in the Netherlands is printed in *TP*, pp. 83–8; cf. p. xlvii.

37. Admiral Edward Herbert (later Earl of Torrington), recently Commander of the Tangier squadron. Though he features sparingly in the journal, the other 'Tangier Papers' contain a relentless indictment of his personal and professional conduct.

38. John Godolphin, Συνηγορος Θαλασσιος. *A View of the Admiral Jurisdiction* (1661; PL 846).

39. *Sc.* the after-dinner recreation in the great cabin.

40. Henry Hordesnel alias Hordsnell, Hortenell: *CTB*, VII, ii, pp. 1299, 1407; iii, p. 1512. 'J. Fordemell' (HMC, *Dartmouth*, I, p. 96) is a misreading partially corrected in *TP*, p. 334 n. 1.

41. Finisterre.

42. Volunteer officer.

43. MS. 'Cont.', usually meaning John Erlisman, Comptroller of Tangier. Chappell, unable to believe that an adult was treated in this way, suggested that the 'young Comptroller' to whom Col. Kirke later made a lewd remark might have been Erlisman's son, for whom 'Cont.' might here stand. Since Erlisman married in 1678, Chappell had further to suppose a previous marriage and an adolescent son from it: *TP*, pp. xlv–xlvi, 93. Application of Occam's razor suggests Erlisman himself was the 'young Comptroller' and also the victim of this prank.

44. Later identified as Dartmouth's servant; perhaps the Thomas *Sessions* entered on the *Grafton* as a gunner: *TP*, pp. 13 n. 2, 94. PRO, ADM 33/1108, f. 31v.

45. Berlenga Islands, off Portugal.
46. Printed in *TP*, pp. 126–9.
47. St Vincent.
48. Richard Gough: cf. Howarth, pp. 155, 160.
49. Commanding the *Mary Rose*, the ship despatched to Cadiz: *TP*, p. 272.
50. Henry Villiers, Second Lieutenant of the *Grafton* (never promoted Captain): PRO, ADM 33/108, f. 13v. *CSO*, p. 452.
51. Reported 10 leagues distant at noon: *TP*, p. 272.
52. Printed in *TP*, pp. 75–83.
53. A dollar was the usual levy; those who preferred might have a ducking from the yard-arm. Similar rites of passage were enacted elsewhere: *Early Voyages and Travels in the Levant*, ed. J.T. Bent (Hakluyt Soc., [1st ser.], LXXXVII, 1893), pp. 105–6. *The Diary of Henry Teonge . . . 1675–1679*, ed. G.E. Manwaring (1927), pp. 47, 54.
54. The *Grafton*'s log recorded anchoring in Tangier Road at 9.30 a.m.: *TP*, p. 272.
55. Ali Benabdala, Alcaïd (Governor) of Alcazar since 1681.
56. St Michel had served as muster-master at Tangier since 1681: Heath, pp. 60 n.1, 164, 174 and *passim*.
57. Minutes are extant only from 14–16 September: Bodl. MS Rawlinson A. 190, f. 4 (printed in *TP*, pp. 333–4). Possibly Pepys overestimated the formality of this 'council of four', and his own part in the overall evacuation plans. An official journal of the more limited duties to which he was actually appointed was begun on 19 September: see below, n. 63.
58. Minutes of council of war (15 September): HMC, *Dartmouth*, I, p. 90.
59. Captain of the *Happy Return*: *CSO*, p. 482. *TP*, p. 272.
60. Including one to James Houblon; the landing was described in his next letter (14 October): Howarth, p. 158–60.
61. The Governor's wife, Lady Mary Kirke from 1689, when her father succeeded as 4th Earl of Suffolk (and Hereditary Visitor of Magdalene).
62. Formerly Attorney-General of Tangier, and now Admiralty Judge there: *TP*, pp. 18 n. 3, 162.
63. Kept from 19 September to 12 November (briefly summarised in HMC, *Dartmouth*, III, pp. 34–5). It is this 'official' journal to which Pepys refers again on 1 and 9 October, and 3 November; the 'private' journal mentioned on 3, 23, 28 October and 5 November is the present text.
64. The clergy of the Portuguese church: HMC, *Dartmouth*, III, p. 34.
65. 'Mighty . . . oracles' occurs at f. 207v dated 17th, but following other addenda for 20th and 21st, and despite uncertain reading of '22nd', its location here seems confirmed by 'this Saturday' *TP*, p. 21 & n. 1.
66. Robert Hooke, *Micrographia* (1665); Pepys bought his copy (PL 2116) in the year of publication: *Diary*, VI, p. 2 n. 2.

67. Thomas Hughes, later so identified (*TP*, p. 96); perhaps also 'the minister' above p. 135.

68. The fortifications, and the area generally, to the west of the city, named by Sir Hugh Cholmley, first engineer of the Mole. He was a native of Whitby, Yorkshire, and had acquired relevant experience from pier construction there: Routh, *Tangier*, p. 344 & n. 2.

69. Submissions from the Mayor and the Portuguese clergy: HMC, *Dartmouth*, III, p. 34.

70. Cf. HMC, *Dartmouth*, I, pp. 87, 88.

71. *TP*, p. 65.

72. The seamen were formed into four battalions of 200 men, who were provided with distinctive new uniforms, weapons and union flags: HMC, *Dartmouth*, III, p. 40. Cf. *TP*, p. 273.

73. Before 8 a.m.: HMC, *Dartmouth*, III, p. 34, which confirms that the commissioners sat from then till after 9 p.m., save for an hour at noon.

74. Booth gave him 21 guns: *TP*, p. 273.

75. Overlooking the week's work: HMC, *Dartmouth*, III, p. 34.

76. John Giles, an army officer, in charge of the drillers: *TP*, pp. 30 n. 1, 69.

77. A common complaint that the proclamation of a free port (1662) had been disregarded: Routh, *Tangier*, pp. 18 & n. 2, 148–50.

78. Isma'il as-Samin alias Mulaï Ismaïl, Sultan of Morocco.

79. Samuel Hunter, muster-master of Dartmouth's fleet: *CTB*, VII, ii, p. 1442.

80. Richard Leake; although bred a seaman, his rank denoted command of a detachment of gunners from the Tower of London: *TP*, pp. 32 n. 1, 69, 228.

81. Charles Duncombe, prominent City financier and Cashier of the Excise: *Hist. Parl.*, II, pp. 242–3.

82. William Gifford, Captain of the *Lark*; Kt 1702: *CSO*, p. 175. Cf. below p. 151.

83. Sunderland argued in 1680 that Tangier must be abandoned if Parliament did not vote supply, and after return to office in 1682 he tried to sell it to the French: HMC, *Ormonde*, V, p. 344. Evelyn, *Diary*, IV, p. 209. J.P. Kenyon, *Robert Spencer, Earl of Sunderland, 1641–1702* (1958), p. 53 n.; Trumbull was Sunderland's 'creature', so he is here regretting that a policy he disliked should have been promoted by his patron and friend: *ibid.*, pp. 120–1, 263.

84. Cf. Hornstein, *Navy*, pp. 157–9, 205–7.

85. Casualties in, respectively, the Third and Second Dutch Wars.

86. Kirke allegedly embezzled the King's stores to build a residence for his mistress, Mrs Collier, and a *bagnio* where he entertained other ladies: *TP*, pp. 90, 92.

87. Henry Killigrew, Captain of the *Mountagu*: *CSO*, p. 256. *ODNB*. *TP*, p. 274.

88. Sheres had published *A Discourse touching Tangier* anonymously in 1680 (Wing S3058; PL 558).

89. Perhaps Josiah Burchett, later Admiralty clerk and (1694) Secretary, thought to be the 'Joseph Burcher' among *Grafton*'s passengers: PRO, ADM 33/108, f. 31v. *TP*, p. 37 & n. 1.

90. The Portuguese clergy reported that the cathedral itself and the *misericordia* belonged to their King, to whom satisfaction was due; on their own account they claimed compensation for their private houses: HMC, *Dartmouth*, III, pp. 34–5.

91. Howarth, pp. 158–60 (though dated 14 October).

92. Robert Cuthbert, merchant and councillor.

93. Attended by several small proprietors: HMC, *Dartmouth*, III, p. 35.

94. Address of the Mayor (William Smith), aldermen and inhabitants (8 October): HMC, *Dartmouth*, I, pp. 96–7.

95. Probably the Nicholson later mentioned (*TP*, p. 179), who may have been the Lt Nicholson sent to the Sultan of Morocco in 1682 (Routh, *Tangier*, p. 231). None such in *CSO* so presumably an army officer.

96. Report on proposal for valuation of properties, signed by Pepys, Bacher and Trumbull (10 October): HMC, *Dartmouth*, I, p. 97.

97. Ensign Thomas Phillips, engineer: see colour plates II–V.

98. The *Lark*, Capt. Gifford, and another ship left on this mission 12 October: *TP*, p. 275.

99. Hamet Lucas, secretary to the Alcaïd Mohammed Ohadu, FRS, during his embassy to England in 1682: Routh, *Tangier*, pp. 211–12, 220–35.

100. Carpenter of the *Turkish Tiger*: *TP*, p. 137.

101. Matthew Aylmer, later Admiral of the Fleet, Baron Aylmer of Balrath: *CSO*, p. 14. *ODNB*. *Hist. Parl. 1690–1715*, III, pp. 96–9.

102. HMC, *Dartmouth*, III, p. 35.

103. Report on objections of Mayor and proprietors, signed by Pepys, Bacher and Trumbull (13 Oct): HMC, *Dartmouth*, I, p. 97.

104. An improvised mixture of French, German and other European languages.

105. Report on the Mole (13 October): HMC, *Dartmouth*, I, p. 97.

106. Dartmouth countermanded his recent prohibition (above, 10 October) by ordering a salute of 15 guns: *TP*, p. 275.

107. Address from the military to the King (14 October): HMC, *Dartmouth*, I, pp. 97–8.

108. The eight private houses of the cathedral clergy rated in sum at £599 12s 9d: HMC, *Dartmouth*, III, p. 35.

109. Capt. Daniel Deering (*CSO*, p. 120) had driven a 12-gun corsair ashore south of Sallee: *TP*, p. 275. Deering's report of the incident is dated 14 October: HMC, *Dartmouth*, I, p. 98.

110. Thomas Silver, an artillery officer: PRO, ADM 33/108, f. 30v. *TP*, p. 90.

111. *TP*, pp. 141–2, 144, 145–6. Pepys abhorred and later tried to prohibit 'Good Voyages' (carriage of plate and other commerce by RN ships).

112. Letters of this date to James Houblon and Thomas Gale (Trumbull's neighbour) are in Howarth, pp. 160–3.

113. The *Swallow*, Capt. Henry Carverth, carried a batch of evacuees. Trumbull was back in Whitehall by 10 November: *TP*, p. 276. HMC, *Dartmouth*, I, p. 99.

114. Col. Marmaduke Boynton.

115. Thomas Atkins.

116. Probably the notes printed in *TP*, pp. 89–104

117. Anthony Wilkinson: PRO, ADM 33/108, f. 31v.

118. John Mings complained of other misfortunes at Tangier and while at Constantinople as servant to the Ambassador, Sir John Finch: *TP*, pp. 97–8. HMC, *Dartmouth*, I, p. 104.

119. The *St David*, Capt. George Rooke, was home by 18 November: *CSPD October 1683–April 1684*, p. 98. Cf. *TP*, p. 276. Rooke would return 21 years later to establish a more enduring British presence in the Straits.

120. Including claims by John Meagher, apothecary (for medicine supplied to soldiers), Stephen Vincent, baker (for bread supplied to the hospital), and the four senior companies of the garrison (for their pay): HMC, *Dartmouth*, III, p. 35.

121. Richard Hakluyt, *The Principal Navigations, Voyages, Traffiques and Discoveries of the English Nation* (1599–1600; STC 12626, 12626a) is retained at PL 2111–12. This classic work is not mentioned in the Diary, but there are extensive references throughout the *TP* and *Naval Minutes*.

122. Thomas St John: *CTB*, VII, ii, p. 1299.

123. Including petition of Solomon Pariente (for 8 years' pay as an interpreter between the Governors and the Moors), received 2 November: HMC, *Dartmouth*, III, p. 35.

124. Lt Ignatius Usher: *CSO*, p. 449.

125. Capt. Sir Francis Wheler: *CSO*, p. 466. *ODNB*.

126. The 'large folio' calendared in HMC, *Dartmouth*, III, pp. 34–9, including the commission journal (concluded 12 November) and much else.

127. That is, the ship's boat came in, as the ship herself could not. Ships from England put into the road the following day: *TP*, p. 278.

128. From Secretary Jenkins: HMC, *Dartmouth*, I, p. 98. His chief news was that Lord Rochester had sprained his ankle.

129. The *Oxford* and *Greyhound* lost their anchors, the former then colliding with the *Mountagu*, wrecking her bowsprit, head and foreyard: *TP*, pp. 56 & n. 1, 103, 279.

130. Sarah Houblon (cf. above pp. 97, 105 n. 6), who is likely to be the S.H. elsewhere mentioned (*TP*, p. 56 & n. 2; Chappell's alternative suggestion is not persuasive).

131. Cement setting under water.

132. *TP*, p. 280.

FIVE

Diary of the Special Commission 3 January–28 April 1686

Pepys's return from the Tangier expedition was soon followed (June 1684) by his restoration to the Admiralty Secretariat. Since Charles II now acted as his own Lord High Admiral, Pepys was this time not the secretary to a board of Commissioners, but the King's immediate minister. The letters patent by which he was appointed reflect that new status. This placed Pepys broadly on a par with the Secretaries of State, though, as shown below, he encroached on the Secretaries' technical functions at his peril. Pepys's position was further strengthened by the accession of the Duke of York as James II in February 1685.

During his years out of office Pepys's resentment against the incumbent administration of the Navy had been steadily accumulating. His displeasure was directed chiefly against the Board of Admiralty constituted in 1679 as part of the King's accommodation with the Whigs. The Board had been remodelled several times, but remained strong with Pepys's political opponents. Pepys took note of every instance of their alleged failings, and plotted his revenge. This process was much accelerated during the Tangier expedition, which gave him plentiful opportunity for discussion with sea officers dissatisfied with the regime. Dartmouth in particular became a strong ally. Their special hate-object was Edward Herbert, Dartmouth's predecessor as C.-in-C. of the Mediterranean squadron, appointed to the Board on his return.[1] Once Pepys had regained his place, it became more than ever his concern to denigrate the record of the 1679–84 Commissioners by contrast with the achievements of his own previous term at the Admiralty (1673–9). He detected a widespread decline in morale, coupled with neglect of the fleet itself and its shore installations. Primarily he accused the Commissioners of allowing the thirty new ships ordered in 1677 to fall into decay. This was a recurring theme in the business related below, and Pepys continued the argument in his retirement. Pepys's views, trenchantly expressed and solidly documented, were long accepted at face value. Only recently have his statistics and overall strategies been queried; as a result a fairer picture of the 1679–84 Commission has emerged.[2]

Pepys was also dissatisfied with the current state of the Navy Board. This department continued in being when there was also a Board of Admiralty. The Admiralty Board (or Commissioners) served in place of a Lord High Admiral; the Admiralty directed operations, and had overall administrative control. The Navy Board (or Commissioners) remained responsible for the Navy's material needs and manning. While the Admiralty Board was almost entirely comprised of politicians,[3] the junior Commissioners were, as before, retired sea officers or professional administrators. Between 1679 and 1684 the Navy Board's staff was cut back as part of the Admiralty's economies. On his return to power Pepys looked with dismay at the resulting inefficiency, all the more painful because of his own efforts at the Navy Office between 1660 and 1673. He decided that a complete overhaul was necessary. After a year of surveys on the ground and through the records, he devised a two-year scheme by which necessary repairs and new work could be achieved on a quarterly budget of £100,000. To implement this he proposed that the existing Navy Board should be replaced by a temporary special Commission. The stages by which this body was created are the subject of the following diary.

As his model Pepys looked to the reigns of James I and Charles I. In 1618 the Navy Board had been replaced by Commissioners responsible directly to Lord Admiral Buckingham. This arrangement lasted for a decade. These earlier Commissioners, however, were trouble-shooters brought in to supersede regular officials suspected of corruption. Two were shipwrights, and two others had worked on Navy accounts; but predominantly they were City men or Treasury officials. Pepys assigned all the credit for the Jacobean Commission's achievement to one of the shipwrights, William Burrell.[4] For his own Commission he wanted only professional naval men. His creation was in any case of a different caste. It was not a commission of enquiry, seeking to detect and admonish those guilty of neglect. The main villains (the Admiralty Board) had already been identified and dismissed. Most of the senior people in the Navy Board would be re-employed in the Special Commission, though some would be given inferior responsibilities. The essence of Pepys's scheme was the cancellation of existing portfolios within the Navy Board, allowing him to bring in some of his own most trusted agents. Pepys himself did not need to sit with them. The Commission went on to perform the greater part of its programme within budget and some months ahead of schedule. The whole fleet was overhauled, new ships and shore facilities were built, and the regular patrols were maintained.

Fundamental to Pepys's scheme was the supply of fixed sums from the Exchequer. James II began his reign with the enthusiastic support of the Tory majority in Parliament, and was voted additional supply to restore the Navy. Customs dues on wine, vinegar, tobacco and sugar were pledged for eight years from 1 July 1685. Some of this revenue also had to go to the Ordnance Office, and to pay off Charles II's debts. The receipts, benefiting from the trade boom of the 1680s, yielded an average £333,000 per annum, which was £55,000 above estimate. These receipts did not have to provide the whole £400,000 per annum which Pepys calculated, since that included items on the Navy's ordinary budget. James's overall finances were put on a solid basis at the start of his reign, and developed gratifyingly.[5] The King's personal interest in the Navy then waved Pepys's scheme into the fast track. Pepys also had the full cooperation of the Lord Treasurer, the Earl of Rochester. The first entries in the diary reflect a relationship between the Crown, the Treasury and the Admiralty lubricated by plentiful access of public revenue.

This also enabled Pepys to get the men he wanted. Principally that meant Sir Anthony Deane, who had taught Pepys about shipbuilding in his early days at the Navy Office, and had subsequently become his colleague there. This close relationship had been reinforced by their shared troubles during the Popish Plot. Deane played a major part in shaping the proposal Pepys presented in January 1686, and Pepys was determined that Deane should be on the Commission which put it into effect. Deane, however, required some persuasion. He had retained his place at the Navy Board despite the charges brought against him in 1679; he resigned in pique the following year, a month after he and Pepys had received their discharge from King's Bench. He now enjoyed a handsome living from private work, and made it clear that the offered salary of £500 per annum was an inadequate inducement to return to public office. Pepys had the awkward task of telling the King that Deane had declined his service; in fact Rochester reacted to the snub more sharply than the King himself.

Pepys was asked to submit alternative names. In the list he duly produced every individual was ruthlessly put down. Some, such as Sir John Tippets, the incumbent Surveyor of the Navy, and Sir Phineas Pett, the Comptroller of Storekeepers' Accounts, were said to be incapable because of age and gout. Others were too young, or without practical experience. Some had built only boats or merchant vessels. Sir Henry Johnson, who had built ships for Pepys before, was now too rich to need the work. A couple of the candidates were dismissed as religious fanatics; rather more were simply drunks or illiterates, or both. The King, of course, knew many of these men very well, and he can scarcely have shared all Pepys's venomous assessments. Pepys was in any case planning to re-engage Tippets and Pett in more limited roles. The King was nevertheless persuaded that Deane must be hired, and authorised the 'encouragement' of an additional £500 per annum.[6]

One of Pepys's nominees did successfully decline the offer. This was the Treasury official John Shales, briefly encountered in the 1680 diary, who was fully occupied as Purveyor-General to the army. Otherwise Pepys was able to assemble the team he had planned. His friend William Hewer was an automatic selection. Within the limits of naval administration it was a step up for him to be a Commissioner, since his last employments had been as Chief Clerk to Pepys and Deputy Judge-Advocate (resigning from the first with his master, and discharged from the second later in 1679). His continuing position as Treasurer of the Tangier Committee had advanced his standing in public affairs, and he had also become a major investor in the East India Company. He had good claim to be appointed to the new Commission in his own right.

Pepys's brother-in-law Balthasar St Michel was a more questionable nominee. He had done good work as a muster-master during the Dutch wars and then at Tangier, but this in itself would not normally have led to a place at the Navy Board. Pepys was showing personal gratitude to St Michel for his recent work in collecting evidence against Scott. The King was scarcely well placed to censure this obvious nepotism, since Lord Treasurer Rochester was *his* brother-in-law. So St Michel was confirmed as Resident Commissioner at Woolwich and Deptford. Another of the old gang, Thomas Hayter, who had been serving as Assistant Comptroller, had to be assured that he would still be employed. The existing Clerk of the Acts (James Southerne), Comptroller (Sir Richard Haddock) and Surveyor (Tippets) were appointed to wind up existing accounts, and Hayter was to assist them. Haddock took the demotion badly, and Pepys had to work hard to mollify him. Haddock, Tippets and Southerne all returned to their former places when the Special Commission's work was completed.

Rear Admiral Sir Richard Beach was retained as Resident Commissioner at Portsmouth, where he had been a forceful presence for seven years. Sir Phineas Pett moved to Chatham yard, from which Sir John Godwin was recalled to serve in the main body of Commissioners. Admiral Sir John

Narbrough likewise relinquished the post of Comptroller of Victualling Accounts to become a general commissioner. The one wholly new appointment was that of Captain (later Vice-Admiral) Sir John Berry. The Navy Treasurer was notionally a member of the Navy Board, and sat in on its meetings from time to time. For the most part he presided over his separate subdepartment. The incumbent Treasurer, Lord Falkland, held his post despite Pepys's dissatisfaction with his neglect of duty. Pepys's direct dealings with the Lord Treasurer side-stepped the Navy Treasurer's function, and he did not find it necessary to reform it. He made his point neatly enough by having Falkland's official residence turned over to Balty St Michel.

The diary presents a fairly bare account of these appointments. Only the interviews with the anxious Hayter and the tetchy Haddock reveal something of the personal tensions which resulted. An observation by the King is built up as a piece of great nautical wisdom, though it proves to be wholly unremarkable. A more impressive report of the sailor king comes in the penultimate entry, describing his visit to the ships at Chatham on 27 April. Here at last is a set-piece, with James moving knowledgeably from ship to ship, feeling their rotted timbers with his own hand. A recurring image in Pepys's reports is here given the royal touch. It is also the final piece of descriptive journalism from the greatest of our diarists.

The text is taken from the sole copy in PL 1490, pp. 7–73, not previously printed. This MS, a small octavo of 445 pages, is devoted to the work of the Commission. It includes Pepys's 'Proposition' outlining the task, copies of several letters and more formal documents contemporary with the diary, and some later material. There are also two larger MSS containing the Commission's reports (to Lady Day 1687 and 1688) shelved separately (PL 2823–4) because of the Library's arrangement of all material by size.

1. Cf. above, pp. 127, 168 n. 37.
2. Pepys's version is summarised in W.A. Aiken, 'The Admiralty in conflict and commission, 1679–1684', in *Conflict in Stuart England: Essays in Honour of Wallace Notestein*, ed. Aiken and B.D. Henning (1960), pp. 203–25; against which see principally J.D. Davies, 'Pepys and the Admiralty Commission of 1679–84', *Historical Research*, LXII (1989), pp. 34–53, and Hornstein, *Navy*, pp. 10–32.
3. Only two of the thirteen Admiralty Commissioners appointed between 1679 and 1684 were seamen (Sir John Chicheley and Edward Herbert). The formal distinction between Civil Lords, i.e. the politicians, and Sea Lords, the

177

professional seamen, was not yet current; only from 1853 until the abolition of the Admiralty Board in 1964 was the First Lord invariably a civilian and the First Sea Lord the senior professional member. When The Queen resumed the office of Lord High Admiral (following Charles II's precedent of 1684), the titles of First and junior Sea Lords were preserved out of regard for tradition.

4. PL 2735, pp. 44–109. *Diary*, IV, p. 96 & n. 4; IX, p. 482. *Naval Minutes*, pp. 95–6, 277–9. McGowan, p. xix & nn.
5. 1 Jac. II c. 1. Chandaman, *Revenue*, pp. 35–6, 257–61.
6. PL 1490, pp. 143–52.

A DIARY OF MY PROCEEDINGS WITH THE KING UPON THE GENERAL PRESENT STATE OF HIS NAVY.

Friday January 3d 1685/6. This day His Majesty was pleased to grant me a solemn hearing upon the general subject of the present state of his Navy, before himself and my Lord Treasurer Rochester[1] in his Present [*Presence*] Closet at Whitehall; and thereupon graciously to express his great satisfaction in the same, and to command my putting together in writing the heads of what I had then opened to him, with my conceptions touching what might be to be done towards the restoring it with £400,000 per annum, the sum he had declared his resolution to assign indivertibly to that, and for answering all the standing occasions of it, with my advice touching the persons fit to be entrusted therewith in the room of the present officers.

Upon which applying myself to it and getting both the one and the other despatched with what haste I could, I demanded of His Majesty a time for my presenting the same to him in company with my Lord Treasurer, who appointed me Friday the 29th of January 1685/6 in his new Closet, where they received it both with extraordinary instances of satisfaction and concurrence, commanding me to be preparing a commission conformable thereto, and all necessary papers, appointing Friday the 5th of February in the afternoon before Council for my presenting the same to him.[2]

Friday February 5th. Attending the King (my Lord Treasurer present) I gave them in discourse my conception of a draft of this commission, grounded generally upon a commission I found on a like occasion in the 18th of K. James 1st,[3] which was read to them by Burchett my clerk,[4] and agreed to both as to the matter and Commissioners (old and new) to be put into the same; but with a distinct notification and limitation of their duties, to be advised

179

upon by me with the Attorney-General;[5] those only to the Commissioners for the yards to be separate.

Accordingly upon discourse with Mr Attorney-General, and several conferences thereon and comparing of ancient commissions both as to Principal Officers and Commissioners, and above all with that of the 18th of K. James, we agreed upon the substance and method both of the joint and separate commissions; he desiring me to take the trouble of preparing the first drafts of both. Which I did, but by reason of his term business and others he could not find leisure to receive and consider of them till the 26th of February, being Friday, when upon perusal and full debate he approved and confirmed them under his hand.

After which I proceeded to the engrossing them for the King's signing, and had them ready the next day, but could not find the King at leisure to give me an audience upon it till Wednesday night, March the 3d, when attending him by his appointment with my Lord Treasurer, I presented him with them, and opening every particular as to the reason of them, he fully approved of the whole, and signed them.

Which done, I acquainted the King and my Lord Treasurer that I had spoke with Capt. Shales[6] and proposed the matter to him (which I did about three days before, at my house in the morning), who I found very thankful for the King's favour to him, and mine in proposing him, and was most willing to accept of it, provided he might hold his present employment in the army, which he said he was so far embarked in that he could not without prejudice both to the King and himself now divest himself it. But, I explaining to him as well the necessity as the King's expectation of his whole time to the Navy, he concluded that if one only could be had, he must abide by his present employment as Purveyor-General for the army; and so he wholly declined it. And the King and Lord Treasurer being satisfied in the reason and ingenuity [*genuineness*] of his proceedings therein, I by the King's command proposed Mr Maddocks[7] as the fittest man to come in his room, if there were present occasion or should [*be*] hereafter; but did rather incline to think that it might save the King one Commissioner's salary to take Sir Jno. Narbrough of the old number into the new,[8] and leave Mr Hayter to assist the old number in the business of the accounts,[9] with condition that if upon experience I found a necessity of having another new one, the King would allow of it, and Mr Maddocks to be the man. Which he and my Lord Treasurer did agree to; and accordingly the King signed the general commission with Sir Jno. Narborough to be one for the new work in the room of Mr Shales.

I then acquainted the King and my Lord Treasurer with what had passed in this interval between Sir Anto. Deane and me, to whom by the King's command upon the 5th of February I communicated his intentions of recalling him to his service by my letter to him Sunday morning the 7th, and carried him the next morning to the King, who then proposed the work to him, and received his answer to the King's said proposal by a letter from him of the 11th, which I now (viz. March the 3d) and no sooner had opportunity of communicating to the King and my Lord Treasurer Sir A.D.'s making difficulty of accepting the same.[10]

The King's determinations thereon with the advice of my Lord Treasurer I communicated to him by a letter the same night, and received his reply to him in writing March 6th.[11] Which I thought fit to communicate first apart to my Lord Treasurer at the Treasury Chamber the same day in the morning, and agreed upon bringing him to my Lord Treasurer in the afternoon. Which was accordingly done &c. at his lodgings, where my Lord expressed his dissatisfaction with Sir A.D.'s backwardness and standing upon terms with the King, with a degree of heat that I was sorry for, as being what was too much to be offered to anybody that was not then in the King's pay, and much more to him that I knew the King could not be without, had he asked ten times as much.

Sunday March 7th. I visited my Lord Treasurer by agreement with him last night, in the morning before church-time, both about Sir A.D. and the general business of the Navy, with a determination that Sir A.D.'s letter should be shown the King.

Which I did on Tuesday morning alone in the Queen's Bedchamber, to his satisfaction, and got a meeting appointed thereon with him and my Lord Treasurer at his return from hunting on Thursday afternoon; but was disappointed by my Lord Treasurer's failing to be there. But had it effectually the next morning Friday the 12th in his closet, where I presented them with the list I had promised the King on Tuesday of all the noted builders at this day in England.[12] To the King's full conviction of the necessity of his prevailing with and satisfying Sir A.D. Which I was commanded to signify to him, and did it the same noon, dining with him and W.H. by ourselves in London.

Memorandum, to preserve by me the several characters of the persons in that list.[13]

Saturday March 13th. I brought Sir A.D. to the King in the morning to kiss his hand, who declared the same to him to his full satisfaction, and afterwards to my Lord Treasurer at the Treasury Chamber, with the same mutual content.[14]

Sunday 14th. I carried Mr Hewer to kiss his hand in the morning in his Bedchamber; and the like to my brother St Michel in the afternoon at the Cabinet, with expression of great kindness and esteem to both.

Memorandum, that both the King and my Lord Treasurer did assure Sir Anto. Deane and Mr Hewer of their being complied with as to the business of money, and supported against any obstructions or uneasinesses they should meet withal from any thing or persons in the execution of this work.

Memorandum, my being directed by the King and Lord Treasurer to draw out my proposition in a paper by itself to be communicated to such as the King should appoint as Commissioners to execute it for their perusing and giving their opinion touching the scope and practicableness of it. The rest of my memorial they thinking unfit to be communicated to any but themselves. As also my giving the King and my Lord Treasurer each of them an original duplicate signed by myself of my whole memorial, as also a copy of my proposition apart to my Lord Treasurer as it is to be communicated to the Commissioners.

Memorandum, that my Lord Treasurer, both to me alone and Sir A.D. afterwards with me, did declare that his forementioned earnestness with Sir A.D. on Saturday afternoon last sprang from no unkindness, but his trouble under the fear he had that the King's services being wholly broke by the difficulty Sir A.D. made in his coming in to it, expressing his extraordinary esteem and value of Sir A.D., and that there was no man in England capable of serving the King in this juncture but he.

Memorandum, that the terms agreed to touching Sir A.D. were his having for his particular encouragement to go through the extraordinary part he was to perform in this service £500 per annum extraordinary by a separate warrant (the less to shock his brethren) over and above the common wages of £500 per annum as a Commissioner in general.

Memorandum, that I first communicated this matter and the result of it to the rest of the Commissioners besides Sir A.D. and Mr Hewer (with whom I consulted all along in the whole) and Capt. Shales, which I have already mentioned, viz.

Sir Jno. Berry soon after Sir A.D. had first been with the King, Sir A.D. first mentioning it to him by my advice, and then I sent for him and did it.

Mr St Michel upon Sunday morning March the 14th, and in the afternoon carried him to kiss the King's hand.

To Sir Phin. Pett[15] Monday March the 15th at my office in the morning.

To Sir Jno. Godwin by a letter to Chatham Tuesday March 16th.[16]

Wednesday March 17th. Sir A.D.'s not being satisfied sooner occasioned the drafts of the several commissions being made without any mention of the salaries, but that being now over, I this day presented the King and he signed one general additional warrant for the salaries of the whole at £500 per annum.[17] What is to be allowed extraordinary to Sir A.D., being (as before) to be done hereafter by particular warrant.

I at the same this morning carried Sir Jno. Berry[18] and Sir Phin. Pett to kiss the King's hand, whom he received kindly.

This morning also Sir Richard Haddock came to me with his complaint of what he heard abroad, and was informed by me in the general of the King's resolutions, being much satisfied with the provision made for him.[19]

Soon after Sir Jno. Narbrough came to me, who thankfully received the advice of the King's favour to him.

Then I carried the several commissions and put them into the hands of Mr Johnson at the Temple, in the absence of Mr Attorney-General.

Thursday March 18th. This day I was visited again by Sir R.H. after his having been with the King, and received little satisfaction thereby, he making great complaints of his being undone if (as he is informed) he be turned out of his employment, making great supplications to me, and begging my pardon for all his misbehaviours towards me, which I told him, and truly, I never had any regard to in the governing myself where the King is concerned, nor had in this occasion. But comforted him with the King's goodness to him in keeping him in commission, adding that no prince in Europe but himself (after such managements) would have done it.

Friday March 19th. This afternoon Sir Jno. Godwin, upon a late summons from me comes to town, to whom opening the whole matter, he expressed himself most ready to submit to His Majesty's pleasure in calling him from thence, but yet, so that if it could otherwise have been, I perceive he would have wished it, upon the score of his health, from the air and exercise he'll want here, with some regard also to the £100 per annum he receives there from the victualling.[20]

Saturday March 20th. I attended the King with my Lord Treasurer at his levee and had his approbation to the advertisement I had with the advice of Sir A.D. and W.H. agreed on for the next *Gazette* inviting people to fell timber.[21] The King also approved of my proposition of having a strict survey of the stores gone in hand with immediately, and for my preparing and ascertaining the duties of the Treasurer of the Navy in order to his enjoining them on him, and appointed Monday next in the afternoon for his being attended by the whole new Commission but for Sir Rd Beach, who is yet at Portsmouth.[22]

I this morning also first presented Sir Jno. Godwin to the King upon this alteration, who was pleased to receive him graciously.

Home, where the gentlemen of the new Commission had their first interview and meeting, viz. Sir Anto. Deane, Sir Phin. Pett, Sir John Narbrough, Sir Jno. Godwin, Sir Jo. Berry, Mr Hewer and Mr

St Michel, whom I entertained for two hours before dinner with opening very particularly the whole grounds of the King's late and present proceedings in the change he is now making in the Navy, together with my proposition for the works to be done therein with £400,000, and the measures upon which the same was grounded; which were largely argued and confirmed by Sir A. Deane without any present objection thereto from any of them, but referred to further debate upon their having time to consider the same.

This evening Mr Hewer brought from Mr Johnson, the Attorney-General's clerk, the foul drafts of the commissions.

Sunday the 21th. In the evening I with Mr Hewer compared Mr Johnson's said drafts with the King's warrants for the commissions, and find them to be no more than the very words of my warrants turned into the style of commissions, without anything to be objected to them, and therefore returned them to him to be finished accordingly.

Monday the 22th. Having of my own accord drawn up in writing some heads of matter for His Majesty to discourse upon to his body of new Commissioners, and read and opened the same to him in presence of my Lord Treasurer in his Bedchamber at St James's at the hour he appointed in the afternoon,[23] and having also conducted thither Sir Anto. Deane, Sir Jno. Narbrough, Sir Jno. Berry, Sir Phin. Pett, Sir Jno. Godwin, Mr Hewer and Mr St Michel, they were called in, where His Majesty (my Lord Treasurer attending) was pleased first himself by a very earnest, plain and serious discourse, and then commanded me [*sc. 'by commanding me'*] to read over and enlarge upon my said paper head by head, to open to them his whole mind therein, owning the difficulties but yet enlarging upon the necessity and importance of it, and their known ability for the work; encouraging them by a promise of good and effectual payment of the £400,000 per annum, and his supporting them against all those difficulties (through ill will and otherwise) which both himself and my Lord Treasurer largely owned their foreseeing they would have to contend with, foretelling them by the parallel of what he used to say upon his discerning a ship's doing ill in time of fight at sea where he knew the ability of the commander, that if this service did not speed under them, he would say the same, viz. that he was sure it did not arise from want of ability or good will, but from some other fault or misfortune.

Hereupon Sir Anto. Deane, in the name of the whole, spake much, and to His Majesty's and Lord Treasurer's satisfaction, declaring his not doubting their giving His Majesty a good account of the service, answerable in every particular to the heads of my proposition, which he observed their having seen and considered; provided their payments were made good to them according to it, which both the King and Lord Treasurer answered them they should be.

Sir A.D. also took occasion of opening the business of E. Country [*Baltic*] timber and plank, and the no reliance to be had upon any sufficient quantities to be had of English; and yet the other not safe to be made use of without an act of state to justify it, because of the late great, though unjust, imputation laid on it relating to the decay of the new ships, which he satisfied the King's demand touching the true rise of, who was thereupon pleased to allow of the reasonableness of Sir A.D.'s proposal touching an act of state to warrant it, and direct me to prepare myself to open the same to him in Council the first Council day after Easter, viz. Friday in Easter week.

Wednesday the 24th. Recollecting that the intimation in the *Gazette* invites all people to bring in tenders of timber and plank to the Navy Commissioners after Lady Day, which will be tomorrow, and that on other regards no time ought to be lost between this and the passing of the great seals, which the absence of the Attorney-General from town occasions some delay to, I thought it necessary to provide and this morning get signed by the King a previous temporary warrant for the setting these gentlemen presently to work, in order to a speedy survey and adjusting the dwelling-houses, offices and the books and papers thereof, &c.[24]

In the evening spoke to my Lord Treasurer for the new Commissioners to have an opportunity of paying their duty to him by a joint visit, and to receive his commands; which he accepted for tomorrow in the afternoon.

Thursday Lady-day March 25th. Accordingly they all attended him this afternoon at his house, where he received them well, voluntarily took notice of the difficulty of their task, saying that he believed it to be the greatest that ever any man undertook; promised them good payments of their money, and desired their demands in the distribution thereof in order to his preparing himself for it; taking notice also of the many eyes that will be upon them, some that it may be would expect too much from them, as well as others who would maliciously endeavour to wrong them; that therefore they must prepare to bear it, and that he would labour to support them through all. Sir Anto. Deane making his reply answerable to what he had done to the King, and with the same satisfaction. Present Sir A.D., Sir J.N., Sir Jno. Berry, Sir P.P., Sir J.G., W.H., B. St M. and myself.

By this night's post I first acquainted Sir Rd Beach with what has been thus doing in the Navy, and more particularly that of his own continuing in his present post, and inviting him to town to understand the rest.[25]

By the same post I also wrote to Mr Battine at Portsmouth, inviting him to prepare himself in order to an establishment to be made about the business of controlling of storekeepers.[26]

Friday March 26th. By agreement last night, and notice sent to the old ones by Sir Jo. Narbrough, I first brought them and the new together this morning at the Navy Office; where, by the King's command intimated in his forementioned previous letter, I opened to them his whole determinations about this change, reading to them the drafts of His Majesty's warrants both for the general commission and those to the out-Commissioners, with the appointment of their salaries, and then read and delivered them the King's letter to the body of them dated the 23th instant setting them to work.[27] With which, and after several interchanges of friendly discourse between them together, and more particularly the old ones with myself, without any show of disagreement or reluctancies in their obliging the King, I left them to their work.

Saturday 27th. This morning I first spoke with Mr [*Tom*] Hayter about the business, he coming to me for information in the share he has in it, solemnly asking me pardon for anything wherein he had given me occasion of being dissatisfied with him, which I told him, whether there were anything or no, or I had any resentments thereof or not, ought not, nor never did, nor should operate at all with me in any matter where the good of the King's service is concerned, and therefore told him His Majesty's gracious intentions of keeping him still in his pay as at present, wherein I had done him no ill office. But that His Majesty had not yet fully determined upon the work he would allot to him, but that I supposed he was indifferently disposed to whatever His Majesty should require from him. Which he readily and thankfully agreed to, with my referring him to my giving him notice when he should know more of the King's pleasure about it.

This morning the bills were returned out of the country from Mr Attorney-General, engrossed in parchment for the King's signing.

Sunday 28th. This evening I presented to His Majesty at the Cabinet the several bills prepared by the Attorney-General, and had them signed.

Monday 29th. This morning the bills were delivered by Mr Hewer at the Signet Office, to be despatched there and at the Privy Seal. And this day I drew up a memorial for the King, by his direction, touching the duty of the Treasurer of the Navy,[28] in order to his delivering and recommending it to him with his own hand.

Tuesday 30th. This morning, by appointment between my Lord Treasurer and me on Sunday night, the new Commissioners went with me to his Lordship, in order to their proposing their methods of payments of the £400,000. But finding him at the Treasury Chamber busy, I proposed to my Lord the respiting of it [*to*] tomorrow morning, which was accordingly agreed, and the body of the Commissioners went directly from thence down together to make their first visit to the yards of Deptford and Woolwich.

Wednesday 31th. This morning according to agreement I accompanied the body of the new Commissioners to my Lord Treasurer, viz. Sir Anto. Deane, Sir Jno. Narbrough, Sir Jno. Berry, Sir Phin. Pett, Mr Hewer and Mr St Michel (Sir J.G. being at Chatham and Sir R.B. at Portsmouth), where at his house they presented him with a copy of my proposition, with a short report under all their hands at the end of it containing their opinion touching the properest division of the payments of the £400,000 per annum, namely by even weekly proportions the year round,[29] which my Lord Treasurer at the first reading did without any hesitation tell them that he approved of it, and it should be made effectually good to them, to begin as they then upon his question told him from the 25th instant. And because he said he was to go out of town, as he did that very afternoon, for a few days during the approaching Easter holy days, he told them he would immediately give order for the gross sum of the first week's payment, viz. £7,000, to be immediately paid them.

He then mentioned two or three reasonable particulars which he thought (and which were yielded to by N.O. [*Navy Office*]) ought to be taken by them in part of this £400,000, namely the moneys that should be paid to the victuallers from the 25th of March (provided as N.O. said that the whole came with this 5*d* and 7*d* per man a day) and what remained unpaid of what the last N.O. were to have for the repair of the thirty ships.

But he observed that in this their report they gave not so strict an answer as might be convenient to the point demanded of them by the King, and desired by himself, as that which he thought indispensably necessary both for the satisfaction of the King and himself, and the doing right to me as the author of the proposition, and to themselves, that it might be remembered what works were expected from them, and no more, what sum and payments they demanded, and no less, and what their giving their opinion in writing under their hands touching the practicableness of the proposition. And this I also seconded my Lord in, and was answered by Sir Anto. Deane in the name of the rest, that they had considered and did declare themselves satisfied in the practicableness thereof, and that with that money those payments and other supports desired by them and promised by the King and his Lordship, they doubted not to give both of them the satisfaction of seeing the works done accordingly; with this only difficulty resting on them, namely of their being able even with money to furnish themselves with materials, and more especially proper timber, plank and masts. This, however, my Lord Treasurer answered, would be to be reckoned a great misfortune but no fault in them. So, he insisting on't, they undertook to give him a written declaration from them concerning this last matter.

This begat a fresh mention of the debate about East-Country goods, which he remembered was appointed to be heard before the King at the Council table upon Friday in Easter week.

Memorandum, that I call upon Mr Hewer for a copy of their report this day touching the payments upon my proposition, to be entered in my collection of the proceedings hereon.

Memorandum, that they being gone, my Lord Treasurer and I passed some time alone together, I acquainting him with the reading to him the state I have prepared for the King of the Treasurer of the Navy's duty, in order to the King's giving it him with his own hand. Which I for divers reasons advised might be done when his Lordship might be present; he agreed to it, but he desired it might be respited till his return to town, which would be in a few days.

He then fell into talk about the state of the Chest,[30] and his having ordered one year's pay to be presently made it; and then of the arrear to pensions and half-pays, and his being solicited much about it – which being all unhinged by the late King's death, is a point now lying before the King, and I undertook to bring to some speedy issue with the King and his Lordship together.

He ended with an extraordinary motion that would encourage him (if it could succeed) to clear all at once the whole arrear to the yards: a thing I allowed to be the most desirable at this juncture for the King's service, as well for the men, because of the necessary purge that must be made therein. Upon which he earnestly recommended it to me to consider how far what he proposed could be made practicable.

Friday April 2d. This day I was given to understand a stop to be put by Mr Bridgeman[31] at the Signet Office to the passing of the commissions there till he had spoken with me upon the score, as is supposed, of his apprehending the Secretaries of State's being overlooked by my passing it thus far without them, which I am prepared both by constant practice and the reason of it to justify. But the devotion of the time will not, I fear, give me opportunity of bringing it into debate before Easter Day be over.

Easter-Tuesday April 6th. Having been given to understand that the stop before mentioned does not arise from the King's original warrant to the Attorney-General passing through my hand, but from my presenting the bills pursuant thereto to the King for his signing, which ought only to be done by a Secretary of State, I am well satisfied of my being (out of a zeal to despatch) fallen into a mistake in that matter, and therefore acknowledged it by a letter this morning to Mr Bridgeman, offering any way to rectify it with least loss of time to the business.

Easter-Wednesday April 7th. Sir Rd Beach being upon my invitation come to town, I accompanied him to the King, who very kindly received him, and he thankfully owned His Majesty's favour in keeping him in his post.

This morning also the King signed and I despatched away to N.O. an additional temporary order to that of the 23th of March and dated it the 25th, to enable N.O. to do the whole work of P.O. [*Principal Officers*] of the Navy from that day till the commissions (which commence then) shall be passed, which now will be in a few days, they being this morning taken out of the Signet and Privy Seal upon the removal of Mr Bridgeman's stop thereto, by paying of the Secretaries' fees. The fear of losing which, I find after all, to have been the only occasion of that stop, and not the point of jurisdiction or strictness of method to be preserved.

Memorandum, that upon my coming out from the King in his Closet at St James's, I met my Lord Treasurer newly returned from his three or four days' recess, who of his own accord put me in mind now of my summoning him to attend the King on occasion of my Lord Falkland's[32] being to be spoken to in the matter, which I told him should soon be brought to an issue. He also asked me whether we had received the first £7,000 (which I could not indeed tell, but presume N.O. had), adding that he would continue it without fail (weekly), proposing to me that because the weekly sum demanded by N.O. in their last paper consists of broken money, which would be a little troublesome to be complied with, he could wish that N.O. would be contented with their receiving weekly the round sum of £7,000, which he would punctually make good, and adjust the broken money (to make up the £100,000 complete) at the end of every quarter. I told him I hoped they would, and would propose it to them and give him their answer, which he desired I would do.

Easter-Thursday April 8. This morning by letter I acquainted N.O. with what my Lord Treasurer said to me yesterday about the £7,000 per week and adjusting of the odd money at the end of each quarter, desiring their opinion thereon, and received their answer in the afternoon, submitting to that proposal of his Lordship's.

Memorandum, to enter both those papers in my collection.

From Thursday April 8 to Sunday 11th. Busy in preparing the several instructions for the commissions, which are engrossed ready to be carried to the Great Seal, but forborne for want of the said instructions to be annexed to them.

The Easter holy days have also prevented my getting a time appointed for the King and my Lord Treasurer's first opening all this negotiation to my Lord Falkland till this night at Cabinet, where the King appointed tomorrow in the afternoon for it, my Lord Treasurer present; whereof I gave notice immediately to my Lord Falkland.

Monday April 12th. This afternoon by appointment I attended the King, where with my Lord Treasurer having first opened to them what I had prepared and was fit to be said to my Lord Falkland, he was called in, where I having first shown the King's respect to his Lordship, both by his provision in behalf of my Lord and his office in the general commission, and in reserving to himself the first opening of this matter to him, which is the reason of my not having yet done it, then I proceeded to observe the King's next thoughts, which were in relation to his own service, by considering the importance of his having the Treasurer's part in this affair well executed, and then enquiring how the present duty and instructions of that officer now stood and was complied with. In answer whereto I by his command had put together what I had to say in writing, giving a deduction, and the present state of this officer's duty, and what was wanting and needful to be now settled with my Lord Falkland, and read the same – *vide* the entry of it, and what I add at the end about his Deptford house for a new Commissioner. Which having done, the King, with great kindness and plainness too, opened the importance of his compliance strictly in his attendance at the Board and giving his whole time to the business, with his desires and expectations that he would do it. My Lord Falkland thankfully received this admonition from His Majesty, excused his imperfect service hitherto from his late want of health, and his having yet done as much as his late predecessors; but that he would now apply himself closely to it. With which, and repetitions thereof in discourse on both sides, the meeting ended satisfactorily, as did also that about the house, he readily submitting it to the King's occasions, declaring his being fully satisfied of the usefulness of having a Commissioner resident upon the place for that yard and Woolwich, and so parted; his Lordship afterwards telling me when alone that he had another reason for his past slackness in his attendances at the N.Bd, which he was loath to name to the King (but had heretofore observed to me), viz. the ill-treatment he had received from Sir Rd Haddock particularly and other gentlemen at the Board, which will be now over, he declaring himself extremely satisfied with those new ones he shall now have to do withal; and so we parted, he telling me that he had been for some time in physic and water-drinking for the gravel,[33] which he should be obliged to continue for about a week longer, but hoped he should then be in condition to give his due attendance at the N.Bd. Upon which I repeated again to him what I had before said before the King, namely that it would be now the more necessary not only from the general consideration of the muchness and importance of the service upon his fellow-officers' hands, but from the danger there will be of wanting a quorum by some of their number's being by the ill state of things forced to be much at the yards, and from the use of his character as Treasurer must be of to the Board in their treating with merchants touching payments.

February April 16th. The commissions having lain several days ready engrossed, but it being this day before I could dispatch to my satisfaction the several instructions to be annexed thereto and get them signed by the King, I sent the general ones which required binding to the binder's, and had them dispatched this night.

Saturday 17th. This morning, it being a seal-day with my Lord Chancellor, the instructions were carried and annexed to the commissions, and the general one had accordingly its receipt put to it and passed,[34] and brought to me to the Navy Office, where I then was upon an appointed conference with the town shipwrights about the present state of England as to plank for shipping. Which holding long, and neither the old Commissioners nor the Lord Falkland present, the opening it was respited till Monday; order being taken there for the advertising the said old Commissioners of it, and I undertaking to do it to my Lord Falkland, which I did Sunday 18th by letter, which is to be entered.[35]

Monday April 19th. According to appointment I met the Commissioners both old and new at the Navy Board, and (my Lord Falkland being by illness prevented in meeting us) the general commissions and instructions annexed were read; and that done, with something said by Sir Rd Haddock to bespeak a dispensing with the limitation therein to the course of payments with respect to their own and clerks' bills, I advised not only as to that, but in general that their whole instructions might be first well perused and considered, and that then what observations they had to make or explanations or dispensations to require in this or any other particulars (as I would not undertake but there might be some) might be presented to the King. Which was yielded to, and I left them to proceed by themselves, these being there Sir J.T., Sir R.H., Sir A.D., Sir J.N., Sir J.B., Sir P.P., Mr S., Mr H., and Mr St M., Sir Rd Beach being at Portsmouth and Sir J.G. not yet returned from Chatham, where he has been for some time fitting himself for his removal thither.

This morning also passed the great seal for the three particular commissions,[36] they being reciped [*received*] (as I suppose) this day; it being necessary from the respect they have to the general commission that they should bear date after that. For which only consideration they were forborne to be sealed with the other. And when passed they were carried to the Navy Office by Mr Walbanke, but came after I was gone. However, coming before the Board was up, I doubt not but they were opened and read. And thus this whole matter is finished. God grant it good speed.

Take notice in due place of Sir J. Godwin's and Sir Rd Beach's answers to my letters of advice touching this change.

Thursday April 22. This morning, at the desire of the old Commissioners, I attended them (viz. Sir R.H., Sir J.T. and Mr S., who brought also with them Mr Hayter) to the King, myself declaring the occasion of it to be their acknowledging and rendering thanks to His Majesty for his favour in continuing them in his service, with the provision made for them both as to work and wages specified in His Majesty's late general commission for the Navy and the instructions annexed thereto, which have now* been opened to them; they repeating severally their thanks, without anything offered at all in relation to the change that had been made therein, either by them or from the King to them. So that after having admitted them to kiss his hand and his recommending to them the applying themselves to the work appointed them, and their answering that they had taken a house upon Tower Hill near the present general office of the Navy for the seat of their action, the King fell to talk of the business of Sir Robert Gordon and Sir Saml Morland's pumps,[37] which had been the day before tried, and were to be repeated this morning if Gordon's could be put in order, which the King seemed to declare his expectation of no success from; and then they parted.

Memorandum, that this morning before this conference, my Lord Treasurer meeting me in the Bedchamber, took me aside, asking me whether there was a necessity of Sir R.H.'s removing from his house in the Office, he having made it his desire that he might not, telling his Lordship there would be a house to spare. I replied that there was a necessity of it, or the King's service must suffer, it being indispensably necessary that the Secretary of the Office must reside there, as the Clerk of the Acts did and had always done; and that this was the house that Sir R.H. could only mean. With which my Lord Treasurer broke off the discourse, as being very well satisfied therein.

Friday April 23d. Memorandum, that this morning my Lord Treasurer was waited on by myself accompanied by Sir A.D., Sir J.N., Sir J.B., Sir P.P., Mr Hewer and Mr St M. by agreement, where he was presented with their subscription of the 30 March last to my proposition touching the practicableness of the same, to the full satisfaction of my Lord Treasurer, who then proceeded to the business of the weekly payment, and his late proposal to me of paying only the round £7,000, and making good the odd money to complete the quarterly £100,000. Whereto I read to him their written submission of the 8th of April 1686, to his like satisfaction.

From thence I proceeded to the giving his Lordship the account he formerly desired and has expected of all the heads of the change now in view for which money is to be provided more than what's included in the works to be performed upon my proposition of £400,000 per annum. By which he had it at once before him to see through the whole of the expense the King was likely to be at for the future. And this I gave him in a scheme, with which he was very well satisfied; the Commissioners at the same time giving him a particular abstract of every of the particular works mentioned in the scheme, with their estimate of their charge and demands of payment. Which amounting to about £23,000 (besides the general arrear of the Navy), his Lordship seemed desirous of lessening it or knowing whether anything could be found towards it out of the works of my proposition that by the forwardness of the year might be spared within this year, and particularly the number of men for the Channel Guard, which he left for me to consider upon conference first had with N.O. what ships could be set forth and within what time, and to give the King and him my opinion of it, when the King may direct also whether what shall be so saved out of the said number of men in sea-pay may be applied to any of these extraordinary works, or for the carrying so much faster on the works of the proposition; my Lord showing great tenderness in the making of any infraction thereon. In the mean time nevertheless (upon Sir A.D.'s largely opening the indispensableness of building the two long storehouses) he promised to allow £2,000 extraordinary, besides the weekly £7,000 (which he says shall not fail them), for the immediate going-in-hand with those storehouses, until we shall see what (if anything) may be saved towards the further charge thereof out of my proposition for this year as before. And so the matter went off.

An occasion followed of their discoursing somewhat concerning their having the constant assistance of the Treasurer of the Navy at the Board; they having not yet seem him once. Upon which I observed (as my Lord also did) that the King had expressly sent for and enjoined that matter upon my Lord Falkland, who promised that he would, and 'tis to be hoped that he will. If not, upon notice, his Lordship was assured the King would remedy it. So we parted, they to their office and I to mine, where by agreement I wrote to my Lord Falkland (Enter the letter),[38] inviting him to meet me at the Board tomorrow morning for the considering and determining in several matters towards the execution of the King's present commission before the present number of them should be separated, as they would now immediately be; and when this is done, nothing else remains that I can think of for the finishing this whole work of settlement of the Navy; and [? sc. 'save for'] the reading solemnly once at the Board, which has never been yet done, the commissions and instructions to those of the out-yards, that the Board may be apprised of that part of the settlement, and those out-Commissioners go immediately to their work.

Accordingly *Saturday the 24th* there was a meeting at the N.Bd, my Lord Falkland present, with A.D., J.N., J.B., P.P., W.H., B. St M. and myself, where the general commission and its instructions, and after[*wards*] Mr St Michel's (as an instance of one of them) and his instructions were deliberately read, and several things occasionally spoken to several points thereof, particularly to what concerned the house of Deptford, which my Lord Falkland very readily accorded to, leaving it to me to signify the King's determination and his assent thereto to Mrs Gunman, who now lives in it in his right. Which done, and some matters adjusted against the Board's attending the King on Monday next at Chatham, I left them at their business and departed.

The same day I wrote a letter to Mrs Gunman about this house (Remember to enter it)[39] and delivered it to Mr St Michel.

Tuesday 27th. This day being at Chatham, myself with Sir A.D., J.N., J.B. and J.G. (Sir P.P. being also there, but bed-ridden by lameness) attended the King there, and in particular had a full opportunity of showing him by inspection the backwardness of the docks (neither of them being likely to be of any use to him this year), the want of a storeroom and consequently the necessity of the long storehouse we are proposing, and the place designed for it; and above all the wretched condition of the hulls of his great ships, as well by showing him the *Grafton* now in dock (notwithstanding her being built in the King's yard, all of English timber and plank, and not hastily built, and having been at sea, which last is now also resorted to in excuse for their decay),[40] but another, I think the *Kent*, on float, the King going upon the stage of her side and seeing and feeling the rotten condition of her timbers and treenails with his own hand;[41] but most of all the *Britannia* herself, not above two years since launched,[42] and not till this day observed by Sir A.D. to the King himself on board of her, to be apparently begun to decay all round her spirketing upon the gun-deck. The King, after this view, had the same and divers other particulars of the Navy largely opened to him by me, and discoursed upon at a solemn council held by him thereon at Mr Gregory's house,[43] with the gentlemen before named together with the Duke of Grafton,[44] Lord Dartmouth, R. Adm. Herbert and the Prince.[45] So that this seems to give a perfect consummation of the late business of our Navy settlement by the King's becoming an ocular witness of the necessity of it, from the state of his ships, besides what was in discourse added as to the stores from the evident want of materials necessary for the repair thereof, especially as to thick stuff, plank and treenails, and those not in view to be had for money; to which His Majesty also had an opportunity of having an account given him upon the place of the universal supineness of his officers, with a proof of it the same evening beyond all expectation or imagination, upon our seeing him on board his yacht in the evening bound for London,[46] and we back again from below Gillingham up the River, in a violent storm of rain all that evening and night, without one port shut upon any one of the ships in our passage but what we by hailing caused to be so, or upon the *St Andrew* and *Grafton* in dock, neither shipwright nor assistant not any other officer minding it till, sending for Dummer,[47] we required him to see it done, with a resolution of calling the whole to a strict account for it; nothing being more evident than the evil that this negligence has brought upon the Navy by ships being kept with their ports either always shut in dry weather or open in wet, to the occasioning that a succession of heat and moisture that has ruined them.

Memorandum here to enter my letter (as soon as I came home Wednesday 28th) to the Commissioners at Chatham, reminding them of the account resolved to be called for of this neglect upon the view which I left Sir J.N. and Sir J.B. to take the next morning of the effects of it from ship to ship, upon sight of their decks after the last night's rain.[48]

Wednesday 28th April 1686. From this day the Commission proceeded in its advances towards the general repair of the Navy, furthered therein by the frequent personal visits of the King to the several yards, and public instances given of his satisfaction in the same, and from the solemn annual representations received in writing from the body of the Commission in the months of August 1687 and 88 of its procedures through every part of the service, too long for this place, but virtually contained in a particular report thereof to him from Sir Anto. Deane in July in the latter year. And so it continued till the October following, when the Commission was determined [*ended*] and another passed, recalling the old officers in conjunction with the same Commissioners.[49] Which alteration happening six months within the time designed for the continuance of the former sprang from a complication of thoughts and considerations which His Majesty was pleased to confine the knowledge of the whole of to himself only and to me; but all built upon the entire and earlier satisfaction given him than was expected of by performance of the work cut out for the Commission, as is largely declared in the patent for its dissolution, and in especial towards Sir Anto. Deane and Mr Hewer by the particular commissions reserved for them therein, though prevented in their passing the seal by the interposition and solicitations of Mr Hewer, made successful by the Revolution following soon after in the State.

The diary concludes here. Pepys adds (pp. 73–9) some comments on the criticism raised against the 1686 Commission after the Revolution, and his publishing his Memoires *in 1690 by way of vindicating the Commission's record by comparison with that of the Admiralty Board of 1679–84.*

1. Lawrence Hyde, 1st Earl of Rochester, younger son of the 1st Earl of Clarendon.
2. Pepys's 'Memorial and Proposition' dated 26 January: PL 1490, pp. 81–121; revised version of the 'Proposition' printed in Pepys, *Memoires* (ed. Tanner), pp. 19–23 and summarised in Tanner, *Naval MSS*, I, pp. 68–75.
3. An error for *16th* year of James I, which began in *1618*. See McGowan, pp. xvii–xxvii, pp. 257–306.
4. Josiah Burchett, Admiralty Secretary 1694–1742: Sainty, pp. 113–14.
5. Sir Robert Sawyer; see above, pp. 9, 32 n. 4.
6. Capt. John Shales (as above, pp. 98, 110 n. 84). In *Pepys and the Navy* I followed Bryant (*SN*, p. 449) in wrongly calling him Henry.
7. Robert Maddocks, Paymaster of the Navy: Collinge, p. 120. He was not in fact required as Commissioner.
8. Adm. Narbrough, whom Pepys admired, was Comptroller of Victualling Accounts in the old Board; he became a Commissioner for Current Business in the new regime, w.e.f. 17 April: Collinge, p. 125.
9. Thomas Hayter had served Pepys as clerk from 1660, and succeeded him as Clerk of the Acts 1673 and Admiralty Secretary 1679; since 1682 he had been Assistant Comptroller. As promised he was made an Assistant to the Commissioners for Old Accounts, w.e.f. 26 March: Collinge, p. 109. *Diary*, X, p. 171.
10. PL 1490, pp. 127–9, 131–4 (Pepys to Deane, 7 February, and reply, 11 February).
11. PL 1490, pp. 135–7, 139–42 (Pepys to Deane, 3 March, and reply, 6 March).
12. 18 names: PL 1490, p. 143, printed in Pepys's *Memoires* (ed. Tanner), pp. 29–30.
13. All but Deane are dismissed as unsuitable because of professional and personal defects: PL 1490, pp. 145–52; extracts printed in Tanner, *Naval MSS*, I, pp. 76–8, and in E. Chappell, *Samuel Pepys as a Naval Administrator* (Cambridge, 1933), pp. 19–20.
14. The King this day set in motion the formal process for dissolving of the Navy Board and appointing the first new Commissioners: PL 1490, pp. 155–90.
15. A member of the family which ran Chatham dockyard for several generations; Master Shipwright there 1660–80, then to the Navy Board as Comptroller of Storekeepers' Accounts; now designated resident Commissioner at Chatham: Collinge, p. 130. *Diary*, X, p. 326.
16. PL 1490, pp. 191–3 (Pepys to Godwin).
17. PL 1490, pp. 195–7 (warrant for salaries).
18. Appointed Commissioner of Current Business: Collinge, p. 86.
19. Haddock was the incumbent Comptroller, and his 'provision' as Commissioner for Old Accounts was a considerable demotion; he recovered his old post in 1688 and retained it until his death in 1715: Collinge, p. 106.

20. Godwin had to resign as Surveyor-General of Victualling on becoming one of the Commissioners for Current Business: Collinge, p. 104.

21. Notice (dated 19 March) that from 25 March the Commissioners would attend daily at the Navy Office to received tenders for felling and cutting timber: *London Gazette*, no. 2123 (22–25 March 1686).

22. Rear Adm. Beach was Resident Commissioner at Portsmouth, and so continued under the new Commission, and afterwards: *Diary*, X, p. 23. Cf. R.V. Saville, 'The management of the royal dockyards, 1672–1678', in *The Naval Miscellany, Volume V*, ed. N.A.M. Rodger (NRS, CXXV, 1984), p. 97 and *passim*.

23. PL 1490, pp. 199–202.

24. PL 1490, pp. 207–9 (warrant as proposed, 25 March). This had already been authorised in a general way by warrant of 23 March (*ibid.*, pp. 203–5).

25. PL 1490, pp. 211–13, 215–16 (Pepys to Beach, 25 March, and reply, 28 March).

26. Edward Battine, a dockyard official, had already given Pepys a substantial dossier on building, rigging and fitting out ships: PL 977.

27. PL 1490, pp. 203–5 (King to Commissioners, 23 March).

28. PL 1490, pp. 227–50 (30 March).

29. PL 1490, pp. 224–6; PLB 83, p. 4 (Commissioners to King, and to Rochester, 30 March).

30. The Chatham Chest, the charitable fund for seamen and their dependants.

31. William Bridgeman, Under-secretary of State: *Hist. Parl.*, 1, pp. 718–19.

32. Treasurer of the Navy.

33. Calculus; of particular interest to Pepys, who had the same complaint throughout his adult life.

34. PL 1490, pp. 261–321 (general commission, 17 April and instructions, 16 April).

35. PL 1490, p. 322 (Pepys to Falkland, 18 April).

36. Pett and St Michel, and Beach; all three patents and instructions in PL 2867, pp. 111–41; PL 1490, pp. 323–49 has those for St Michel, and note of variants in the other two.

37. Morland, Fellow of Magdalene, spy, bigamist and engineer; the pump he devised to bring water to Windsor Castle earned him the title 'master of mechanicks' from Charles II: H.W. Dickinson, *Sir Samuel Morland, Diplomat and Inventor, 1625–1695* (Cambridge, 1970), pp. 56–73. Cf. R. Luckett, 'Sir Samuel Morland: engineer-royal or uxorious gadgeteer?', *MCMR*, new ser. no. 40 (1995–6), pp. 26–30. Some of Gordon's gadgets were equally quirky, but James II took him seriously. Unfortunately, the pump broke again when demonstrated before him on 22 April; but in the following year two were tried in the Navy, for which Pepys authorised payment of £318: *Passages from the Diary of General Patrick Gordon of Auchleuchries. A.D. 1635–A.D. 1699*,

[ed. J. Robertson], (Spalding Club [XXXI], Aberdeen, 1859), pp. 128–9. HMC, *6th Report* (1877), p. 687 (Pepys to Gordon, 24 May, 10 June 1687).

38. PL 1490, pp. 351–2 (Pepys to Falkland, 23 April).

39. PL 1490, pp. 353–4 (Pepys to Mrs Gunman, 24 April).

40. Built at Woolwich by Thomas Shish, 1679: Fox, *Great Ships*, p. 175. Pepys had personal experience of her being at sea: above, pp. 121–32, and plate 11.

41. The *Kent* was a 3rd-rate, built 1679: *ibid.*, p. 175.

42. The only 1st-rate of the 1677 programme, built by Sir Phineas Pett at Chatham, 1682: *ibid.*, pp. 169–70, 174. See plate 10.

43. Edward Gregory, Clerk of the Cheque (later Kt and Commissioner at Chatham); Pepys had admired the house when Gregory's father occupied it: *Diary*, III, pp. 155–6; X, p. 161.

44. Son of Charles II.

45. Prince George of Denmark, the King's son-in-law.

46. Pepys fails to mention that the King's yacht then ploughed into one of the great ships and broke her bowsprit: Robertson, *Diary of General P. Gordon*, pp. 130–1.

47. Edmund Dummer, Assistant Shipwright at Chatham, later (1692–8) Surveyor of the Navy: Collinge, p. 98. *Hist. Parl. 1690–1715*, III, pp. 931–3. One of those whom Pepys rejected (on account of inexperience) as an alternative to Deane on the Special Commission. But his MS compositions (including fine technical drawings) would be incorporated in Pepys's library: PL 1074, 2934. Cf. 'Edmund Dummer's "Account of the general progress and advancement of His Majesty's new dock and yard at Plymouth", December 1694', ed. M. Duffy, in *The Naval Miscellany, Volume VI*, ed. Duffy (NRS, CXLVI, 2003), pp. 93–147.

48. PL 1490, pp. 356–60 (Pepys to Godwin, Narbrough and Berry, 28 April).

49. PL 1490, pp. 369–82 (dissolution of Commission, 12 October 1688).

Diplomatic Notes

Key

[. . .]   uncertain text

[ship]   text supplied where MS is corrupt, illegible or mutilated

[*ship*]   editorial interpolation for fluency, or in explanation of immediately preceding word(s)

?   qualifies supplied or interpolated matter

*   indicates a comment in the diplomatic annotation below

Text 1: Brooke House Journal

5 January]	the: MS 'that'
7 January]	hold: MS 'would' (misheard in dictation)
20 January]	'tis: MS 'his' (likewise)
24 January]	which: MS 'with'
17 February]	at: MS 'and' (misheard)

Text 2: King's Bench Journal

9 July]	by: MS 'but'
	have: MS 'a' (possibly a false start to 'as plainly have said it')

Text 3: Proceedings with James and Harris

24 January]	words of mine: corrected from 'my words'
27 January]	to: corrected from 'of'
	go: corrected from 'gett'
	which: followed by otiose 'when' (false start to construction)
30 January]	bade: corrected from 'told'
	of any of his: 'corrected from 'of his', with extraneous 'of h[is]' inserted then deleted
	my: corrected from 'our'
11 March]	which should be: corrected from 'instead of'

203

18 March]	has: corrected from 'had'
20 March]	as: corrected from 'and'
27 March]	his: MS 'with', wrongly corrected from 'his'

Text 4: Tangier Journal

See Introduction, pp. 118–19. This section has selective reference to typescript transcripts by W. Matthews (M) and E. Chappell (C) deposited in the PL reference collection. Notes to words flagged * but not bracketed in the text give those M readings rejected by C which seem plausible to the present editor *on grounds of sense and syntax*. MS denotes readings agreed by M and C, or so annotated in Chappell's published edition

13 August]	supposed: M 'heard', prompting C to query his 'supposed'
	pilot's: so M; here preferred for sense to C's conjectured 'poulterer'
17 August]	beard: M 'back'
	Wyndham's: M: 'Wind's'; C 'Winter's' but prints 'Wyndham's' for sense
19 August]	the miners: M 'that went'; C prints 'the [?]'; but sense clear (cf. footnote)
23 August]	linen: M 'men'
26 August]	business: M 'designs'
27 August]	my notes: M 'minutes'
29 August]	do: M 'draw'
	quite: M 'in the [*blank*]'
2 September]	weather: M 'wind'
	wind: M 'weather'
6 September]	shoal: M 'school'
8 September]	quite through: M 'in the (thwarts?)'
	bottle: C's conjecture (none from M)
9 September]	awed: M 'ado'
	&c.: M 'ale &c.', queried by C but not printed
	drunk: so M; queried by C
13 September]	these: M 'evening'
14 September]	deserted: M 'destroyed'
15 September]	actions: M 'occasion'
17 September]	an: MS 'and'
20 September]	stuff: M 'faced', noted by C as possible alternative
	[. . .]: M: 'k. . .'; C rejected his own 'socks'
21 September]	public: M 'private'
23 September]	leapt: MS 'left'

admired: M 'remarked'

a little: M 'lately'

24 September] declare: M 'proclaim'

28 September] small: M 'several'

half: M 'quarter'

above: MS 'about'

granadoes: so M, here preferred to C's 'grenades'

about: M: 'above'

contented: M 'condemned'

29 September] So: so M, here preferred to C's 'as'

1 October] principally: M 'particularly'

him: 'them'

2 October] promises: M 'presently'

send: M *blank*, prompting C to reject his conjectured 'give', but sense clear

3 October] me: so M, here preferred for sense to C's 'him'

7 October] vats: MS 'fats'

14 October] carried: MS 'carry'

under: MS 'order'

never: MS 'ever'

trouble: M, C no suggestions

24 October] yacht: so M; C gives as conjecture

25 October] glad: M 'willing'; C gives 'glad' as conjecture

24 November] plainness: M 'playing'

25 November] to: so M, but C conjectured 'for' before noting MS 'from'

would: MS 'could'

Text 5: Diary of the Special Commission

22 April] now: MS 'new'

Index

Peers and holders of courtesy titles are indexed under their surnames, and are identified by date of death unless the date of creation or succession is specified. Some titles and offices achieved after 1688 are supplied in square brackets. The entry London is to the City proper and the suburb of Southwark; places in the early modern metropolis to the west of Temple Bar are indexed under Westminster. P stands for Pepys in numerous entries. Almost all the matter indexed stands in some relation to him, and the entry under his own name is therefore confined to a few key details. The swung dash (~) introduces general sequences in some longer entries, or to mark a break in the alphabetical arrangement of sub-entries.

—, Anne, Mrs Hewer's kinswoman, 79
—, Richard, joiner, 98, 99, 100
—, Thomas, W. Hewer's clerk, 99, 104
Admirals, Lord High, monarchs as, 178
   n. 3
   see also James II; Villiers, George (I)
Admiralty:
   Commission/Commissioners: Board
     of 1679–84 criticised by P, 173–4,
     199; Commissioners generally, 35,
     36, 52, 85, 91, 101; individuals,
     5, 32 n. 9, 33 n. 21, 105 n. 11,
     177 n. 3; premises (Derby House),
     38, 72, 75, 78, 79, 80, 93, 104
     n. 1; subsequent history, 178 n. 3
   minor officials: clerks, 73, 75, 105
     n. 5, 106 n. 26; head messengers,
     67, 104 n. 3; porters, 67, 104 n. 1
   Secretary: P as (1673–9), 35, 36,
     115; (1684–9), 173; successors,
     105 n. 11, 106 n. 26, 200 nn. 4, 9
Admiralty Court, 167 n. 19;
   jurisdiction, 126, 126–7
Albemarle, Duke of see Monck, George
Alcazar (Alcassar) Bay, Morocco, 162
Alcazar, Alcaïd of see Ali Benabdala
Aldeburgh (Alborough), Suff, by-
   election, 9, 32 n. 1

Ali Benabdala, Alcaïd of Alcazar:
   belligerence expected/provoked,
   131, 145, 153, 164, 165; facade,
   146; gifts/courtesies exchanged
   with, 133, 160, 164; openness
   with proposed/rejected, 137;
   parley with Dartmouth, 140–1;
   servants, 134; son, 141–2; ~ also,
   117, 132, 133, 142, 143, 144,
   148, 153, 162, 163, 165, 169
   n. 55
Allin, Adm. Sir Thomas, 65, 90
animals and insects (except as food,
   q.v.): cat, 168 n. 33; glow-worm,
   153; lizards, 135; locust, 135–6;
   mosquitoes ('clinches'), 132, 133,
   137, 138, 150, 151; porpoises,
   128; spider, extraordinarily large,
   136
apothecary, 172 n. 120
Arlington, Lord see Bennet, Henry
Armenia, men of, 152
Armorer, Sir Nicholas, 95, 109 n. 70
army: appointments, 108 nn. 44, 49;
   finances, 3, 12
Arundell, Henry, Baron Arundell of
   Wardour (d. 1694), 87, 108
   n. 54

Ashburnham, William, Cofferer of the Household, 98, 110 n. 83

Ashby, Capt. John [Kt 1689], 123, 130, 167 n. 16

Ashley, Lord *see* Cooper, Anthony Ashley

Astrey (Astry), James, Clerk of the Crown, 53, 58

Atkins, Samuel, P's clerk, 35–6, 73, 81, 82, 97, 105 n. 5, 108 n. 59, 139, 162

Thomas, Dartmouth's cook, 158

Atlantic Ocean, 114

Aylesford, Earl of *see* Finch, Heneage

Aylmer (Elmer), Capt. George, 124, 125, 167 n. 23

Capt. Matthew [Baron Aylmer of Balrath 1718], 151, 171 n. 101

Ayloffe (Ayliff), Joseph, 9, 32 n. 4

Baber (Babor), Sir John, physician, 93, 100, 109 n. 66, 111 n. 95

Bacher (Beecher), Frederick, Admiralty judge at Tangier, 133, 138, 169 n. 62

baker, 172 n. 120

Baltic (East Country), timber, 186, 190

Banck, Pieter van der, engraver, plate 3

Banks (Bankes), Elizabeth, Lady Banks, 100, 111 n. 91

Sir John, Bt, 67, 98, 110 n. 85

banks/bankers, 66, 68, 80, 106 n. 18, 109 n. 59

Barbary: coast, 130; corsairs, 113, 117, 171 n. 109; states/power of (generally), 145, 153; *see also* Moors

Batten, Sir William, Surveyor of the Navy (1660–7), 1, 6, 15, 16, 25, 33 n. 16

Battine, Edward, 187, 201 n. 26

Beach, Adm. Sir Richard, Navy Commissioner, Portsmouth (1679–90), 176, 184, 187, 188, 191, 194, 201 nn. 22, 25, 36

Beckett, Isaak, artist, plate 7

Beckford, Sir Thomas, 49, 62 n. 34

Beckmann (Beckman), Maj. Martin, engineer, 114, 125, 126, 138, 156, 167 n. 27

Beckwith, Thomas, 72, 73, 78

Belasyse, John, Baron Belasyse (d. 1689), 87, 108 n. 54

Belbin, Nicholas, Navy Office clerk, 72

Bennet, Henry, Baron Arlington [Earl 1672], Secretary of State (1662–74), 10, 12–13, 32 n. 8

Berkeley (Berkely, Berkley), George, Earl of Berkeley (d. 1698), Elizabeth his Countess, and Lady Elizabeth their daughter, 100, 110 n. 89

Sir William, 147, 170 n. 85

Berry, Capt. Sir John, Commissioner of the Navy (1686–90): Captain in Tangier fleet, 121, 123, 128, 136, 148, 166 n. 5; Special Commission, 177, 183, 184, 185, 187, 188, 194, 195, 197, 199, 200 n. 18, 202 n. 48

Bertie (Bartie), The Hon. Charles, Treasury Secretary (1673–9), 98, 110 n. 84

Bethell (Bethel), Sir Hugh, MP, 79, 106 n. 16

Betterton, William, actor, 107 n. 39

Beverley, Yorks, MP, 110 n. 75

Bible, P reads, 128

Blackwall, Midd, 100, 111 n. 92

Blake, Adm. Robert, 113

Blathwayt (Blathwaite), William, Clerk of the Privy Council, 96, 110 n. 74

Blayney (Blany), Robert, 91, 109 n. 59

Blood, Col. Thomas, 98, 110 n. 82

books and MSS:

   printed works mentioned in the texts: Bible, 128; Butler, *Hudibras*, 125, 167 n. 28; Charles II, *Declaration . . . concerning the treasonable conspiracy*, 126, 168 n. 32; Godolphin, *Admiral Jurisdiction*, 127, 168 n. 38; Hakluyt, *Principal Navigations*,

160, 162, 171 n. 121; Hooke, *Micrographia*, 135, 169 n. 66; Witsen, *Aeloude*, 96, 109–10 n. 74; Zouch, *Jurisdiction of the Admiralty*, 26–7 (*ter*), 167 n. 31

principal extant MSS compiled by P mentioned in the texts (except the texts themselves): characters of shipwrights, 182, 200 nn. 12, 13; 'Defence of the Navy Board' (1669), 3–4, 13–14, 33 n. 13; letters, 81, 106 n. 24, 122, 149, 155, 166 n. 11, 169 n. 60, 171 n. 91, 172 n. 112, 181, 183, 187, 194, 197, 199, 200 nn. 10, 11, 16, 201 nn. 25, 35, 202 nn. 38–9, 48; 'Memorial and Proposition' (1686), 179, 200 n. 2; other Special Commission business, 185, 201 n. 23; Tangier business, 127, 129, 130, 131–2, 133, 143, 150, 158, 161, 163, 166 n. 7, 168 n. 36, 169 nn. 46, 52, 57, 63, 172 nn. 116, 123, 126; witness depositions &c., 100, 104, 111 nn. 97, 102

other principal works compiled by P: Diary (1660–9), xxi, xxii, xxiii, 1, 3, 71 n. 6, 168 n. 33; *Memories* (1690), 199, 200 nn. 2, 12; 'Mornamont', 38, 41 n. 4, 67, 71 n. 5, 105 n. 7; 'Navy White Book', 8 n. 10; 'Parliament Notes', xxiii; 118; Spanish papers, 117, Tangier papers, 118–19, 168 n. 37

other printed books owned by P: Dangerfield, *Second Narrative*, 63 n. 51; Littleton, *Dictionarius Quadripartitus*, 107 n. 31; Oates, *Narrative of the Horrid Plot*, plate 2; Seller, *English Pilot*, plate I; Sheres, *Discourse touching Tangier*, 170 n. 88; Sprat, *History of the Royal-Society*, and other works, 107 n. 34; *Transactions of Sir Robert Peyton*, 63 n. 51; *Tryal . . . For the riot at Guild-hall*, 63

n. 52; *Tryal . . . of Sir John Fenwick* (1697), and other works, 109 n. 68

other MSS owned by P: Battine, 'Method of building . . . ships of war', 201 n. 26; Blayney, 'Case . . . of Samuel Atkins', 109 n. 59; Dummer, writings on shipbuilding, 202 n. 47; *Hue & Cry after P. & H.* (in MS), 108 n. 56

for newspapers see London Gazette *and* Mercurius Anglicus

Booth, Sir William, Captain of the *Grafton*, 126, 127, 128, 129, 130, 132, 137, 152; log, 116, 166 n. 1, 170 n. 74

Boteler (Buttler), Elizabeth, Lady Boteler, 111 n. 90

Sir Francis, 100, 111 n. 90

Boynton, Col. Marmaduke, 156

Brampton (Bramton), Hunts, 104, 111 n. 103

Breames (Breame), Walter, JP, 48, 61 n. 31

Brereton (Breereton), William, Baron Brereton (d. 1680), chairman of the Brooke House Commission: clashes with P, 5, 10, 11–12; fraud allegation, 7, 27, 29–30; irritates King, 12, 18; musical, 19, 33 n. 23; ~ also, 9, 14, 24–5, 26, 27, 29, 30, 31

Bridgeman, Sir Orlando, Lord Keeper (1667–72), 10, 17, 32 n. 8

William, Clerk of the Privy Council and Under-secretary of State, 9, 190, 191

Bridgwater, Earl of *see* Egerton, John

Brisbane, John, Admiralty Secretary (1680–4), 105 n. 111

Brooke House Commission; appointment, 3, 32 n. 10; members, 5, 8 n. 7, 32 n. 9, 33 nn. 15, 21, 34 nn. 35, 37

'Observations': (1) [contracts with merchants], 14–18; (3, 5) [defects in Navy Treasurer's accounts],

18–19, 20–1; (7) [supervision of under-officers], 21; (8) [storekeepers' accounts/surveys], 21–2; (9) [musters], 23; (10) [boatswains' and carpenters' accounts], 23; (11–13) [payment of seamen by ticket], 24–5; (14) [short rations], 25–7; (15, 16) [favouring certain merchants], 27–8; (17) [paying off ships], 28–9; (18) [prizes], 30–2; [*nos 2, 4, 6 not covered in this edition*] *other issues*: diversion of war funds to 'other uses', 10, 11–12, 17–18; opening date of hostilities, 11, 32 n. 10, 19; ticket fraud alleged against P, 25, 27, 29–30

Brooke House Journal: MS and publication history, xxi–xxii, 7–8, 203; synopsis *see preceding entry*; text, 9–32

Brouncker, William, Viscount Brouncker (d. 1684), Commissioner of the Navy (1664–80) and Admiralty (1681–4), 9, 14, 17, 18, 27, 28, 32 n. 2, 84, 85, 86, 101, 109–10 n. 74

Bruges, *prov.* Flandre-Occidentale, Belgium, 62 n. 45

Brussels, 38, 62 n. 45

Bryant, Sir Arthur Wynne Morgan, author, xxii, xxv, xxvi n. 9, 105 n. 6, 108 n. 48

Buckingham, Dukes of *see* Villiers, George (I) and (II)

Budgeon, —, ship's carpenter, 151, 171 n. 100

Burchett, Josiah, Admiralty clerk, [Secretary 1694–1742], 170, 200 n. 4; ? as 'Jos.', 149; ? as 'Joseph Burcher', 171 n. 89

Burghley, Lord *see* Cecil, William

Burlings [Burlenga Islands], 129, 169 n. 45

Burrell, William, shipwright, 174

Butler, James, Duke of Ormond (d. 1688), 10, 32 n. 8, 109 n. 71

Samuel (d. 1680), author, 125, 167 n. 28

Thomas, *called* earl of Ossory (Ormond's heir, d. 1680), 95, 109 n. 71

see also Boteler

Byron, Lt Richard, 99–100, 110 n. 87

Cadiz (Cadiz, Cales), *prov.* Cadiz, Spain, 117, 129, 139, 148, 149, 158, 165, 166, 169 n. 49

Calais, *dép.* Pas-de-Calais, France, 36, 48

Cambridge University, Magdalene College: members, 32 nn. 4, 8, 201 n. 37; Pepys Library, xxii, 7, 41, 70, 119, 177; plates 1–8, I–V; [*see also books and MSS*]; Visitor, 169 n. 61

Cambridge University Library, mistaken for PL, 105 n. 7

candles, 122, 132

Capell, Arthur, Earl of Essex (d. 1683), 104

Capps (Capp), John, seaman, 29, 34 n. 36

cards, P wins at, 166

carpenter, ship's, 171 n. 100

Carteret (Carterett), Sir George, Treasurer of the Navy (1660–7), 1; accounts examined, 3, 4, 9, 10, 18, 19, 20, 33 n. 25; private organ, 33 n. 23

Cary, Anthony, Viscount Falkland (d. 1694), Treasurer of the Navy (1681–9), 177, 191, 192–3, 194, 196–7, 201 n. 35, 202 n. 38

Carverth, Capt. Henry, 172 n. 113

Castle Rising, Norf, constituency, 61 n. 27

Castleton, —, lawyer, 68, 81

Catherine of Bragança, Queen of Charles II, 113

Catholicism/Popery, 35, 38, 39, 44, 48–9, 63 n. 50, 68, 88, 91, 95, 103, 108 nn. 53–5, 110 n. 76

Cavelier, Jean, artist, plate 1

Cecil, William, Baron Burghley
(d. 1598), and his son Thomas,
Earl of Exeter (d. 1623), 108
n. 52

Chappell, Edwin, editor, 118–19, 120
n. 12, 168 n. 43, 172 n. 130,
204

Charles I, King: execution
commemoration, 77, 105 n. 15;
navy, 174

Charles II, King:
*Privy Council debate on Brooke
House report*: amused/sarcastic, 7,
19, 23, 30; angry, 12, 18; chairs
proceedings; 4, 6–7, 8, 11–32
passim; mastery of detail, 15, 23,
34 n. 29

relations with P: appoints as
Admiralty Secretary (1673), 35;
(1684), 173; assists/supports P at
Privy Council debate, 5, 6–7, 10,
11, 12, 15, 17, 18, 19, 20, 21,
22–3, 26, 28, 30, 31, 32; calls P
'his advocate',12; commissions
published defence, 12–13;
dismisses fraud allegation, 30; P
attends/ reports to, 4, 10, 13–14,
14–15, 33 n. 13; P's continued
access to during Popish Plot,
43–4, 49–50, 56–7, 61 n. 15, 111
n. 103; supposed readiness to
believe P's guilt, 78

various: criticism of wartime
leadership, 2, 3, 4, 12; death, 190;
debts, 175; dines in City, 84, 107
n. 43; dockyard visit, 111 n. 92;
evacuation of Tangier, 114–15,
121, 126, 146–7, 152; Lord High
Admiral, 173, 178 n. 3; marriage
treaty, 113; players, 105 n. 7;
plots against/deliverance from, 61
n. 20, 126, 128–9, 168 n. 32;
political skills/manoeuvres, 3, 4,
6, 8 n. 9, 36; present from New
Englanders, 16; ~ alluded to, 50,
62 nn. 44, 67, 85, 98, 106 n. 25,
108 n. 47, 111 n. 103, 142, 145,
148, 153, 171 n. 107, 201 n. 37

Chatham, Kent, dockyard, 21, 82, 88,
90, 176, 183, 188, 194, 199, 200
n. 15, 202 n. 42, 47; Clerk of the
Cheque, 202 n. 43; Commissioner
see Pett, Peter; defensive chain, 2;
Dutch raid (1667), 22; royal visit
(1686), 177, 197–8; ship built at,
plate 10

Chatham Chest, 80–1, 106 n. 20, 201
n. 30

Chelsea (Chelsey), cottage at Parsons
Green used by P, 76, 96, 97, 105
n. 13; neat-houses, 110, 111 n.
96; tavern keeper, 95

Chicheley, Rear Adm. Sir John,
Commissioner of the Admiralty
(1677–9), 177 n. 3

Chiffinch (Shevins), William, Page of
the Bedchamber, 57, 63 n. 49

Childs, John, author, 119–20 n. 1

Cholmley, Sir Hugh, engineer, 170 n. 68

Christmas carols, 117

Clare, —, servant of AG, 42, 50

Clarendon, Earls of *see* Hyde, Edward;
Henry

Clarges (Clergis), Sir Thomas, MP, 50,
62 n. 40

Clifford, Sir Thomas, 17

Closterman, Johann Baptist, artist,
plate 5

clothiers, 62 n. 34, 91, 97, 110 n. 79

coaches: Hewer to be abducted in, 85,
92; P's, 92, 100; sale, 98

coachmaker, P visits, 101

coachman, P's, 76

coffee-houses, 48, 74, 95; King
deprecates gossip in, 19

Coladon (Colodon), Dr —, physician,
91, 96, 97, 98

Collier, — Mrs, Kirke's mistress, 170
n. 86

Collins, John, engraver, plates II–V

Collinson (Coleson), Capt. Robert, 38,
52, 62 n. 45

Commonwealth/Protectorate ('the late
times'/'the State'): civil service, 32
nn. 2, 5; naval management, 18,
19, 20, 24, 26, 32 n. 9, 33 n. 21

Constantinople [*modern* Istanbul], 172 n. 118
convoys, 15
Conyers (Coneirs, Coniers), George, SJ, 44, 61 n. 20
Cooper, Anthony Ashley, Baron Ashley, Earl of Shaftesbury (1672), 17, 36, 92, 98, 109 nn. 59, 61
Coote, Stephen, author, xxvi n. 10
cork, 136
Cotter, —, 84
Council, Privy: Cabinet [*principal PCs attending King*], 127, 182, 188; Clerk, 9; debate on Brooke House report, 4–5, 11–32; Lords of the Committee [*PC committee*], 73, 104 n. 4; Office, 90; power to imprison, 54; ~ also, 179, 186, 190
Counsel, King's, 11–12, 13, 43
Court, 34 n. 34, 35, 40, 84, 85, 147
Coventry, The Hon. Sir William, Commissioner of the Navy (1662–7) and Treasury (1667–9), 9, 13, 32 nn. 2, 7, 65
Cranfeild, Edward, gentleman usher, 98, 110 n. 81
crimes and offences: buggery, 122; forgery, 45–6; murder, 35–6; mutiny, 26, 166; piracy, 36–7, 43, 68, 76, 105 n. 12, 106 n. 16; rape, 159; treason/espionage, 36, 37, 38, 40–1 & n. 9, 43, 51, 53, 54, 55, 62 n. 47, 126, 168 n. 32
Cromwell, Oliver, Lord Protector (1653–8), 2, 17, 33 n. 21, 107 n. 38, 167 n. 21
  Richard, Lord Protector (1658–9), 5, 33 n. 21
Cumberland, Duke of *see* Rupert, Prince
Curle, Dr —, physician, 84, 91, 92
customs (dues), 175
Cuthbert (Cutberd), Robert, merchant, 149, 162, 171 n. 92; wife, 149, 160

Damort, —, 95
dancing, 27, 128, 132

Dartmouth, Baron *see* Legge, George
Davies, John David, author, 177 n. 2
Deane, Sir Anthony, shipwright, Commissioner of the Navy (1675–80, 1686–9): career, 41 n. 2, 52, 62 n. 44, 84, 85, 92, 96, 97, 98 109 n. 63
  charges against: arrest, 42, 61 n. 14; attends AG in chambers, 50; bail, 49, 59; damages claimed against, 79, 90, 106 n. 16; King's Bench appearances, 42, 43, 44, 53; matter for assizes 43, 47, 52, 54, 56, 61 n. 14; ~ also, 36, 37, 38, 39, 40, 68, 87, 105 n. 12
  Navy Commission (1686): appointment engineered by P, 175, 176, 181, 182–3, 200 nn. 10, 11, 13, 202 n. 47; attendance, 184, 185, 187, 188, 194, 195, 197; recommendations, 186, 189, 196, 198, 199, 199, 202 n. 47
  various: portrait, plate 6; servant boy, 73; social/correspondence with P, 72–3, 83, 84, 85, 86, 94, 124
  Christian, Lady Deane, 85
Deane Sands, off Portsmouth, 122
Deering (Dering), Capt. Daniel, 154, 171 n. 109
Deptford, Kent, dockyard, 106 n. 21, 176, 188, 192, 197
Derby, —, 78
des Moulins, —, Mlle, 61 n. 30
d'Este, Laura, Duchess of Modena, 100, 111 n. 94
d'Estrées (D'Estree), *Comte* Jean, Vice-Admiral of France, 46, 61 n. 26
Dieppe, *dép.* Seine Maritime, France, 48
dissenters, 69, 84, 98
Dolben (Dolbin), Sir William, JKB (1678–83, 1689–94), 39–40, 46, 53, 57, 58, 61 n. 25
Donluis *alias* Lewis, Phelix, P's clerk, 48, 61 n. 32, 66, 71 n. 4, 97, 98, 100, 110 n. 80
Dover, Kent, 48, 107 nn. 30, 42

Downing, Sir George, Treasury
      Secretary (1667–71), 10, 32
      n. 5
Downs, South, 123
Drapentier [? Drapentière], John,
      engraver, plate 8
dress and personal appearance: Arab
      costume, 135, 140, 152, 158;
      drawers and sleeves pinned
      against mosquitoes, 151; feet
      warmers, 163; female, 143; sailors
      disguised as soldiers, 140, 170 n.
      72; shaving, 135; slops, 62 n. 34,
      110 n. 79; suit, 133; washing of
      linen, 123
drills (for mining), 133–4
Dummer, Edward, [Surveyor of the
      Navy 1692–9], 198, 202 n. 47
Du Moulin, Pierre, 48, 61 n. 30
Duncombe (Duncomb), Charles,
      Cashier of the Excise, 145, 170
      n. 81
   Sir John, Commissioner of the
      Treasury (1667–72), 10, 13, 32
      n. 7
Dunkirk, *dép*. Nord, France, 36
Dunnose (Dunoze), [*headland*], Isle of
      Wight, 122
Dunster, Giles, Commissioner of
      Accounts, 8 n. 7
Dutton (Dotton), Sir Richard, 49
Duval (Du Vall), Claude, highwayman,
      17, 33 n. 20

East India Company, 176
Edgcumbe (Edcomb), Sir Richard and
      Lady Anne, and Richard their son,
      later Baron Edgcumbe (d. 1758),
      123–4, 167 n. 20
Egerton, John, Earl of Bridgwater
      (d. 1686), 17
Elizabeth I, Queen: accession
      anniversary, 106 n. 25; navy,
      20–1, 22, 32 n. 35
Elizabeth II, Queen, Lord High Admiral
      (from 1964), 178 n. 3
engineers, 114, 117, 154, 156, 160,
      170 n. 68, 201 n. 37; lack tools,

138; varied estimates for Tangier
      demolition, 133, 141, 165
English Channel (Narrow Seas): guard,
      186; musters, 23; short rations in,
      25
Erlisman, John, Comptroller of Tangier,
      129, 150, 152, 168 n. 43; son,
      168 n. 43
Essex, Earl of *see* Capell, Arthur
Etherege, Sir George, playwright (*She
      Would if She Could*), 67, 74, 105
      n. 7
Evelyn, John, and Mary his wife, 33
      n. 25
Exchequer, court of, 20, 32 nn. 5, 6, 33
      n. 25, 34 n. 37, 175
Exclusion crisis, 40, 62 n. 35, 114
executions, 12, 33 n. 20, 109 n. 68; P in
      danger of, 40

Fairfax, Capt. the Hon. Thomas, MP,
      85, 86, 87, 108 n. 49
Faithorne, William, jun., engraver, plate
      5
Falkland, Viscount *see* Cary, Anthony
Fenn, Jack, Paymaster of the Navy
      (1660–8), 25
Fenwick, Sir John, Bt, 94, 109 n. 68
Fez, Morocco, 152
Finch, Sir Heneage [Earl of Nottingham
      1681], SG (1660–70), 20, 33 n.
      24
   Heneage [*son of the above*; Earl of
      Aylesford 1714], SG (1679–86),
      42, 60 n. 4
   Sir John, ambassador at
      Constantinople, 172 n. 118
Finisterre, Cape (North Cape), 128
fishing (sport), 162
FitzRoy, Henry, Duke of Grafton
      (d. 1690), 167 n. 26, 198, 202 n.
      44
flags, 170 n. 72
Flanders, 52, 100
food and drink:
   customs/cuisine: Arab eating habits,
      135; Italian, 136; Spanish, 149,
      160

fish: ling, 90, 123; lobster pie, 85; pilchards, 166

various: boar, 133; bread, 172 n. 120; fowl, 133, 164; grapes, 132, 133, 136; meat, stinking, 137; milk, 123, 134, 141; onions, 133; pomegranates, 132, 133, 136; sugar (customs), 175; sweetmeats, 133; syllabub, 123; turkey, 165–6; vinegar (customs), 175

water: medicinal, 193; Tangier supply inadequate, 132, 141; with wine, 130

wine: brandy (medicinal use), 166; champagne, 92, 109 n. 62; civic, bad, 107 n. 43; cooled in saltpetre, 133, 136; customs, 175; diluted, 130; punch, 129; tent, 83, 107 n. 35; toasts, 129, 155

Fox, Sir Stephen, Commissioner of the Treasury (1679x1702), 75, 105 n. 9

France:
   naval affairs: Admiralty, 38; Admiralty Court, 37; Navy, 125; stores better furnished than English, 138; Treasurer *see* Pellissary, Georges; Vice-Admiral *see* d'Estrées, Jean

   P's contacts: visit, 9, 32 n. 1; witnesses from, 39, 40, 51, 52, 83, 84, 106–7 nn. 28–30, 42

   relations with England: ally, 36; ambassador from, 37; potential enemy, 43, 51; Tangier offered to, 170 n. 83

Frankish (language), 152, 171 n. 104
friar (so described), at Tangier, 134

Gainsborough (Gaynsb'), Earl and Countess of *see* Noel, Edward and Mary

Gale, Samuel, P's godson, 111 n. 98
   Dr Thomas, 101, 111 n. 98, 172 n. 112

Gargrave, —, servant of Dartmouth, 135

Garraway *alias* Garway (Garaway), William, MP, 76, 80, 105 n. 14

Garter, Order of the, insignia, plate 2

Gauden, Sir Denis, Navy Victualler, 25, 26, 91, 109 n. 59

George, Prince of Denmark, [Lord High Admiral 1702–8], 198, 202 n. 45

German (language), 171 n. 104

ghosts, 130, 135, 168 n. 33; Arab dress suggestive of, 158

Gibraltar, 164; capture (1704) alluded to, 172 n. 119

Gibraltar, Straits of, 130, 131

Gibson, Richard, P's clerk, 81, 106 n. 21

Gifford, Capt. William, 145, 146, 170 n. 82, 171 n. 98

Giles, Capt. John, 143, 170 n. 76

Gillingham, Kent, 198

Gladman, John, tobacconist, 44, 61 n. 19

Gleréaux, sieur des *see* Thévenin, Paul

Godalming (Godilman), Surr, 121

Godfrey, Sir Edmund Berry, JP, murder, 36, 37, 105 n. 5

Godolphin, John, author, 127, 167 n. 38

Godwin, Sir John, Commissioner of the Navy (1686–8), 176, 183, 184, 185, 187, 188, 194, 197, 200 n. 16, 201 n. 20, 202 n. 48

Goldsbrough, —, 83, 84

Gonson, Benjamin, Treasurer of the Navy (1549–77), 33 n. 25

Goodenough, Richard, attorney, 57, 59, 63 n. 52

'Good Voyages', 155, 171 n. 111

Gordon, Sir Robert, 195, 201–2 n. 37

Gothenburg [Göteborg], *reg.* Vaster-Götland, Sweden, 14, 16, 33 n. 16

Gough (Goffe), Richard, merchant, 130, 169 n. 48, 139

Grafton, Duke of *see* FitzRoy, Henry

Gravesend, Kent, 76

Green Ribbon Club, 82, 106 n. 25

Gregory, Edward, Clerk of the Cheque, Chatham, 198, 202 n. 43

Edward, father of the above, 202
    n. 43
John, Commissioner of Accounts, 8
    n. 7, 30, 31, 34 nn. 35, 37
Griffith [*or* Griffiths], —, merchants, 49
Griffith, —, tavern-holder, Chelsea, 95
Grimston, Sir Harbottle, MP, 91, 109
    n. 60
Grundy, Dr —, 121
Guards, 12
Gunman (Gunmon), —, Mrs, 197, 202
    n. 39
    Capt. Christopher, 121, 166 n. 2
gunners, 170 n. 80

Haddock, Capt. Sir Richard,
    Commissioner of the Navy
    (1673–1715): demoted, 176, 183,
    195, 100 n. 19; disgruntled in
    consequence, 184, 195; other
    quarrels, 193, 194; portrait, plate
    5
Hakluyt (Hacklewitt, Haklewt),
    Richard, author, 160, 162, 172
    n. 121
Haley, Kenneth Harold Dobson, author,
    36, 41 n. 11
Halifax, Viscount *later* Marquess of *see*
    Savile, George
Hall, —, 98
Hamburg (Hambrough), *Land*
    Hamburg, Germany, 14
Hamet Lucas, secretary to Moroccan
    embassy, 151, 171 n. 99
Harbord (Herbert), Sir Charles
    (d. 1672), 66
    William, brother of Charles, MP:
    chairman of Miscarriages
    Committee (1679), 60 n. 6,
    103–4, 110 n. 75; 106 n. 18;
    family, 66; marshals evidence
    against P, 36, 37, 42–3, 50, 51,
    53, 54, 55, 56, 62 nn. 36, 42; 68,
    83, 84, 93, 95–6, 97, 98, 103, 108
    n. 55; payments to witnesses, 66,
    69, 79–80, 86–7, 88, 90, 91–2,
    95, 99, 100, 101, 102; proposes
    conference/resolves differences

with P, 68, 69, 85, 86–9; willing
    to sustain quarrel in print, 94
Harford (Hartford), Robert, printer, 97,
    99, 100, 101, 110 n. 77
Harris, Alexander, Admiralty head
    messenger (1666–82): approaches
    to P/information from, 66–7, 68,
    69, 70, 72–3, 74–5, 77, 78, 79,
    80, 81, 82, 83, 84, 85, 89, 90, 91,
    92, 93, 94, 95, 96, 97, 101, 102,
    103, 104; dismissal/claim for
    compensation, 76, 104 nn. 1, 3;
    divulges Hewer kidnap plan,
    84–5; 92; mother, 95; replies 'very
    scurvily', 87; reviled by Russell as
    likely perjurer, 96, 99
    Benjamin, printer, 108 n. 56
    John, brother of Alexander,
    Admiralty porter (1676–8):
    dismissal/claim for compensation,
    68, 72, 76, 104 nn. 1, 3;
    interviews with P/Deane, 73, 94,
    101; involved in Hewer kidnap
    plan, 92; ~ also, 78, 79
    Mary, wife of Alexander, 44, 61
    n. 16, 78, 89, 91, 95
Harwich, Ess, dockyard, 21; MPs: (P),
    61 n. 27; (another), 100, 110
    n. 88
Hatfield Woodhall, Herts, 111 n. 90
Hayes, John, P's solicitor, 40, 43, 47,
    48, 49, 50, 52, 53, 58, 59, 69, 82,
    86, 87
Hayter, Thomas, P's clerk, Admiralty
    Secretary (1679–80): attends
    King's Bench, 48; P retains
    services, 176, 177, 181, 200 n. 9;
    reassuring interview, 187–8;
    ~ also, 75, 105 n.11, 195
health:
    ailments: calculus (gravel), 193, 201
    n. 33; cold, 100, 127, 150; cold in
    throat (P speechless from), 151,
    158, 159, 160, 161, 162, 163;
    (improves with coming of rain),
    164; fall, 149; flux, 152;
    headache, 127, 143, 162, 164;
    ingestion of phlegm, 162;

injuries/deaths from explosion,
159; seasickness, 126; sprained
ankle, 172 n. 128; tuberculosis
(consumption)/effects of, 65, 84,
96, 98; vomiting, 123, 127
medicines and treatments: bleeding,
148, 149; inhalation ('fume'), 92;
powder for cold, 162; washing
feet in brandy, 166; waters, 193;
~ also, 193, 172 n. 120
Henry VIII, King, 8 n. 9
Herbert, Adm. Arthur [Earl of
Torrington 1689], Commissioner
of the Admiralty (1683–4, First
Lord 1689–90), 127, 168 n. 37,
173, 177 n. 3, 198; 'young
fellows' of, 152
Elizabeth, Countess of Powis, 57, 63
n. 51
William, Earl of Powis (d. 1696), 87,
108 n. 54
see also Harbord
Heriot, Harboard, goldsmith-banker,
106 n. 18
James, goldsmith-banker, 80, 106
n. 18
Heroüard, Louis, *sieur* de La Piogerie,
major de marine, 45, 46, 61 n. 22
Hewer, Anne, mother of William, 78,
93
William, P's clerk, Commissioner of
the Navy (1686–9): career, 115,
176, 199
assists P during Popish Plot: attends
King's Bench, 53; canard of
unspecified fraud, 73; libel against
him and P, 90, 108 n. 56; gathers
information/interviews witnesses,
68, 69, 74, 77, 78, 79, 80, 81, 82,
83, 84, 85, 86, 87, 90, 91, 92, 96,
97, 98, 99, 100, 101; P uses his
name on false receipt, 104
Navy Commission (1686):
appointment, 176, 182, 183;
attendance, 184, 185, 187, 188,
194, 195, 197, 199; reports to P,
190; unwilling to undertake
residuary work, 199

Tangier business: appointed P's
successor as Treasurer, 91, 106 n.
58; with P on voyage/during stay,
115, 123, 126, 127, 128, 132,
143, 149, 150, 162
various: Chatham Chest business,
80–1; communicates, 84;
excursion to Spain, 117–18, 155,
163, 164, 166; health, 85, 90,
126, 164; kidnap plan, 69, 84–5,
85, 92, 101; lodgings shared with
P, 38; P solicitous for welfare,
161, 164
Higgins (Higgins), —, Mrs, 84, 101,
107 n. 37
Hill, George, founder, 44, 61 nn. 18, 20
Holland regiment, 108 n. 44
Holmes (Homes), Sir John, 84, 91, 107
n. 36
Adm. Sir Robert, brother of Sir John,
107 n. 36
Holt, Sir John, 51, 62 n. 43
Hooke, Robert, author, 135, 169
n. 66
Hordesnel *alias* Hordsnell, Hortenell,
Henry, Recorder of Tangier, 128,
150, 168 n. 40
Hornstein, Sari Ruth, author, 120 n. 1,
177 n. 2
Hoskins, Benjamin, Master of the
Grafton, 126
Hotham (Hothum), Sir John, Bt, MP,
96, 100, 101–2, 110 n. 75
Houblon, family, 67, 105 n. 13
Houblon (Houblin), James [Kt 1691],
merchant: bail for P, 49, 62 n. 34;
correspondence, 110 n. 74, 121,
149, 166 nn. 6, 11, 169 n. 60,
172 n. 112; credit arranged for
Tangier/Spain journey, 130; house,
107 n. 41; livery as disguise in
Hewer kidnap plan, 92; social, 96,
101, 105 n. 6
Sarah, wife of James, 85, 97, 105
n. 6, 110 n. 78, 165, 172 n. 130
Wynne (Gwin), son of James and
Sarah, 74, 101, 105 n. 6, 111 n.
100

Household, Royal: Cofferer, 110 n. 83;
    Gentlemen of the Privy Chamber,
    109 nn. 66, 68; Grooms of the
    Bedchamber, 63 n. 48, 166 n. 13;
    Page of the Bedchamber, 63
    n. 49
Howard, George, Earl of Suffolk
    (d. 1691), Visitor of Magdalene
    College Cambridge, 169 n. 61
    Henry, Duke of Norfolk (d. 1684),
    servant of, 93, 94
    Sir Robert, Treasury Secretary
    (1671–3), 98, 110 n. 84
    William, Viscount Stafford (d. 1680),
    87, 108 n. 54
Howarth, Robert Guy, editor, xxii, 118,
    120 n. 11
Hughes, Thomas, Anglican minister
    at Tangier, 135, 170 n. 67, 143,
    152, 156, 170 n. 67; garden,
    136
Huguenots, 61 n. 30, 62 n. 34, 106
    n. 27
Hunter, Samuel, muster-master at
    Tangier, 136, 143, 150, 170
    n. 79
hunting, 133, 160, 181
Hyde, Edward, Earl of Clarendon
    (d. 1674), 62 n. 41, 200 n. 1
    Henry, Earl of Clarendon (d. 1709),
    50, 62 n. 41
    Lawrence, brother of Henry, Earl of
    Rochester (1682), First Lord of
    the Treasury (1679–84), Lord
    Treasurer (1684–7): assists
    establishment of Special
    Commission, 175, 176, 177, 179,
    180, 181, 182, 184, 185, 186,
    188, 189, 190, 191–2, 195, 196,
    197, 200 n. 1, 201 n. 29; sprains
    ankle, 172 n. 128; ~ also, 85, 108
    n. 45, 137; plate 7

interpreters, 134, 140, 172 n. 123
Ireland: budget, attempt to finance
    Tangier from, 114; coast, 126;
    ~ also, 87, 88, 95, 107 n. 33, 109
    nn. 70–1, 145

Isma'il as-Samin *alias* Mulaï Ismaïl,
    Sultan of Morocco, 143, 144,
    146, 148, 164, 171 n. 95
Italy, cuisine, 136

James I, King, navy of, 174, 179, 180,
    200 n. 3
James II, King:
    (1) *as Duke of York and (to 1673)
    Lord High Admiral:*
    Admiralty business: commissions for
    purchase of goods, 32 n. 17;
    instructions to Navy Board
    (General 1662, and Additional),
    6, 21–2, 24, 26, 34 n. 26; Navy
    Board reports to, 27; resignation,
    35, 61 n. 23; ~ also, 29
    relations with P: accord at Privy
    Council debate, 4, 15, 17, 26, 28,
    31; business meetings, 10, 12, 67,
    85; P reports to, 3, 4, 9, 13–14,
    33 n. 13, 62 n. 42, 66; P retained
    as his unofficial agent, 31, 45, 93;
    social, 13, 100
    various: assassination attempt, 168
    n. 32; birthday marked at Tangier,
    152; court business/movements,
    84, 85, 108 n. 47, 111 n. 94;
    equerry, 166 n. 12; Exclusion
    crisis, 40, 114; mother-in-law,
    100, 111 n. 94; players, 107
    n. 39; return from Scotland
    celebrated, 107 n. 39, 107–9
    n. 43
    (2) *as King:*
    Navy business: approves/appoints
    Special Commission, 175, 176,
    179–98 *passim*, 200 n. 14, 201
    nn. 27, 29; concern for decayed
    ships, 186, 198; nautical wisdom,
    177, 185–6; P attends, 179, 180,
    181, 182, 183, 184, 185, 186,
    188, 190, 191, 192, 195, 197–8; P
    submits list of shipwrights to,
    175–6, 182; urges Navy Treasurer
    to his duty, 192–3, 197; visits to
    fleet/yards, 177, 197–8, 199;
    yacht in collision, 202 n. 46

various: accession, 173; levée, 184; 201 n. 37; portrait, plate 3; revenue, 175; water pumps, 195, 201 n. 37

James, Elizabeth mother of John, 65, 69, 70, 82, 83, 84, 87, 89, 91, ?95, 97, 98, 101, 102–3, 104

Elizabeth, sister of John, 65, 70, 81, 82, 85–6, 87, 96, 99, 100, 103–4

John, P's former butler:

career: butlering, 102; debts, 104; employment/dismissal by P, 37–8, 61 n. 17, 66, 68, 70 n. 2, 75; libel against P and Hewer, 90, 108 n. 56; Navy, 65–6, 70 n. 1; other employments/past villainies, 66, 75, 78, 88, 89, 91, 95, 101–2; payments to, 68, 79–80, 85, 86, 87, 88, 90, 91–2, 93, 94, 95, 99, 103; plot to kidnap Hewer, 69, 84–5, 92; visit to Holland, 70 n. 3, 75; Whig connections, 66, 81–2, 92, 102

charges: James against P, 37–8, 43, 44, 60 n. 10, 66–7, 76, 85, 88, 91, 95, 103, 110 n. 76; P against James, 66, 68, 75, 91

meetings with P: arranged by intermediary, 66–7, 73–4, 94; attempts to make deal, 68–9, 74–8, 79–80; conference with Harbord &c. 69, 85–90, 98

retractions: contrition prompted by illness, 81, 82–3, 102–3; first statement agreed/signed, 69, 84, 87–9, 90, 91; further statement extracted by Harbord, 69, 93, 94, 96, 97; newspaper reports, 69, 94, 96, 98–9, 100, 101, 103, 109 n. 69, 111 n. 101, 103

terminal illness: ailing/medical attention, 81, 83, 91, 92, 96, 98, 99; death/burial, 99, 100, 101

various: charity from P, 69, 70, 85, 89, 104; godfather, 101–2; Duke of York's interest, 100; mother's pride, 102; pocket book, 68, 69, 82–3, 94, 96, 99; sacrament, 83,

84, 88; ~ P declines to debate issues in print, 93, 94–5; his Journal of Proceedings with James and Harris: MS, 70, 203–4; text, 72–104

Jeffreys, Sir George, Baron Jeffreys of Wem (1685), LCJ, Lord Chancellor (1685–8), 39, 193

Jenkins, Sir Leoline, Secretary of State (1680–4), 122, 133, 155, 159, 172 n. 128

Jesuits, real and imagined, 38, 44, 61 n. 20, 80, 106 n. 19

Jews, 97, 98, 165

Johnson, —, clerk to AG, 184, 185

Sir Henry, shipwright, 111 n. 192, 175–6

Jones (Joanes), Sir Thomas, JKB (1676–83): sympathetic to P/Deane, 53, 56, 58; ~ also, 39, 40, 62 n. 46; plate 4

Sir William, AG (1675–9): lacks evidence, 43, 44, 46, 47; opposes bail, 44, 45, 48; resignation, 49, 62 n. 35; ~ also, 40, 42, 45, 49, 50, 56

Jordan, —, messenger, 83

Joyne, John, watchmaker, 71 n. 5, 83, 106 n. 29, 107 n. 30

Ken (Kenn), Thomas, chaplain to Dartmouth's fleet, [Bishop of Bath and Wells 1685]: belief in ghosts, 130, 135; critical of Tangier vices, 143, 160; nervous at sea, 136; senior Chaplain, 166 n. 4; sermons, 121, 129, 143, 149, 152; ~ also, 123, 153, 156, 159, 162, 166 n. 4; plate 8

Kent, 76

Kerne, Dr —, 97

Killigrew, Capt. Henry, 148, 157, 161, 165, 170 n. 87

King, Thomas, MP, 100, 110 n. 88

King's Bench, court of, P/Deane appearances before:

chronology: commitment to Tower/ transfer to Marshalsea, 42, 43;

court appearances (*entries begin*),
42, 43, 49, 50, 51, 53, 57, 59;
discharge, 59–60; ~ comment and
later references, 36, 38–41, 103,
175
issues: bail/sureties for, 39, 43, 44,
45, 46–7, 48, 49, 50, 57, 58, 59,
62 n. 34; felony triable before
lower court, 43, 47, 51–2, 54, 56;
Habeas Corpus, 39, 42, 51, 53,
54, 60 n. 2; King's interventions,
43–4, 56–7, 61 n. 15;
parliamentary privilege/session,
47, 53, 55, 58–9; P's handwriting,
45–6, 61 n. 24; warrant of
commitment, 39, 42–3, 53, 54
evidence/witnesses:
affidavits/depositions, 42–3, 44–5,
48–9, 56, 60 nn. 8, 9, 61, nn. 16,
18, 19, 33; evidence insufficient,
43, 44, 51, 54, 57, 60, 62 nn. 36;
evidence ruled inadmissible, 57–8;
papers withheld from defence, 48,
49; prosecution loses witnesses,
50, 51, 54–5, 57; single witness
insufficient in treason trial, 40–1,
43; witnesses for defence
contacted/brought from abroad,
39, 40, 51, 52, 52–3, 83, 84, 62 n.
45, 106–7 nn. 28–30, 42
*P's relations with Judges/Law
Officers*: clashes with AGs, 45,
47, 48, 49–50, 51; encouraged by
LCJ and some colleagues, 39, 45,
46–7, 47–8, 51, 52, 53, 55, 56,
58; hostility of other Judges,
39–40, 42, 47, 51, 53–4, 55–6;
interview with AG in chambers,
40, 50–1
King's Bench Journal, MS, 41, 203;
text, 42–60
King's Bench prison (Marshalsea) *see
under* London
Kirke, Mary, wife of Percy, [Lady Mary
1689], 132, 136, 169 n. 61
Col. Percy, acting Governor of
Tangier: belligerence, 131, 153;
garden, 143; shows P Roman

ruins, 149; vices/villainy, 136,
143, 158, 160, 168 n. 43, 170
n. 86; ~ also, 121, 132, 140, 141,
142, 144, 145, 148, 155, 156,
161, 162
Kneller, Sir Godfrey, artist, plates 3, 6, 7
Knightsbridge, Midd, 85, 108 n. 48

Lambert, Maj.-Gen. John, 124, 167 n.
21
Lambeth, Surr, 121
Land's End, in Sennen, Cornw, 124
Langham, Sir James, Bt, Commissioner
of Accounts, 8 n. 7
La Piogerie (La Piogery), *sieur* de *see*
Heroüard, Louis
Latham, Robert Clifford, editor, xxiv,
xxvi n. 1, 7, 8 & n. 10, 119
Lauderdale, Earl *then* Duke of *see*
Maitland, John
Lawrence, Dr Thomas, 123, 135, 138,
157, 166 n. 15
Lawson, —, P's clerk, 160
Leake, Capt. Richard, 144, 154, 155,
170 n. 80
Lee, Sir Thomas, Bt, Commissioner of
the Admiralty (1679–81,
1689–91), 70 n. 1, 75, 85, 104,
105 n. 11
Legge (Legg), George, Baron
Dartmouth (d. 1691), Admiral of
Tangier squadron 1683–4: boards
Grafton, 121
commission/instructions: confided to
P, 122; later to others, 127–8,
128, 131; reminded of details by
P, 137–8; prevents news from
England, 139; also ~ 115, 116,
117, 121, 124, 125, 129, 166
n. 7
miscellaneous business: address from
military, 152; appoints senior
chaplain, 166 n. 4; dealings with
townsmen, 116, 144, 149, 151,
153; orders all hands to Mole,
156, 157, 157–8; password, 158;
prohibits/orders salutes, 151, 171
n. 106

relations with Moors: bravado, 145, 146, 164; considers revealing withdrawal plan, 117, 133, 137–8; correspondence, 147–8, 153, 160, 163–4; examines renegade, 134, 135; meetings, 132, 142, 151; parley with Alcaïd, 140–1; supplies gunpowder, 151; treaty, 140, 141, 142, 165

relations with P: confidences, 122, 137–8, 141, 147, 149, 150, 154, 158, 164, 173; critical of delay, 136; drafting papers &c., 116, 125, 127, 128, 129, 144, 148, 150, 153; expeditions, 132, 161; leave granted to P, 164, 165; observing demolition, 156, 160, 161, 162; P reports to, 143–4, 159, 163; social, 124, 126, 130, 133, 138, 151, 155, 160, 166

various: attends James II, 198; cook, 158; courted by Portsmouth burghers; 123; health, 143, 144, 148, 149, 150, 164; laughter, 151, 155; melancholy/anxiety, 137–8, 149; not suicidal, 147; papers, 116; portrait, plate 9; servants, 157–8

Capt. William, brother of George, 123, 166 n. 13

Leghorn [Livorno], reg. Livorno, Italy, 114

Levinz (Levins, Lewins), Sir Creswell, AG (1679–80): appointment, 49; comments to P/Deane in chambers, 50–1; inadequately briefed, 54–5; paper disallowed in evidence, 57–8; withdraws charges, 59–60; ~ also, 40, 52, 53, 56, 62 nn. 35, 42

Lewis *see* Donluis Phelix

Lidoct, ? John, 90, 108 n. 57

Lisbon, 129

liturgies and prayers: Arab, 135; burial (RC), 144; Charles I execution anniversary, 77; Charles II deliverance from murder plot, 128–9; communion, 69, 83, 84,

88; shipboard, 121, 123, 124, 126, 127, 128–9; ~ also, 87, 135, 136, 142, 143, 144, 149, 152, 156, 160

Littleton, Adam, Canon of Westminster, 69, 83, 84, 86, 88, 96, 97, 98, 107 n. 31

Lloyd, Christopher, author, xxiii (quoted), 119 n. 1

Logan, Lt Andrew, 65, 70 n. 1

London:

  churches: St Pancras Cheapside, 19, 33 n. 22; St Paul's Cathedral, 19

  City/Corporation: charter, 40; civic banquet, 84, 107–8 n. 43; Lord Mayors, 33 n. 15, 109 n. 59

  Companies: Clothworkers, plate 1; Shipwrights, 194

  Inns of Court: Gray's Inn, 32 n. 4, 40, 50, 60 n. 7, 62 n. 43; Inner Temple, 62 n. 43

  prisons: Marshalsea, Southwark, 43, 61 nn. 14, 15; Newgate (New Gate), 80; Tower, 38, 41 n. 5, 42, 43, 48, 48, 66; gunners, 170 n. 80; 'lords in' (Catholic prisoners), 87, 108 n. 54

  streets/other locations: Arch Row, Lincoln's Inn Fields, 111 n. 91; Cornhill, 101, 110 n. 77; Crane Court, off Fleet St, 111 n. 90; Devonshire House, 44; Dorset Garden theatre (Duke's Company), 107 n. 39; Fenchurch St (Fanchurch), Mitre tavern, *formerly* Rawlinson's, 68, 79, 106 n. 16; Fleet Bridge, 106 n. 18; Fleet St (Fleete), Naked Boy (Heriot's bank), 66, 68, 80, 106 n. 18; Great Winchester St, 84, 85, 86, 90, 92, 95, 107 n. 41; Holborn, Brooke House, 3, 11; Houndsditch, 44; Lime St, 106 n. 16; Little Britaine St (Little Brittany), Smithfield, 101, 111 n. 100; Old Fish St, 97; Portugal Row, 92; Royal Exchange, 90, 98; St Paul's School, 111 n. 98;

Salisbury Court, off Fleet St, 86;
Tower Hill, 195
various: Great Fire (1666), 33 nn.
15, 22; picture dealers, plates II–V
London Gazette, 63 n. 54, 168 n. 32,
184, 186, 201 n. 21
Long, Sir Robert, Bt, Treasury official,
10, 13, 17, 32 n. 6
Lorrain, Paul, P's library clerk, 83, 106
n. 27
Louis XIV, King of France, 36; admires
same girl as P, 110 n. 89
Lowestoft, battle of (1665), 1

Maddocks (Maddox), Robert,
Paymaster of the Navy (from
1671), 180, 181, 200 n. 7
Mahon, Port, Majorca, 114
Maitland, John, Earl of Lauderdale
[Duke 1672], 27, 31–2
Malta, 114
Mansell, Col. Roderick, Whig agent:
creature of Shaftesbury, 92, 98,
109 n. 61; Green Ribbon Club,
82, 106 n. 25; history/rogueries,
83, 95, 102; originator of P's
troubles, 80, 90; payments to
J. James, 79, 99; proposes
lampoon, 108 n. 56; P meets for
first time, 86, 89; ~ also, 68, 85,
87, 106 n. 17
maps: P accused of passing to French,
37, 38, 51, 62 n. 45; Tangier: (P's
collection), 116, plate I ;
(modern), 112
Mariott, —, Duke of Norfolk's servant,
93, 94, ?98 [*? confusion with
next*]
Marratt, Richard, Admiralty porter, 72,
?98, 99, 104 n. 3, 109 n. 67
Marshall, Andrew, author, quoted, 37
Mason, Sir Richard, 44, 61 n. 17, 65,
75, 95, 105 n. 9
Matthews, Sir John, MP, 100, 111
n. 93
William, xxvi n. 3, 119, 204
Meagher, John, apothecary, 172 n. 29
'meal-tub' conspiracy, 63 n. 51

Mediterranean (the Straits), 65, 113,
114, 130, 169 n. 53, 172 n. 119;
P enters, 131
Medway, River, Dutch raid (1667), 1–2,
3, 22, 33 n. 27
Mennes, Sir John, Comptroller of the
Navy (1661–71), 1, 14, 17, 33
n. 14
Mercurius Anglicus, 69, 94, 96, 98, 99,
100, 101, 103, 109 n. 69, 110
n. 77, 111 n. 101
Meres, Sir Thomas, MP, 57, 63 n. 50
Messina, reg. Messina, Italy, 65
Middleton, Charles, earl of Middleton,
Secretary of State (1684–8),
190
Col. Thomas, Surveyor of the Navy
(1667–72), 14, 33 n. 14
minerals: cement (tarras), 165, 172
n. 31; lime, 132; saltpetre, 133,
136
mines (military)/miners/drillers, 117,
118, 123, 133, 143, 144, 145,
149, 163, 167 n. 18, 170 n. 76; P
views workings, 153–4, 154–5,
156–7, 158, 160
Mings, John, 159, 172 n. 118
Modena, Duchess of *see* d'Este, Laura
Mohammed Ohadu, *alias* Ben Hadu,
Moroccan ambassador, 113;
secretary to, 151, 171 n. 99
Monck, George, Duke of Albemarle
(d. 1670), General-at-Sea, 26, 34
n. 32
Monmouth, Duke of *see* Scott, James
Montagu, Edward, Earl of Sandwich
(d. 1672), 66, 114, 115, 147, 170
n. 85; daughter *see* Edgcumbe,
Lady Anne
Moon (Moone), Capt. Samuel, 36, 37,
43, 54, 60 n. 9, 79, 94, ?97
Moors:
customs/beliefs: boat mending, 151;
dress, 135, 140, 152, 158; eating,
135; equestrianism, 141; huts,
157, 158; martial skills/ drill, 132,
140; patience, 150; prayers, 135;
~ also, 140, 150, 152

forces: army, 117, 131, 134, 140–1,
  145, 146, 164; fleet, 140, 145;
  sentries, 116, 150, 151, 163
P's sightings: observes from distance,
  116, 131, 132; ventures closer,
  150, 151, 156, 157, 158, 163
relations with England: defector,
  supposed, 134–5; embassy from
  (1682), 113, 151, 171 n. 99;
  espionage, 144; history, 113–14,
  150, 156; hostages, 164, 165;
  hostility expected, 114, 117, 132,
  137–8, 145–6, 154, 158, 165;
  hostility provoked, 153; hostility
  temporarily unlikely, 162, 165;
  interpreters, 140, 172 n. 123;
  interviews with Dartmouth, 132,
  134–5, 140–1, 144, 145;
  meetings/access to Tangier
  restricted, 145, 148, 160; powder
  sent to, 151, 165; presents from,
  153; revelation of withdrawal
  plan suggested/rejected, 117, 133,
  137–8; sentries frightened by
  explosion, 163–4; treaty, 140,
  141, 142, 143, 144, 164, 165
surprises for: booby trap, 156;
  mortars, 158
for rulers see Ali Benabdala; Isma'il
  as-Samin; *see also* Barbary
Mordaunt, Sir Charles, Bt, 107 n. 37
  Elizabeth (Mrs Francis Godolphin),
  Lady Mordaunt, 84, 85, 98, 99,
  100, 101, 107 n. 37, 108 n. 48
Moreau, Claude, 106 n. 28
Morelli (Morelly), Cesare, P's
  household musician, 37–8, 66, 70
  n. 2, 76, 80, 88, 91, 110 n. 76,
  111 n. 103
Morland, Sir Samuel, Bt, Fellow of
  Magdalene College, Cambridge,
  195, 201 n. 37
'Mornamont' [*fict.*], 41 n. 2; *see also*
  books (4)
Morocco: modern kingdom, 113;
  Sultan *see* Isma'il as-Samin; *see*
  principally Moors
Mount Edgcumbe, Devon, 123–4

Muddiman (Muddyman), Henry, 94,
  95, 109 n. 69
Mulaï Hamet (Mulay Hamet), 145, 151
music: flutes, 130; guitar, 132; harp,
  125, 132, 160; organ, 33 n. 23;
  song, 125; trumpets (military),
  163; violin, 128; ~ also, 19, 35,
  123, 126, 127, 128; *see also*
  dancing

Narbrough, Adm. Sir John,
  Commissioner of the Navy
  (1680–8), 176–7, 180–1, 184,
  185, 187, 188, 194, 195, 197,
  199, 200 n. 8, 202 n. 48
National Maritime Museum, 116
navigation/steering, 128, 129, 167
  n. 25
Navy Board/Navy Office [*as constituted*
  1660–86]:
  Commission (generally):
    joint/corporate functions, 15;
    officials, 106 n. 21, 109 n. 63;
    premises, 194, 195, 201 n. 21;
    wartime strains, 26–7, 28–9;
    ~ later history, 178 n. 3, 199
  Commissioners (particular): *Clerk of*
    the Acts: P as, 1–24 *passim*;
    residence, 195; *Comptroller*:
    duties, 1, 4, 17, 21–2; *Surveyor*:
    duties, 21–2; *see also* Batten, Sir
    W.; Middleton, T.; *Treasurer*:
    accounts, 18–19, 20–1; duties, 2,
    177, 184, 188, 190, 192–3,
    196–7, 201 n. 28; Exchequer fees,
    20–1, 33 n. 25; *see also* Carteret,
    Sir G.; Cary, A.; *without portfolio*:
    see Coventry, Sir W.; Penn,
    Sir W.
  functions: contracts, 2, 6, 14–17, 21,
    27–8, 33 nn. 16–18; fitting out
    ships, 23; musters, 23; payment of
    seamen, 2, 24–5, 28–30;
    stores/surveys/supervision of
    under-officers, 21–2, 23, 31–2;
    victualling, 24–6
  Instructions from Lord High
    Admiral: (1662: General), 6,

21–2, 24, 26, 34 n. 26; Additional, 26

Navy Commission ['*Special Commission' superseding Navy Board 1686–8*]:

Commissioners: appointment/warrants, 175–7, 180–4, 185, 187, 188, 190, 191, 192, 193, 194, 197, 200 n. 18, 201 nn. 24, 34, 36; appointment declined, 176, 181; first meeting, 184–5; instructions, 192, 193–4, 195, 197, 201 nn. 34, 36; redeployment of existing Commissioners/officials, 176–7, 180–1, 187–8, 195, 200 nn. 8, 9, 15, 19; 201 nn. 20, 22; residences, 195, 197; salaries, 183, 187, 200 n. 17; winding-up, 199, 202 n. 49; *see individually*: Beach, Sir R.; Berry, Sir J., Sir R.; Deane, Sir A.; Godwin, Sir J.; Haddock, Sir R.; Hewer, W.; Narbrough, Sir J.; St Michel, B.; Southerne, J.; Tippets, Sir J.

finance: budget by P, 174, 179, 185, 196; instalments, 188–9, 191–2, 195–6; parliamentary support, 175; Treasurer's work evaluated/by-passed, 177, 184, 190, 192–3, 196–7

functions: design by P, 179–80, 185, 200 n. 2; pay, 190; shore installations, 186, 197–8; repair of ships, 189, 198; supervision of stores/surveys, 184, 186, 187; victualling, 189; visits to fleet/yards, 188, 197–9

P's Diary: MS, xxii, 177, 205; text, 179–99

various: Jacobean precedent, 174, 179, 180, 200 n. 3; list of shipwrights submitted to King, 182, 200 nn. 12, 23; King's inaugural address, 185–6; P impedes fees to Secretaries of State, 190–1; timber fellers invited to tender, 184, 186, 201 n. 20

Navy Records Society, xxi–xxii, xxiii, 7, 116, 118, 119

Nedham (Needham), John, Receiver-General of Westminster Abbey, 93, 109 n. 64

Netherlands, The, United Provinces of [*loosely* Holland]: Admiralties, 23, 34 n. 28; intelligence gathering proposed, 127, 168 n. 36; J. James in, 75; P visits, 32 n. 1; P's witnesses from, 38, 52; war expenses, 6, 34 n. 29; *see also* War, Dutch

Neve, —, lawyer, 94

Neville (Neville), *alias* Scarisbrick, Edward, SJ, 80, 106 n. 19

New England, 37; masts from, 16, 33 n. 16

Newman, Richard, JP, 87, 103

Newmarket (New Markett), Suff, palace, 85, 100, 103 n. 111, 168 n. 32

Nicholson, Lt —, 150, 171 n. 95

Noel, Edward, Earl of Gainsborough (d. 1689), and Mary his Countess, 121

Norway, masts from, 33 n. 16

Norfolk, Duke of *see* Howard, Henry

North Cape [Finisterre], 128

Norwich, —, P's coachman, 76

Nottingham, Earl of *see* Finch, Heneage

Oates, Titus, 61 n. 20, 80; plate 2

Ollard, Richard Laurence, author, xxii, 167 n. 21

Ordnance Office, 2, 3, 12, 175

Orford, Earl of *see* Russell, Edward

Ormond, Duke of *see* Butler, James

Osborne, Col. Henry, Commissioner of Accounts, 8 n. 7

Ossory, Earl of *see* Butler, Thomas

Ostend, *prov.* Flandre-Occidentale, Belgium, 111 n. 94

Otway, Thomas, playwright (*The Orphan*), 67, 84, 107 n. 39

Oxford, Bodleian Library, Rawlinson MSS, 41 n. 4, 63 n. 53, 67, 108 n. 56, 118

Pallavicini (Palavicini), Peter, 49, 62
  n. 34
Pariente, Solomon, interpreter, 172
  n. 123
Paris, 37, 46, 106 n. 29
Parliament:
  assembly: prorogation/dissolution,
    50, 58, 60 n. 2, 62 n. 39, 73;
    evidence withheld until session,
    53, 55, 73; session anticipated,
    58–9
  House of Commons [*often
    'Parliament'*]: *committees*:
    miscarriages (1667), 2, 3; (1679),
    36, 38, 60 n. 6, 66, 68, 79, 110
    n. 75; Navy accounts, 4; Popish
    Plot, 62 n. 40, 63 n. 50; *various*:
    elections 9, 32 n. 1, 35, 166 n. 13,
    123; privilege, 47; Sergeant at
    Arms, 38, 42; supply, 2, 3, 4, 11,
    34 n. 29, 114, 170 n. 83, 175;
    tacking, 3; ~ also, 13, 37, 38, 42,
    45, 46, 51, 53, 54, 56, 60 n. 10,
    65, 66, 75, 76, 88, 100, 105 n. 9,
    108 n. 55
  House of Lords: committee (Navy
    accounts), 4, 9, 32 n. 3; King's
    attendance, 3, 8 n. 9; ~ also, 3
  statutes: 13 Car. II st. 1. c. 1
    (sedition), 41 n. 9; 19 & 20 Car. II
    c. 1 (Commissioners of Accounts),
    3, 4, 11, 17, 18, 32 n. 10; 25 Car.
    II c .2 (Test), 35, 61 n. 23; 31 Car.
    II c. 2 (Habeas Corpus
    amendment), 39, 50, 51, 53, 54,
    60 n. 2, 62 n. 47; 1 Jac. II cc. 3–5
    (excise), 175
Parsons Green *see under* Chelsea
Paz, Samuel de (Depaz, Du Pas, Du
  Passe), Dartmouth's Spanish
  secretary, 127, 142, 148, 151,
  156, 164, 168 n. 36
Pearce, Capt. John, 65, 70 n. 1
Pearse (Pierce), James, surgeon, 67, 84,
  107 n. 38
Pedro II, King of Portugal, 147, 171
  n. 90
Pellissary, Georges, *seigneur* de,

Treasurer-General of the French
  Navy, 45, 47, 61 n. 21, 106 n. 28
Pemberton, Sir Francis, JKB (1679–80),
  39, 41 n. 6, 42, 47, 51, 53, 55,
  58, 60 n. 5
Penn, Sir William, Commissioner of the
  Navy (1660–9), 1
Penny, —, slopseller in Surinam, 97
—, Mrs, P's tailor in London, 91
Pepys, family, 107 n. 37
  Elizabeth, wife of Samuel, death, 3,
    9, 32 n. 1, 107 n. 37
  John father of Samuel, 111 n. 103
Pepys, Samuel, Clerk of the Acts
    (1660–73), Admiralty Secretary
    (1673–9, 1684–9):
  career (*main stages*): (pre-1660:
    Exchequer clerk), 32 n. 2;
    (1660–73: Clerk of the Acts),
    1–34; (1662–79: Tangier
    Committee), 115; (1673–9:
    Admiralty Secretary), 35–6;
    (1679–80: fall/under cloud),
    36–111; (1683–4: Tangier visit),
    115–72, 173; (1684–9: Admiralty
    Secretary), 173–99
  charges against: piracy, 36–7, 68, 76,
    105 n. 12; Popery, 35, 36, 38,
    48–9, 63 n. 50, 68, 88, 91, 95,
    103, 106 n. 27, 108 n. 55, 108
    n. 76; ticket fraud, 25, 27, 29–30,
    34 n. 36; treason, 36, 37, 40, 43.
    51, 53, 54, 55, 67
  circle: cronies, 32 n. 2; 107 n. 38,
    109 n. 59; godson, 111 n. 98;
    Magdalene room-mate, 9, 32 n. 4;
    women friends, 37, 84, 85, 97,
    98, 99, 100, 101, 105 n. 6, 107
    n. 37, 108 n. 48, 110 n. 78, 165,
    172 n. 130
  household: coachman, 76;
    housekeeper, 66, 75; library clerk
    see Lorrain, P.; musician *see*
    Morelli, C.
  houses: Brampton, 104, 11 n. 103;
    Parsons Green, Chelsea, 76, 96,
    97, 105 n. 13; York Buildings,
    Westminster, 38

various: arrest/imprisonment, 42–4,
61 nn. 14, 15; finances (personal),
129–30, 139; oratory, 2, 20, 35,
48; parliamentary career, 9, 32
n. 1, 35, 36, 61 n. 27, 110 n. 85;
protestancy asserted, 48; school,
111 n. 111

writing: drafting/recording
(selective), 28, 125, 126, 127,
129, 131–2, 136, 137, 142–3,
146, 147, 148, 150, 156, 159,
161, 163, 169 n. 57, 172 n. 126,
197, 199; handwriting, 45–6, 61
n. 24; literary style, 13;
shorthand, xxiii–xxiv, 38, 100,
118, 119, 124, 130; *for texts here
printed see* Brooke House
Commission/ Journal; King's
Bench/Journal; James, John; Navy
Commission; Tangier Journal; *for
other principal compositions and
books owned see* books and MSS

Pessaro, Cape, Sicily, 65

Petersfield, Hants, 121

Petre, William, Baron Petre (d. 1684),
87, 108 n. 54

Pett, family, 200 n. 15

Pett, Peter, Navy Commissioner,
Chatham (1660–7), 2, 16

Sir Phineas (Kt 1680), Commissioner
of the Navy (1680–6), 175, 176,
183, 184, 185, 187, 188, 194,
195, 197, 200 n. 15, 201 n. 36,
202 n. 42; kinswoman, 95, 109
n. 72; ship built by, plate 10

Peyton (Payton), Sir Robert, 57, 63
n. 51

Phillips (Philips), Col. Robert, 56, 63
n. 48

Ensign Thomas, 118, 151, 156, 171
n. 97; plates II–V

Pierrepont, William, Commissioner of
Accounts, 8 n. 7

piracy, 43, 68, 76, 105 n. 12, 106 n. 16

Plain Truth [satire on P and Hewer],
90, 108 n. 56

plays: Etherege, *She Would if She
Could*, 74, 105 n. 7; Otway, *The*

Orphan, 84, 107 n. 39;
unidentified, 101

Plymouth, Devon: citadel, 123;
St Nicholas Island, 124, 167
n. 21; Sound, 123; ~ also,
123–4, 125, 137, 166 n. 5, 167
n. 18

Pollexfen (Polyxphen), Henry [Kt
1689], lawyer, 51, 62 n. 43

Pope, the, 61 n. 29; burnt in effigy, 106
n. 25

Popish Plot, 35–64 *passim*, 115, 175

Portland, Dors, 123

Portsmouth, Hants: dockyard, 36, 41
n. 2, 60 n. 11, 176, 184, 187,
188, 194, 201 n. 22; Mayor and
corporation, 123; MPs, 166 n. 13;
~ also, 115, 121, 122

Portugal: coast, 129; subjects of at
Tangier, 133, 147, 151, 153, 169
n. 64, 170 n. 69, 171 nn. 90, 108;
~ also, 80, 113, 115

Povey (Povy), Thomas, 68, 69, 81, 82,
83, 84, 86, 87, 88, 89, 90, 91, 95,
96, 98, 99, 100, 106 n. 23, 108
n. 58

Powis, Countess of *see* Herbert,
Elizabeth

Powis, Earl of *see* Herbert, William

Presbyterians, 111 n. 95

Priestman (Preestman), Capt. Henry,
99, 110 n. 86, 127, 161

printing: newspapers, 97, 99, 100, 101,
110 n. 77, 111 n. 101, 184, 201
n. 21; pasquinades, 62 n. 34, 108
n. 56; pay tickets, 24

privateering, 36, 37

Privy Council, debate on Brooke House
report, 4, 11–32

Privy Seal Office, 188, 191

Prize Commissioners, 30–2

Puckle, James, 38, 52, 62 n. 45

pumps, 195, 201 n. 37

Putney, Surr, 101

Revenue officers, 154, 170 n. 81

Revolution (1688–9), 40

Rich, Capt. Peter, MP, 79, 106 n. 16

Richards, —, kinswoman of Pett,
    ? husband of Solomon, 95, 109
    n. 72
Richmond, Surr, 83, 88, 91, 95;
    apothecary of, 95
Robinson, Sir John, Bt, Lieutenant of
    the Tower, 42, 43
Rochefort (Rochfort), *dép*. Charente-
    Inférieure, France, 46
Rochester, Kent, 83
Rochester, Earl of *see* Hyde, Lawrence
Rolt, Capt. Edward, 67, 84, 107
    n. 38
Rooke, Capt. George [Kt 1693], 172
    n. 119
Roper, Col. William, 48, 49, 61 n. 33
Routh, Enid Maud Grace, author, 119
    n. 1
Royal Horse Guards, 166 n. 13
Royal Society, 5; *History* (1667), 107
    n. 34
Rupert, Prince, Duke of Cumberland,
    General-at-Sea, 26, 34 n. 32
Russell, Capt. Edward [Earl of Orford
    1697], 85, 87, 93, 96, 97, 99, 108
    n. 50; servant, 103, 107 n. 31
Rye House plot, 63 n. 52, 126, 128–9,
    152, 168 n. 32

St George's Channel, 126
St Helens (St Ellens), Isle of Wight, 121,
    122, 166 n. 3
St John, Capt. Thomas, Paymaster of
    Tangier, 160, 161, 162
St Michel (St Michell), Balthasar
    ('Balty'), P's brother-in-law, Navy
    Commissioner, Deptford and
    Woolwich (1686–8): assists P
    during Popish Plot, 37, 38, 41
    n. 5, 97, 98, 101, 107 nn. 30, 42;
    at Tangier, 131, 169 n. 56; Special
    Commission, 176, 177, 182, 183,
    184–5, 185, 187, 188, 194, 195,
    197, 201 n. 36
St Vincent, Cape (South Cape), *dist*.
    Faro, Portugal, 129
Sallee [*modern* Salé] (Salli, Sally),
    Morocco, 145, 171 n. 109

Sandwich, Earl of *see* Montagu,
    Edward
salutes, 121, 131, 132, 140–1, 152, 170
    n. 74, 171 n. 106; forbidden for
    want of powder, 151; P accorded
    despite ban, 157
Santa Cruz, W. Africa [*unidentified*],
    145, 151
Savile, George, Viscount Halifax [Earl
    1679, Marquess 1682], 5
Saunders (Sanders), Edmund [Kt 1683],
    lawyer, 51, 55, 56, 62 n. 43
    Capt. Francis, 99, 110 n. 86
Sawyer, Sir Robert (Kt 1677), AG
    (1681–7), 9, 32 n. 4, 180, 184,
    186, 188, 191
Scarisbrick *see* Neville
Scott, James, Duke of Monmouth and
    Buccleuch (d. 1685), conspiracy,
    63 n. 5
    John, P's accuser: court appearance,
    42–3, 48; disappears, 50, 51, 56,
    57; history/villaines, 37, 41 nn. 3,
    4, 60 n. 8, 61 n. 21, 62 n. 45, 97,
    98, 106 n. 29; new accusations
    expected, 76; Popish goods said to
    be P's, 48; sole witness against P,
    40, 44, 54; speechless in face of
    P's defence, 46; ~ also, 38, 45,
    47, 49, 58, 61 n. 33, 68, 90, 94,
    176
Scroggs (Scrogs), Sir William, LCJ
    (1678–81): allows P/Deane bail,
    45, 47–8, 50; asserts right of
    Englishmen, 46–7; calls for
    evidence or discharge, 51, 52,
    54–6, 57; disallows prosecution
    evidence, 57–8; grants discharge,
    59–60; ~ also, 39, 41 n. 6
    William [Kt 1681] son of LCJ,
    lawyer, 51, 53, 56, 62 n. 43
seal, great, 122, 192
seamen: pay, 2; payment by ticket, 7,
    24–5, 27–30, 34 n. 39; short
    rations, 25–7, 137, 166;
    supernumeraries, 26
sea officers: half pay/pensions, 190;
    volunteer (reformado), 128

Secretaries of State: P accorded
  equivalent status, 173; P impedes
  fees, 190–1; *see also* Jenkins, Sir
  Leoline; Spencer, Robert
Seignelay, *Marquis* de, 37
Seller, John, cartographer, 168 n. 30;
  plate I
Sellers, John, volunteer officer [*if not
  the above*], 126, 168 n. 30
Sennen, Cornw, Land's End in, *q.v.*
Session, —, *perhaps* Sessions, Thomas,
  gunner, 129, 168 n. 44
Shaftesbury (Shaftsbury), Earl of *see*
  Cooper, Anthony Ashley
Shales, Capt. John, Treasury clerk, 98,
  110 n. 84, 176, 180, 181, 183,
  200 n. 6
Shelton, Thomas, stenographer,
  118
Sheres (Shere), Henry [Kt 1685],
  engineer at Tangier: council of
  four, 132; estimates for
  demolition, 133, 165; garden,
  132–3; Good Voyages
  condemned, 155; meeting with
  Alcaïd, 133; mines dug/detonated,
  144, 156, 157, 158; survey of
  fortifications, 154; unhappy, 137;
  work in arrears, 160, 164;
  writings, 148, 179 n. 88; ~ also,
  115, 117, 123, 127, 128,
  130,149, 152
shipbuilding: Dutch manual, 96,
  109–10 n. 74; P instructed in,
  175; thirty ships of P's programme
  (1677), 35, 116, 173, 189, 198,
  202 nn. 40, 42; ~ also, 201 n. 26,
  202 n. 47; plates 10–11
ships and boats:
  accidents: collisions/near misses, 124,
    165, 172 n. 129, 202 n. 46; leaks,
    125, 148, 167 n. 25; run aground,
    122, 154
  features: awning, 128; bowsprits,
    172 n. 129; 202 n. 46; capstan,
    122; maintop, 129; masts, 6,
    14–15, 16, 33 n. 16; ports, 198–9;
    rigging, 201 n. 201; spirketing,

198; timbers, rotten, 198; wings
  cleared for fight, 26
types: barge, 162; boat, able to go
  where ship could not, 164, 172
  n. 127; brigantine/galley, 136;
  flyboat, 123; merchantmen, in
  Tangier fleet, 167 n. 22; yachts,
  122, 166 n. 12, 187, 202 n. 46;
  see further by list following
various: convoys, 15; gunnery
  practice, 128; launching, 91,
  100, 111 n. 92; models, 37;
  pays, 2, 28–9; prizes, 30–2,
  37, 154; punishment aboard,
  122
ships and boats named [identified from
  and by number in *Lists of Men-of-
  War 1650–1700*, Part I, *English
  Ships 1649–1702*, comp. R.C.
  Anderson, 2nd edn (Society for
  Nautical Research Occasional
  Publication no. 5, 1966); rates for
  pre-1660 ships as in Fox, *Great
  Ships*, pp. 174–7]:
Anne yacht [Anderson 297], 124,
  125, 167 n. 25; *Bonaventure
  (Bonadventure)* 4th-rate
  [Anderson 636], 161, 167 n. 22;
  Britannia 1st-rate [Anderson 630],
  198, 202 n. 42; plate 10;
  Catherine (Katherine) of London,
  merchantman, 37, 76, 105 n. 12,
  106 n. 16; *Cleveland* yacht
  [Anderson 463], 121; *Dartmouth*
  5th-rate [Anderson 235], 162;
  Delight flyboat, 123, 167 n. 18;
  Dover 4th-rate [Anderson 217],
  154; *English Tiger see Tiger*;
  Exeter 3rd-rate [Anderson 623],
  launching, 100, 111 n. 92
Grafton 3rd-rate [Anderson 614],
  116, 142, 152, 157, 167 nn. 8,
  22, 25–7, 168 n. 44, 169 n. 50,
  171 n. 89, 198, 202 n. 40; plate
  11; Captain *see* Booth, Sir
  William; Chaplain, 166 n. 4; log,
  166 n. 1, 169 n. 54; Master, 126;
  P aboard, 121–32

Greyhound 6th-rate [Anderson 467], 165, 167 n. 22, 172 n. 129; *Happy Return* 4th-rate [Anderson 214], 169 n. 59; *Henrietta* 3rd-rate [Anderson 206], 128, 148, 166 n. 5, 167 n. 22; *Hunter* privateer, 36–7, 40, 60 n. 9, 68, 105 n. 12; *Kent* 3rd-rate [Anderson 615], 198, 202 n. 41; *Lark* 6th-rate [Anderson 578], 170 n. 182, 171 n. 98; *Lion (Lyon)* 3rd-rate [Anderson 278], 29; *Mary* yacht [Anderson 585], 166 n. 2; *Mary Rose* 4th-rate [Anderson 216], 123, 167 n. 22, 169 n. 49; *Mountagu (Mountague)* 3rd-rate [Anderson 208], 157, 159, 161, 166, 167 n. 22, 170 n. 87, 172 n. 129; *Oxford* 4th-rate [Anderson 569], 122, 165, 167 n. 22, 172 n.129

St Andrew 1st-rate [Anderson 453], 198; *St David* 4th-rate [Anderson 432], 124, 160, 167 n. 22, 172 n. 119; *Sapphire* 4th-rate [Anderson 110], 65; *Swallow* 4th-rate [Anderson 179], 150, 151, 153, 172 n. 113; *Tiger* distinguished from next as English *Tiger (English Tyger)* 4th-rate [Anderson 627], 162; *Turkish Tiger* 4th-rate, Algerine prize [Anderson 596], 171 n. 100; *Welcome (Wellcome)*, merchantman, 124; *Woolwich* 4th-rate [Anderson 575], 167 n. 22

shipwrightry, Dutch book of (Witsen), 96, 109–10 n. 74

shipwrights: City of London company, 194; Irish, 109 n. 70; listed/maligned by P, 182, 200 nn. 12–13

Shish, Thomas, shipwright, 202 n. 40; plate 11

Signet, Clerk of, 167 n. 19

Signet Office, 188, 190, 191

Silver (Sylver), Capt. Thomas, 154, 171 n. 110

Simmons *see* Symons

Skinner, Mary, P's mistress, ?85, 108 n. 48, 111 n. 90

Slingsby, Henry, Master of the Mint, 27, 34 n. 34

Smith, —, watchman, 78

Adm. Sir Jeremy, 15

John, first transcriber of the great Diary and Tangier Journal, 118, 119 n. 1

William, mayor of Tangier: business 132, 133, 134, 135, 150, 151; 171 nn. 94, 103; sails for home, 159, 160; wife, sister, and sister-in-law of, 135

Smyrna (Smirna) [*modern* Izmir], Turkey, 152

soldiers: mutiny over pilchards, 166; sailors as proficient with small arms, 140

Sole Battle, battle of (1672), 66

soundings, 128

Southerne (Southern), James, Admiralty clerk [Secretary 1690–4], 83, 106 n. 26, 176, 194, 195

Southwell, Sir Robert, Clerk of the Privy Council, 50, 62 n. 37

Spain: food/cuisine, 132, 133, 149, 160; literature, 117, 120 n. 6; P/Hewer holiday, 117, 118, 155, 163, 164, 166; rain in, 165; relations with England, 113, 115, 145; women, 149; ~ also, 160, 163

Spanish (language), 80, 133, 142, 148, 168 n. 36

Spartel (Spartell, Spratt), Cape, Morocco, 130, 131, 169 n. 51

Speke, John, 61 n. 14

Spencer, Robert, earl of Sunderland, Secretary of State (1679–81, 1683–8), 44, 61 n. 15, 85, 146, 170 n. 83

Spithead, off Portsmouth, 121

Sprat (Spratt), Thomas, Canon, later Dean, of Westminster, 83, 85, 86, 87, 88, 95, 107 n. 34

Stafford, Viscount *see* Howard, William
stars: P learns, 128; Pole Star, 132
Start Point, in Stokenham, Devon, 123
Stephens (Stephen), Anthony, Navy
    Treasury clerk, 30, 34 n. 36
Stewart (Stuart), — , Mrs, sister of
    Lady Mordaunt, 84, ?85, 101,
    107 n. 37, 108 n. 48
Stokenham, Devon, Start Point in, *q.v.*
Strickland, —, 82
Sunderland, Earl of *see* Spencer, Robert
Surinam, 97, 98, 110 n. 81
Swayne, Capt. Thomas, 37
Symons (Simmons), Will, 9, 32 n. 2

Tangier (Tanger), Morocco:
    administration (home): committee,
        115; finance, 114, 121;
        treasurership, P resigns/succeeded
        by Hewer, 80, 85, 90, 91, 106 n.
        23, 108 nn. 45, 58; ~ also, 66, 80
    administration (local): clerks, 134;
        council of four, 132; garrison,
        114, 135, 156, 172 n. 120; Mayor
        (W. Smith) and aldermen/leading
        burghers, 132, 133, 134, 135,
        150, 151, 159, 160, 170 n. 69,
        171 nn. 94, 103; naval chaplain,
        166 n. 4; officials, 131, 143;
        Recorder, 128, 150, 168 n. 40;
        security/passwords, 153, 158;
        supplies/victualling, 121, 133,
        137, 165–6
    evacuation process: compensation
        for residents (P's main work), 115,
        124, 125, 127, 129, 130, 136,
        138, 139, 141–4, 150, 151, 152,
        153, 154, 159, 160, 171 nn. 90,
        96, 103, 108; demolition, 125,
        126, 127, 130, 133, 137, 141,
        144, 145, 146, 148, 149, 152,
        153–4, 154–5, 156, 157–8, 159,
        160–1, 163, 164, 165, 167 n. 27,
        169 n. 27; withdrawal, quasi-
        ceremonial, 118
    topography (general): difficulties of
        defence, 113–14, 116, 131, 132,
        150; hills blue as in paintings, 167

    topography (particular): baths
        (*bagnio*), 132, 170 n. 86; bay,
        131; castle, 132, 150, 153;
        cathedral (RC), and its
        clergy/houses, 133, 134, 144, 147,
        169 n. 64, 171 nn. 90, 108;
        church of King Charles the
        Martyr (CofE), 135, 143, 144,
        149, 152, 156; Devil's Tower, 138;
        fields, 150, 151, 153, 154, 156,
        158, 159, 162, 163, 165;
        fortifications/earthworks, 114,
        115, 116, 154, 167 n. 27;
        Fountain Fort, 150; hospital, 172
        n. 120; Irish Battery, 158;
        Malabata (Malabat) Point, 157;
        Marine Battery, 162; Mole, 114,
        117, 132, 136, 137, 144, 145,
        148, 149, 152, 154, 155, 156,
        157, 158, 159, 160, 161–2, 163,
        165, 170 n. 68, 171 n. 105; old
        city, 157, 161; Parade, 133, 140;
        Peterborough (Peterborow) Tower,
        117, 154; Pole Fort, 149, 156;
        river, 157; Roman aqueducts,
        149; stockade, 150, 152; Town
        House, 133, 143, 144, 149, 153;
        Whitby, 136, 170 n. 68; York
        Castle, 135
    various: commerce, 11, 143, 145,
        170 n. 77; history, 113–15, 143;
        maps, 112, plate I; prices, 133,
        165–6; siege (1680), 114; vices
        condemned in sermon, 143; water
        supply, 132, 141
Tangier Journal, MS and publication
    history, 115, 118–19, 204;
    composition, 148, 153, 160, 162;
    reliability, 116; text, 121–66
Tanner, Joseph Robson, editor, 200
    n. 2
Taylor (Talor), Capt. John, merchant,
    16, 33 n. 18
telescope, 131, 133, 158
Tetuan, Morocco, 165
Thames, River, 100, 101, 198
Thévenin, Paul, *sieur* des Gléreaux, 83,
    106 n. 28

Thomson (Tomson), Col. George,
    Commissioner of Accounts:
    clashes with P, 9, 29, 31; cites
    Elizabethan precedent, 19–20, 22;
    Commonwealth service, 18, 24,
    32 n. 9, 33 n. 21; mocked by
    King, 19, 23; other quarrels, 14,
    16, 18–19, 23; ~ also, 5, 11,30
Tompson, Richard, engraver, plate 2
Thornhill, Capt. —, 100
timber, 184, 186, 190, 194, 198, 201
    n. 21
Tippets, Sir John, Surveyor of the Navy
    (1672–86, 1688–92),
    Commissioner (1686–8), 175,
    176, 194, 195
tobacco, customs on, 175
tobacconist, 44
Tomalin, Claire, author, xxiii (quoted),
    xxv, 105 n. 6, 108 n. 48
Torrington, Earl of *see* Herbert, Arthur
Treasury, 4, 32 n. 9, 175, 181, 182,
    188; Commissioners, 10; officials,
    32 nn. 5, 6, 98, 105 n. 9, 110
    n. 84
Trevor, Sir John, Secretary of State
    (1668–72), 10, 32 n. 8
Trumbull, Sir William (Kt 1684), Judge-
    Advocate for Tangier evacuation,
    [Secretary of State 1695–7]:
    official: business with P/Dartmouth,
    115–16, 124, 129, 130, 132, 133,
    138, 142, 146, 147, 148, 153;
    told purpose of mission, 127–8,
    128, 131; upset by criticism, 136,
    137, 139, 149
    relations with P: church crawl, 144;
    dining arrangements, 134, 135;
    excursions, 123, 145; good
    companions at first, 125, 126,
    126–7, 150; P increasingly critical:
    149, 150, 153, 155; P supposedly
    does all the work, 150, 154
    return: requested: 151, 152–3, 154;
    sails home, 155–6, 167 n. 19
    various: health, 152; Sunderland's
    creature, 146, 170 n. 83
Tunis, men of ('Tuniseens'), 133

Turks, 152
Turner, Sir William, Commissioner of
    Accounts, 8 n. 7, 14, 33 n. 15
Turpin, Richard, highwayman, alluded
    to, 33 n. 20
Tyburn, Midd, 33 n. 20
Tyrrell, Capt. John, 100, 110 n. 87

Usher, Lt Ignatius, 162

Vaughan, Edward, 70 n. 1, 104
Vaxhall (Foxhall), Surr, 99, 101
Velde, Willem van de, the Elder, artist,
    plate 10
    Willem van de, the Younger, artist,
    plate 11
Verdun, Abel de, midshipman
    extraordinary (the 'French
    Lieutenant'), 125, 167 n. 26
Villiers (Villers), George, Duke of
    Buckingham (d. 1628), Lord High
    Admiral, 174
    George, Duke of Buckingham
    (d. 1687), 36, 40, 66, 70 nn. 1, 2,
    102, 104, 111 n. 102
    Lt Henry, 120, 169 n. 50
Vincent, Stephen, baker, 172 n. 120
Vyner (Viner), Sir Robert, Bt, 67, 91,
    109 n. 59

Walbanke (Walbanck, Walbank), John,
    Admiralty clerk, 75, 81, 99, 105
    n. 11, 194
Waller, Sir William (d. 1668),
    parliamentary commander, 108
    n. 53
    Sir William (d. 1699), MP, 86, 87,
    89, 108 n. 53
War, First Dutch (1652–4), 2, 6, 22–3,
    24, 26, 34 n. 29, 65, 170 n. 85
War, Second Dutch (1665–7), 11,
    17–18, 19, 22, 33 n. 27, 34
    n. 28
    operations: (1665) Lowestoft, 1, 2;
    (1666) division of the fleet, 2;
    Four Days' Fight, and St James's
    Day Fight, 1; (1667) Chatham
    raid, 1–2, 2, 3

post-war enquiry issues: date of
   opening, 4, 11, 17, 19;
   funding/alleged misappropriation,
   2, 4, 11–13, 17–18; Navy Board
   duties, 1–34 *passim*; *see synopsis
   under* Brooke House Commission
War, Third Dutch (1672–4), 35, 36, 46,
   61 n. 26, 170 n. 85
Warcup, Edmund, JP, 68, 81–2, 106 n.
   22
Ward, —, 98
Warren, Sir William, merchant,
   accounts investigated, 14, 15, 16,
   28, 33 nn. 16, 18; *douceur* to P, 6
Warwick, Sir Philip, Treasury Secretary
   (1660–7), 10, 13, 17, 32 n. 6
watchmakers, 83, 106 n. 29
weapons: bombs, 155; fuses, 154;
   grenades ('granadoes'), 141, 205;
   gun carriage, accident to, 141;
   guns, 141, 156; gunnery practice
   aboard ship, 128; lances, 140,
   141; mortars, 158; powder, 151,
   154, 157, 158, 164, 165; shot,
   140–1, 152; small arms supplied
   to sailors ashore, 140, 170 n. 72
weather (exceptional): calm, 128;
   climate change south of Finisterre,
   128; cold, 162; damp/dry, damage
   to ships if ports left open/closed,
   198–9; evening dew, 154; floods,
   164, 165; good, lasting beyond all
   imagination, 160; hail, 164, 165;
   hot, 128; levantine ('levant'), 130,
   131; moonshine, 123, 125, 152,
   153, 156, 157, 158, 163; rains
   (Tangier), 141, 145, 148, 149,
   154, 163, 164, 165; rainy and
   thick/hazy rainy, 126, 163; sea
   running high, 125, 127; storms/bad, 124, 126, 127, 148,
   166; sunset, hills above Tangier
   blue at, 157; thunder/lightning,
   163, 164, 165; very foul, 145
Westminster (and environs), Midd:
   Collegiate Church of St Peter
      (Westminster Abbey): bell, 65, 86;
      clergy, 107 nn. 31, 34; cloisters,

85; lay officer, 93, 109 n. 64;
   ~ also, 69, 89
other churches: Broadway (New)
   Chapel, 83, 107 n. 32; Christ
   Church, 107 n. 32; St Giles in the
   Fields, 100; St Margaret's, 93, 107
   nn. 32, 34, 109 n. 65; St Paul's,
   Covent Garden, 84, 92, 93, 100,
   109 n. 66
palaces: St James's, 67, 100; (King's
   Bedchamber, 185; King's Closet,
   191); Whitehall, 4, 43, 61 n. 15,
   91, 104 n. 1, 172 n. 13; (Chapel,
   84, 101; Council Chamber, 11,
   14, 49, 56; Presence Chamber,
   179); ~ unspecified: King's
   Bedchamber, 182, 195; Queen's
   Bedchamber, 181
places: Ashburnham House, Little
   Dean's Yard, 110 n. 83; Covent
   Garden, 44, 84; Derby House
   [Admiralty Office], 72, 75, 78, 79,
   80, 93, 104 n. 1; Exeter House,
   Strand, 86, 108 n. 52; Hyde Park
   (Hide), 92, 101; King St, Covent
   Garden, 109 n. 66; Mall, The, 13;
   new buildings, 86; St James's
   Park, 13, 82, 100; Savoy, 86;
   Strand, 38, 101; Strutton Ground,
   108 n. 53; Theatre Royal, Drury
   Lane, 105 n. 7; Westminster Hall,
   49, 57, 65, 103, 139; Westminster
   School, 110 n. 83; York Buildings,
   Strand, 38
various: JP, 108 n. 83; picture
   dealers, plates II–V
Wheeler, — [? Francis Wheler], 84
Wheler, Capt. Sir Francis (Kt Aug.
   1683), ?84, 108 n. 44, 162
Whigs, 66, 68, 106 nn. 16, 17, 25, 109
   nn. 60–1, 173
Whitby, Yorks, pier, 170 n. 68
White, Robert, engraver, plate 4
Wilkinson, Anthony, P's servant, 158
William III: as Prince of Orange, 61
   n. 30, 70 n. 2, 75, 105 n. 9; as
   King: assassination attempt, 109
   n. 68

William of Occam, canonist, razor of, applied, 168 n. 43

Williams, William [Kt 1687, Bt 1688], MP, 42, 60 n. 7

Williamson, Joseph [Kt 1672], Under-secretary of State, [Secretary 1674–9], 34 n. 37

Wimbledon (Wimbleton), Surr, 75, 105 n. 11

Winch, Sir Humphrey, Bt, Commissioner of the Admiralty (1679–84), 75, 105 n. 11

Winchester, Hants, 121: assizes, 40, 43, 47, 52, 54, 60 n. 11, 61 n. 14; Cathedral, Canon of, 166 n. 4; College, 121

Windsor [Castle], Berks, 57, 121

Witsen, Nicolaas, author, 96, 109–10 n. 74

Witt, Johan de, Grand Pensionary of Holland, 34 n. 28

women, P's evaluations, 110 n. 89, 132, 135, 136, 149

Wood, —, Mrs, 73
    William, shipbuilder, 15, 16, 33 nn. 16, 18

Woolwich, Kent, dockyard, 66, 176, 188, 193, 202 n. 40; plate 11

Wormall, Bartholomew, curate of St Margaret's Westminster, 93, 109 n. 65

Wright, Robert [Kt 1680], lawyer, 42, 60 n. 12

writs: *habeas corpus*, 42, 60 n. 2; *quo warranto*, 40

Wyborne (Wyburne), Capt. Sir John, 132, 169 n. 59

Wylde (Wilde), Capt. Charles, 122

Wyndham, Col. Sir Francis, 123, 162 n. 12, 104

Yeates, Nicholas, engraver, plates II–V

York, Yorks, Minster, Dean of, 111 n. 98

York (Yorke), Duke of see James II

Yorkshire, militia, 108 n. 49

Zouch, Richard, author, 126, 127, 168 n. 31